P9-BAW-219

Please remember that this is a library book,
and that it belongs only temporarily to each
person who uses it. Be considerate. Do
not write in this, or any, library book.

Harriet E. Gross
Marvin B. Sussman
Editors

WITHDRAWN

Families and Adoption

Pre-publication
REVIEWS,
COMMENTARIES,
EVALUATIONS . . .

"**A** n impressive and timely anthology richly endowed with empirically based and well-researched articles on contemporary issues in adoption, contributed by eminent authors in the field. Written in a lucid and easy-to-read style, this volume will make an invaluable contribution to the adoption literature. A commendable job by. Gross and Sussman."

Paul Sachdev, PhD
Professor of Social Work
Memorial University
of Newfoundland,
St. John's, NF

The *Marriage & Family Review* series:

- *Cults and the Family*, edited by Florence Kaslow and Marvin B. Sussman
- *Alternatives to Traditional Family Living*, edited by Harriet Gross and Marvin B. Sussman
- *Intermarriage in the United States*, edited by Gary A. Crester and Joseph J. Leon
- *Family Systems and Inheritance Patterns*, edited by Judith N. Cates and Marvin B. Sussman
- *The Ties That Bind: Men's and Women's Social Networks*, edited by Laura Lein and Marvin B. Sussman
- *Social Stress and the Family: Advances and Developments in Family Stress Theory and Research*, edited by Hamilton I. McCubbin, Marvin B. Sussman, and Joan M. Patterson
- *Human Sexuality and the Family*, edited by James W. Maddock, Gerhard Neubeck, and Marvin B. Sussman
- *Obesity and the Family*, edited by David J. Kallen and Marvin B. Sussman
- *Women and the Family*, edited by Beth B. Hess and Marvin B. Sussman
- *Personal Computers and the Family*, edited by Marvin B. Sussman
- *Pets and the Family*, edited by Marvin B. Sussman
- *Families and the Energy Transition*, edited by John Byrne, David A. Schulz, and Marvin B. Sussman
- *Men's Changing Roles in the Family*, edited by Robert A. Lewis and Marvin B. Sussman
- *The Charybdis Complex: Redemption of Rejected Marriage and Family Journal Articles*, edited by Marvin B. Sussman
- *Families and the Prospect of Nuclear Attack/Holocaust*, edited by Teresa D. Marciano and Marvin B. Sussman
- *Family Medicine: The Maturing of a Discipline*, edited by William J. Doherty, Charles E. Christianson, and Marvin B. Sussman
- *Childhood Disability and Family Systems*, edited by Michael Ferrari and Marvin B. Sussman
- *Alternative Health Maintenance and Healing Systems for Families*, edited by Doris Y. Wilkinson and Marvin B. Sussman
- *Deviance and the Family*, edited by Frank E. Hagan and Marvin B. Sussman
- *Transitions to Parenthood*, edited by Rob Palkovitz and Marvin B. Sussman
- *AIDS and Families: Report of the AIDS Task Force Groves Conference on Marriage and the Family*, edited by Eleanor D. Macklin
- *Museum Visits and Activities for Family Life Enrichment*, edited by Barbara H. Butler and Marvin B. Sussman
- *Cross-Cultural Perspectives on Families, Work, and Change*, edited by Katja Boh, Giovanni Sgritta, and Marvin B. Sussman
- *Homosexuality and Family Relations*, edited by Frederick W. Bozett and Marvin B. Sussman

- *Families in Community Settings: Interdisciplinary Perspectives*, edited by Donald G. Unger and Marvin B. Sussman
- *Corporations, Businesses, and Families*, edited by Roma S. Hanks and Marvin B. Sussman
- *Families: Intergenerational and Generational Connections*, edited by Susan K. Pfeifer and Marvin B. Sussman
- *Wider Families: New Traditional Family Forms*, edited by Teresa D. Marciano and Marvin B. Sussman
- *Publishing in Journals on the Family: A Survey and Guide for Scholars, Practitioners, and Students*, edited by Roma S. Hanks, Linda Matocha, and Marvin B. Sussman
- *Publishing in Journals on the Family: Essays on Publishing*, edited by Roma S. Hanks, Linda Matocha, and Marvin B. Sussman
- *American Families and the Future: Analyses of Possible Destinies*, edited by Barbara H. Settles, Roma S. Hanks, and Marvin B. Sussman
- *Families on the Move: Migration, Immigration, Emigration, and Mobility*, edited by Barbara H. Settles, Daniel E. Hanks III, and Marvin B. Sussman
- *Single Parent Families: Diversity, Myths and Realities*, edited by Shirley M. H. Hanson, Marsha L. Heims, Doris J. Julian, and Marvin B. Sussman
- *Exemplary Social Intervention Programs for Members and Their Families*, edited by David Guttmann and Marvin B. Sussman
- *Families and Law*, edited by Lisa J. McIntyre and Marvin B. Sussman
- *Intercultural Variation in Family Research and Theory: Implications for Cross-National Studies*, edited by Marvin B. Sussman and Roma S. Hanks
- *The Methods and Methodologies of Qualitative Family Research*, edited by Jane F. Gilgun and Marvin B. Sussman
- *Families and Adoption*, edited by Harriet E. Gross and Marvin B. Sussman

These books were published simultaneously as special thematic issues of *Marriage & Family Review* and are available bound separately. For further information, call 1-800-HAWORTH (outside US/Canada: 607-722-5857), Fax 1-800-895-0582 (outside US/Canada: 607-771-0012) or e-mail: getinfo@haworth.com

Families and Adoption has also been published as *Marriage & Family Review,* Volume 25, Numbers 1/2 and 3/4 1997.

The development, preparation, and publication of this work has been undertaken with great care. However, the publisher, employees, editors, and agents of The Haworth Press and all imprints of The Haworth Press, Inc., including the Haworth Medical Press and Pharmaceutical Products Press, are not responsible for any errors contained herein or for consequences that may ensue from use of materials or information contained in this work. Opinions expressed by the author(s) are not necessarily those of The Haworth Press, Inc.

Cover design by Thomas J. Mayshock Jr.

The Haworth Press, Inc., 10 Alice Street, Binghamton, NY 13904-1580 USA

Library of Congress Cataloging-in-Publication Data

Families and adoption / Harriet E. Gross, Marvin B. Sussman, editors.
     p. cm.
    Includes bibliographical references and index.
    ISBN 0-7890-0322-8 (alk. paper)
    1. Adoption. I. Gross, Harriet. II. Sussman, Marvin B.
HV875.F1446 1997
362.73'4–dc21   97-25269
                                                                    CIP

Families and Adoption

Harriet E. Gross
Marvin B. Sussman
Editors

The Haworth Press, Inc.
New York · London

INDEXING & ABSTRACTING

Contributions to this publication are selectively indexed or abstracted in print, electronic, online, or CD-ROM version(s) of the reference tools and information services listed below. This list is current as of the copyright date of this publication. See the end of this section for additional notes.

- *Abstracts in Social Gerontology: Current Literature on Aging,* National Council on the Aging, Library, 409 Third Street SW, 2nd Floor, Washington, DC 20024

- *Abstracts of Research in Pastoral Care & Counseling,* Loyola College, 7135 Minstrel Way, Suite 101, Columbia, MD 21045

- *Academic Abstracts/CD-ROM,* EBSCO Publishing Editorial Department, P.O. Box 590, Ipswich, MA 01938-0590

- *Academic Search: database of 2,000 selected academic serials, updated monthly,* EBSCO Publishing, 83 Pine Street, Peabody, MA 01960

- *AGRICOLA Database,* National Agricultural Library, 10301 Baltimore Boulevard, Room 002, Beltsville, MD 20705

- *Applied Social Sciences Index & Abstracts (ASSIA) (Online: ASSI via Data-Star) (CDRom: ASSIA Plus),* Bowker-Saur Limited, Maypole House, Maypole Road, East Grinstead, West Sussex RH19 1HH, England

- *CNPIEC Reference Guide: Chinese National Directory of Foreign Periodicals,* P.O. Box 88, Beijing, People's Republic of China

- *Current Contents: Clinical Medicine/Life Sciences (CC:CM/LS) (weekly Table of Contents Service), and Social Science Citation Index. Articles also searchable through Social SciSearch, ISI's online database and in ISI's Research Alert current awareness service,* Institute for Scientific Information, 3501 Market Street, Philadelphia, PA 19104-3302 (USA)

- *Expanded Academic Index,* Information Access Company, 362 Lakeside Drive, Forest City, CA 94404

- *Family Life Educator "Abstracts Section,"* ETR Associates, P.O. Box 1830, Santa Cruz, CA 95061-1830

(continued)

- *Family Studies Database (online and CD/ROM)*, National Information Services Corporation, 306 East Baltimore Pike, 2nd Floor, Media, PA 19063

- *Family Violence & Sexual Assault Bulletin,* Family Violence & Sexual Assault Institute, 1121 East South East Loop #323, Suite 130, Tyler, TX 75701

- *Gay & Lesbian Abstracts,* National Information Services Corporation, 306 East Baltimore Pike, 2nd Floor, Media, PA 19063

- *Guide to Social Science & Religion in Periodical Literature,* National Periodical Library, P.O. Box 3278, Clearwater, FL 34630

- *IBZ International Bibliography of Periodical Literature,* Zeller Verlag GmbH & Co., P.O.B. 1949, d-49009 Osnabruck, Germany

- *Index to Periodical Articles Related to Law,* University of Texas, 727 East 26th Street, Austin, TX 78705

- *INTERNET ACCESS (& additional networks) Bulletin Board for Libraries ("BUBL"), coverage of information resources on INTERNET, JANET, and other networks.*
    - JANET X.29: UK.AC.BATH.BUBL or 00006012101300
    - TELNET: BUBL.BATH.AC.UK or 138.38.32.45 login 'bubl'
    - Gopher: BUBL.BATH.AC.UK (138.32.32.45). Port 7070
    - World Wide Web: http: / / www.bubl.bath.ac.uk./BUBL/ home.html
    - NISSWAIS: telnetniss.ac.uk (for the NISS gateway)
  The Andersonian Library, Curran Building, 101 St. James Road, Glasgow G4 ONS, Scotland

- *MasterFILE: updated database from EBSCO Publishing,* 83 Pine Street, Peabody, MA 01960

- *PASCAL, c/o Institute de l'information Scientifique et Technique. Cross-disciplinary electronic database covering the fields of science, technology & medicine. Also available on CD-ROM, and can generate customized retrospective searches. For more information:* INIST/CNRS-Service Gestion des Documents Primaires, 2, allee du Parc de Brabois, F-54514 Vandoeuvre-les-Nancy, Cedex, France [http//www.inist.fr]

- *Periodical Abstracts, Research I (general & basic reference indexing & abstracting data-base from University Microfilms International (UMI), 300 North Zeeb Road, P.O. Box 1346, Ann Arbor, MI 48106-1346),* UMI Data Courier, P.O. Box 32770, Louisville, KY 40232-2770

(continued)

- *Periodical Abstracts, Research II (broad coverage indexing & abstracting data-base from University Microfilms International (UMI), 300 North Zeeb Road, P.O. Box 1346, Ann Arbor, MI 48106-1346),* UMI Data Courier, P.O. Box 32770, Louisville, KY 40232-2770

- *Population Index,* Princeton University Office Population, 21 Prospect Avenue, Princeton, NJ 08544-2091

- *Psychological Abstracts (PsycINFO),* American Psychological Association, P.O. Box 91600, Washington, DC 20090-1600

- *Sage Family Studies Abstracts (SFSA),* Sage Publications, Inc., 2455 Teller Road, Newbury Park, CA 91320

- *Social Planning/Policy & Development Abstracts (SOPODA),* Sociological Abstracts, Inc., P.O. Box 22206, San Diego, CA 92192-0206

- *Social Science Source: coverage of 400 journals in the social sciences area, updated monthly,* EBSCO Publishing, 83 Pine Street, Peabody, MA 01960

- *Social Sciences Index (from Volume 1 & continuing),* The H.W. Wilson Company, 950 University Avenue, Bronx, NY 10452

- *Social Work Abstracts,* National Association of Social Workers, 750 First Street NW, 8th Floor, Washington, DC 20002

- *Sociological Abstracts (SA),* Sociological Abstracts, Inc., P.O. Box 22206, San Diego, CA 92192-0206

- *Special Educational Needs Abstracts,* Carfax Information Systems, P.O. Box 25, Abingdon, Oxfordshire OX14 3UE, United Kingdom

- *Studies on Women Abstracts,* Carfax Publishing Company, P.O. Box 25, Abingdon, Oxfordshire OX14 3UE, United Kingdom

- *Violence and Abuse Abstracts: A Review of Current Literature on Interpersonal Violence (VAA),* Sage Publications, Inc., 2455 Teller Road, Newbury Park, CA 91320

(continued)

SPECIAL BIBLIOGRAPHIC NOTES

related to special journal issues (separates)
and indexing/abstracting

☐ indexing/abstracting services in this list will also cover material in any "separate" that is co-published simultaneously with Haworth's special thematic journal issue or DocuSerial. Indexing/abstracting usually covers material at the article/chapter level.

☐ monographic co-editions are intended for either non-subscribers or libraries which intend to purchase a second copy for their circulating collections.

☐ monographic co-editions are reported to all jobbers/wholesalers/approval plans. The source journal is listed as the "series" to assist the prevention of duplicate purchasing in the same manner utilized for books-in-series.

☐ to facilitate user/access services all indexing/abstracting services are encouraged to utilize the co-indexing entry note indicated at the bottom of the first page of each article/chapter/contribution.

☐ this is intended to assist a library user of any reference tool (whether print, electronic, online, or CD-ROM) to locate the monographic version if the library has purchased this version but not a subscription to the source journal.

☐ individual articles/chapters in any Haworth publication are also available through the Haworth Document Delivery Services (HDDS).

Families and Adoption

CONTENTS

ABOUT THE EDITORS

Harriet E. Gross, PhD, is Professor of Sociology Emerita at Governors State University in University Park, Illinois, where she taught for over 20 years. Recently retired, she continues her research in a longitudinal study of open adoption families. She obtained her doctorate in sociology from the University of Chicago and has researched and written extensively on family issues throughout her career. An early contributing Coeditor of *Marriage & Family Review*, she coedited *Alternatives to Traditional Family Living*, the second volume in this long series. Dr. Gross is now working on a ten-year update of *Work and Family* with Professor Naomi Gerstel of the University of Massachusetts.

Marvin B. Sussman, PhD, is UNIDEL Professor of Human Behavior Emeritus at the College of Human Resources, University of Delaware. He is also a member of the CORE Faculty of the Union Graduate School of Union Institute, Cincinnati, Ohio. A member of many professional organizations, he received the 1980 Ernest W. Burgess Award of the National Council on Family Relations. In 1983, Dr. Sussman was elected to the prestigious Academy of Groves for scholarly contributions to the field, and, in 1984, he was awarded a lifelong membership for services to the Groves Conference on Marriage and the Family. A recipient of the Distinguished Family Award of the Society for the Study of Social Problems (SSSP), he was honored with the Lee Founders Award, the SSSP's highest professional award, in 1992. The author or editor of 30 books and more than 220 articles on family, community, rehabilitation, health and aging, and organizational transformation, Dr. Sussman's contributions to research and education in the family and aging fields were recognized in 1992 with the State of Delaware Gerontological Society Award.

Introduction

Harriet E. Gross
Marvin B. Sussman

Understandably, the literature about adoption has tilted to the professionals who orchestrate, counsel and control the principals involved—with
a clear emphasis on policy directives. However, by the nineties, adoption
practice had responded to changes reflecting greater tolerance for variations in family lifestyles. Not only adoption counselors and parties took
notice of these arrangements; students of family life and the general
public also did. The selections in this edition, the majority of which are
data-based, continue this policy-directed heritage. There is a growing
literature addressing two additional foci: (1) renewed interest in adoption
from researchers in other behavioral disciplines; and (2) research which
challenges traditional adoption practices. There are new circumstances—
including greater tolerance for variation in adoption possibilities.
Together these changes in the practice and study of adoption render
nearly anachronistic yesterday's construction of normative adoption as
closed and involving a "healthy, white infant." The first two articles deal
with the challenge to past and prevailing definitions which required adoption to keep the two sets of birth and adoptive families from being able to
contact or even know very much about each other. The propellants for
adoption which allow and even encourage such contact today in "open
adoptions" began nearly twenty years ago (Sorosky, Baran & Pannor,

Harriet E. Gross is Professor of Sociology Emerita, Governors State University, University Park, Illinois. Marvin B. Sussman is UNIDEL Professor of
Human Behavior Emeritus at the College of Human Resources at the University
of Delaware.

[Haworth co-indexing entry note]: "Introduction." Gross, Harriet E., and Marvin B. Sussman.
Co-published simultaneously in *Marriage & Family Review* (The Haworth Press, Inc.) Vol. 25, No. 1/2,
1997, pp. 1-6; and: *Families and Adoption* (ed: Harriet E. Gross and Marvin B. Sussman) The Haworth
Press, Inc., 1997, pp. 1-6. Single or multiple copies of this article are available for a fee from The Haworth
Document Delivery Service [1-800-342-9678, 9:00 a.m. - 5:00 p.m. (EST). E-mail address:
getinfo@haworth.com].

1

1978). These parallel forces reflected and contributed to the changing adoption marketplace enabling older birth mothers to voice feelings long suffered individually that, when shared, forged group-based appeals for social acknowledgment (Lindsay, 1987; Solinger, 1992). At the same time the changing cultural climate allowed contemporary birth mothers greater leverage in determining the conditions under which they would place their children (McRoy, Grotevant & White, 1988; Reitz & Watson, 1992) and encouraged the children they had placed, now adult adoptees, to begin contesting—as inimical to their civil rights and psychological well-being—the pre-conditions of secrecy and closed records for their own adoptions (Lifton, 1975; Aigner, 1986).

Still another interested party, the social workers who had been and continue to be the official mid-wives of adoption, also added their voice to the controversy surrounding adoption practice (Modell, 1994). Some of these who arranged these earlier adoptions began to listen to the appeals of older birth mothers and to those of inquiring adult adoptees. Their analysis of the reasons for the laws closing records revealed the circumstances surrounding this imposition of legally bound closure and secrecy. They argued it was largely a mid-century development which resulted from a reworking of an earlier but less rigid concern with these requirements. By the late forties, Freudian-inspired constructions of "neurotic" birth mothers and Bowlby's (1969) derivative, influential "bonding" thesis influenced social work ideology—requiring the adoptive mother to cement her "bond" with her adopted infant (Bowlby, 1969). In such a context, there was to be no "interference" from biological family members (Iwanek, 1987; see Watson in this volume about the need to distinguish bonding from attachment).

These mid-century social workers, perhaps defending their relatively young, professional turf from the omnipresent forays of physicians, lawyers and clergy, argued that only they could insure the necessary protection adoptive families needed (Gross, 1991). In the midst of the era when adoptive mothers, particularly, but fathers too, were to act "as if" the child was just like a biological offspring, the threads of social work ideology contributed to the normative tapestry making legal adoption secret and closed. By the early seventies, however, at first only a few but later many more adoption professionals became advocates of change as they came to reject the logic behind these criteria. All of these forces together with national news stories about problematic adoptions focused attention on the controversy over contact between birth and adoptive parents. In this climate, parallel calls to open records of adult adoptees and to allow greater openness in newly forming relationships between birth and adoptive families gained momentum. However, though some adoptions as early as fifteen years ago were "opened," it was not until the nineties that notable empirical research about such arrangements was added to discussions based on insight and speculation from clinical observation. The first article by Cushman, Kalmuss and Namerow (one of two in this volume) examines birth mothers' response to openness. It is particularly valuable because its findings add to the small, but growing, list of studies indicating benefits for birth mothers when they know something about the families with whom they place their children. This study's value also stems from its relative methodological sophistication: a larger than usual sample, control group and longitudinal design. The second article about openness, by Gross, using data from a longitudinal study about families who were early participants to open adoptions, details three patterns that characterize the early years of these families who entered into adoptions intentionally "open"–in the late eighties when, as yet, no other private agency in their locale offered this option. For two of the patterns she describes among these families who had pre-placement training about openness, a basically positive connection develops and endures over time between members of the birth and adoptive families. However, the nature and intensity of the connection can change as the years pass. Openness appears to be a developmental phenomenon that can lead to new definitions and extensions of family ties. The development of involving and satisfying ties between birth and adoptive family members among a small but significant sub-group of the study's original 41 families (Embracers) may result in the creation of lifelong resource exchanges. One example would be where adoptees make college plans on the basis of proximity to either or both families. Another might be their care of elderly relatives from both families. Certainly the bonds these birth and adoptive families are forging extend the possibility of family reciprocities, not typically expected in our society. A new family form is emerging!

Two articles follow about the growing trend to overcome the limitations imposed by the restrictions of closed records. As with the move towards open adoption, they deal with another more prevalent family relationship made possible when adult adoptees and/or birth parents seek each other. Typically called "reunion" the term refers to the contact between an adult adoptee and some members of his/her birth family. Modell points out that the term can mean not only the initial contact, but also subsequent events. A relationship may or may not develop. There has been little systematic research about such developments. Continuing her analysis of kinship ramifications among principals to adoption, Modell extends her analytic eye to these reunion relationships—once again offering the valuable historical and legal background that made her earlier book (1994) so useful. Fraser, who is himself an adult adoptee and trained sociologist, comes to similar conclusions—from a subjective vantage point—about different stages characterizing the post-contact, reunion relationship.

Next, there follow three articles about additional sources of contemporary variation from traditional adoption—called in the field "special needs" adoptions. These vary from the "healthy white infant" prototype and extend understandings of viable adoptions rarely considered just a decade ago. More possibilities are available in response to the dwindling availability of the "preferred" adoptee; increased publicity about the availability of foreign children needing families; and government willingness to help subsidize families who care for developmentally vulnerable or abandoned and neglected children. More and more parents are building families with these children of a race different from their own, or children with disabilities, or from other countries and cultures. Goldberg, also a sociologist and adoptive mother like those in her study, provides a thoughtful discussion of the problems families in the early nineties experienced in adopting Romanian children. Goldberg's analysis is useful not only for these families but also for other prospective adoptive parents and for the professionals who help arrange these foreign adoptions. Such children, from many more countries today, are unable to be cared for by their impoverished biological families. This is often because parents are unsupported by their own governments in their efforts to keep these children. Whatever the reasons for their circumstances, these children will continue to be sought by families from more prosperous and stable countries. Hollingsworth carefully selected from a number of comparable studies and used statistical techniques to compare findings about the controversial issues of identity and self-esteem among transracially/transethnically-adopted children. Her conclusions highlight the complexity of this body of research, the importance of such qualifiers as age, and the need to exercise caution when framing policy-directives about such adoptions. The next article by Hoopes, Alexander and their colleagues addresses another category of adoptions that promises to become more visible. Though the sample is extremely small, this ten-year follow-up of developmentally vulnerable, African-American adoptees and their families indicates that such families can contend successfully with the special problems of such children.

Reflecting the upheaval in adoption work is the call by Daly and Sobol for legal changes that are needed to "catch up" to contemporary practice realities. They discuss the legal issues raised by consent and openness and argue that legislation governing the implications for all parties should be guided by the growing body of available research about these issues. The next article focuses on distinctions and definitions to the developing debate about the implications and consequences of these changes overtaking adoption practice. Watson calls for a more consistent approach to the use of two key concepts, bonding and attachment, associated with adoption. These terms should not be used interchangeably. Clarifying the distinction in their referents, Watson says, can help avoid misconceptions that have added to confusion among birth and adoptive parents. Clinicians and researchers who deal with adoption and fostering can also benefit from this clarification.

Two empirical reports examine the consequences of adoption for birth mothers and for adult adoptees. Though clinicians' assessments of birth mothers have provided useful guideposts, there have been few studies comparing the differences among those who do and do not place their children for adoption. The work of Namerow, Kalmuss and Cushman fills this gap. Their results focus on benefits to young, unmarried women who place their children for adoption as compared to those who opt to parent. Feigelman's article is also based on an understudied comparison between adult adoptees raised in intact two-parent families with their counterparts both in attenuated nuclear families (step-families) and in intact, bio-parent families. His findings suggest that adoptees (especially boys) may experience increased stress during adolescence. Yet, adoptees in their late twenties and early thirties are more similar than not—to young adults raised in conventional families—on most indices of personal accomplishment and marital stability.

We end this volume with a response by a well-known early adoption researcher to a widely discussed 1994 research report from the Search Institute in Minneapolis, Minnesota. David Kirk takes issue with this report's implication that "all is well with present-day adoption." He argues that not only does this contradict the findings of much previous research, but also the claim rests on questionable research methods. He faults the search Institute's contention on two specific counts: (a) inappropriate comparisons of their finding with Kirk's own by-now-classic formulation of adoptive families' "acknowledgment-of-difference" dynamic, and (b) the Institute's difficult-to-explain lack of attention to its earlier, more critical findings about adoption consequences. This carefully reasoned critique deserves close attention. Yet, in the last analysis, the import of the argument between critics like Kirk and the Search Institute authors hinges on how data inform what we want to know about adoptees and their families. Kirk's argument concerns not only data but also values that enter into the interpretation of data. Much as we want reassurance about the outcome of legally contrived families, we cannot eliminate their distinctiveness. Even if future studies were to confirm a lessening of stigma attached to adoption, that itself would not indicate a lessening of cultural emphasis on procreation. Thus Kirk's critique suggests that we must not lightly abandon what the bulk of other research and clinical impressions about adoption have argued for—sensitivity to the special issues that adoption presents in a culture like ours that puts a premium on biological family formation. Above all, this critique argues that the question of whether adoption presents a lower threshold of problems for adoptees remains open.

REFERENCES

Aigner, Hal J., Jr. (1986) *Adoption in America: Coming of Age.* Greenbrae, CA: Paradigm Press.

Bowlby, John. (1969) *Attachment and Loss Vol. I: Attachment.* New York: Basic Books.

Gross, Harriet E. (1991) "Secrecy in Adoption: Its History and Implications for Open Adoption." Paper presented to the 86th Annual Meetings of the American Sociological Association, Section on Sociology of the Family, Cincinnati, OH.

Iwanek, M. (1987) *A Study of Open Adoption Placements.* 14 Emerson Street, Petone, New Zealand.

Lindsay, Jeanne W. (1987) *Open Adoption: A Caring Option.* Buena Park, CA: Morning Glory Press.

McRoy, R., Grotevant, H. & White, K. (1988) *Openness in Adoption: New Practices, New Issues.* Westport, CT: Praeger Publications.

Modell, Judith. (1994) *Kinship with Strangers: Adoption and Interpretations of Kinship in American Culture.* Berkeley, CA: University of California.

Reitz, Miriam & Kenneth W. Watson. (1992) *Adoption and the Family System.* New York: Guilford.

Solinger, Rickie. (1992) *Wake Up Little Susie: Single Pregnancy and Race Before Roe v. Wade.* New York: Routledge.

Sorosky, A., Baran A. & Pannor, R. (1978) *The Adoption Triangle.* New York: Anchor Press.

Openness in Adoption: Experiences and Social Psychological Outcomes Among Birth Mothers

Linda F. Cushman
Debra Kalmuss
Pearila Brickner Namerow

SUMMARY. This article describes the experiences of young, American birth mothers with regard to openness in adoption process and arrangement. Generally, larger proportions of the sample have experienced moderate, or semi-open, arrangements than those involving direct contact with the adoptive family. The associations between these experiences and a series of social psychological outcomes are examined at four years post-relinquishment. The data reveal that features of open adoption, e.g., visiting/phoning the adoptive family, have strong associations with long-term, positive outcomes for birth mothers. Perhaps equally important is the finding that several moderately open features which do not require direct or ongoing contact between birth mothers and adoptive families, e.g., birth mothers having a role in choosing the adoptive couple, are also strongly associated

Linda F. Cushman is Assistant Professor of Public Health, Debra Kalmuss is Associate Professor of Public Health, and Pearila Brickner Namerow is Associate Professor of Public Health, in the Center for Population and Family Health at the Columbia University School of Public Health.

This research was supported by Grants APR-000942 and APR-000960 from the Office of Population Affairs, U.S. Department of Health and Human Services.

[Haworth co-indexing entry note]: "Openness in Adoption: Experiences and Social Psychological Outcomes Among Birth Mothers." Cushman, Linda F., Debra Kalmuss, and Pearila Brickner Namerow. Co-published simultaneously in *Marriage & Family Review* (The Haworth Press, Inc.) Vol. 25, No. 1/2, 1997, pp. 7-18; and: *Families and Adoption* (ed: Harriet E. Gross and Marvin B. Sussman) The Haworth Press, Inc., 1997, pp. 7-18. Single or multiple copies of this article are available for a fee from The Haworth Document Delivery Service [1-800-342-9678, 9:00 a.m. - 5:00 p.m. (EST). E-mail address: getinfo@haworth.com].

7

with positive outcomes. Policy implications are discussed. *[Article copies available for a fee from The Haworth Document Delivery Service: 1-800-342-9678. E-mail address: getinfo@haworth.com]*

Historically, adoptions in the United States have been "closed," characterized by sealed legal records and no contact between birth parents and adoptive families. During the past several decades this approach has gradually shifted to include arrangements which are more "open." As described in an earlier article, (Cushman, Kalmuss, & Namerow, 1993) openness in adoption is now characterized by a spectrum of practices, including: the birth mother helping to choose, and perhaps meeting, the adoptive couple prior to the child's birth; the adoptive family providing pictures and updates about the child; ongoing contact between the birth mother and the adoptive family through an agency or personally; and the accessibility of nonidentifying or identifying information regarding the birth mother, adoptive couple, and adoptee. Thus, today, adoption is characterized by a continuum of processes and arrangements. Moderately or semi-open adoptions incorporate a varying number of the aforementioned characteristics, but usually exclude the exchange of identifying information, and ongoing personal contact between birth parent and adoptive family (McRoy, Grotevant & White, 1988). These latter features are the defining characteristics of fully open adoption (Lindsay, 1987; Pannor & Baran, 1984).

Despite the consistent trend toward more openness in adoption, debate continues regarding the merits of such practices. Some professionals advocate completely open arrangements, others continue to favor closed adoption, and still others recommend the moderate, semi-open approach which allows the exchange of some information, and perhaps some contact, between birth parents and adoptive families, while still safeguarding the privacy rights of each party involved (Sachdev, 1991).

Research has traditionally focused on the structure and functioning of the adoptive family (Kirk, 1964; McWhinnie, 1967; Richmond, 1957; Schechter et al., 1964). Much of the research in the area of open adoption has maintained this focus (Ryburn, 1994), although several accounts document that openness in adoption does have positive consequences for birth mothers (Lindsay, 1987; McRoy, Grotevant, & White, 1988). These in-depth interviews with birth mothers offer rich, detailed data regarding the experience of openness in adoption from the birth mothers' viewpoint. Larger, quantitative studies regarding the impact of openness in adoption on birth mothers are scant. One study conducted with a sample of birth mothers in New Zealand (Field, 1991) found that those who had some information about the child they relinquished had significantly better psychological well-being than those who did not have access to information. Moreover, birth mothers who had had "reunions" with their adopted children felt more positively about the adoption than did others. Other recent studies have examined the impact of placing an infant for adoption on a variety of sociodemographic and social psychological outcomes for birth mothers (Kalmuss et al., 1992; McLaughlin, Manninen, & Winges, 1988; McLaughlin et al., 1988). However, these investigations do not include openness in the adoption arrangement as a predictive variable. Thus, despite a number of recent inquiries regarding birth mothers' well-being after placing a child for adoption, and a growing body of literature regarding the forms and advantages of open adoption, there have been few empirical investigations linking these two factors. Specifically, we lack systematic data which examine the relationship between openness in adoption and social psychological outcomes for birth mothers.

This article describes the experiences of 171 young, American birth mothers who placed an infant for adoption approximately five years ago, and describes whether these experiences reflect openness in adoption processes and arrangements. We will focus on two components of the adoption process: helping to choose, and meeting the adoptive couple. Four features of openness in the adoption arrangement are examined: (1) having the ability to get information about the child/family through an agency; (2) receiving pictures/updates regarding the adopted child; (3) being able to contact the adoptive family directly; and (4) having visited or talked on the phone with the adoptive family since placement. Additionally, we explore the attitudes of women who did not have these experiences to assess whether they wish that they did, or believe that the more closed processes and arrangements which they experienced suited their needs. Finally, we will assess the relationships between these specific features of openness in adoption process and arrangement, and several social psychological outcomes for the birth mothers at four years postbirth. These outcomes include current levels of: grief, regret regarding the adoption decision, worry about the child, sadness, relief, and feeling "at peace" with the adoption decision.

METHOD AND SAMPLE

The data for this article were gathered as part of a longitudinal study of the determinants and consequences of placing an infant for adoption versus parenting among unmarried, adolescent women. The study design for the larger project called for three rounds of interviews with pregnant adolescents: one during the third trimester of pregnancy, one at approximately six months post-birth, and one when the child was approximately four years of age. Women planning to parent their babies, as well as those planning to place, were recruited for the larger project. This article focuses on those who placed their infants for adoption.

Since the rate of relinquishment is only 5-6% among pregnant teenagers, generating a sizeable sample of placers was a significant methodological challenge. Working with the National Committee on Adoption, we identified sites in 13 states, aiming for those that served the largest number of pregnant teens. Twenty-three maternity residences, some of which also functioned as adoption agencies or were affiliated with agencies, and seven non-residential agencies, were ultimately recruited as data collection sites for young women planning to place their babies.

In order to be eligible to participate in the study, the respondents had to be age 21 years or younger, and unmarried at the time of the first interview. We recruited only African-American and white women because there would not have been an ample number of Hispanic respondents to allow for three-way race/ethnic comparisons in analyses. At Round 1, we recruited 272 women who were planning to place their babies for adoption. At Round 2 (six months post-birth), only 215 had actually placed their babies *and* were located for follow-up. At Round 3, 171 (80%) of those who had placed and were interviewed at Round 2 were recontacted and interviewed again for the four year follow-up.

As shown in Table 1, the mean age of the sample is now 22.9 years. Reflecting both the comparatively low rate of placement among African-American versus white teens (Kalmuss, 1992), and the racial composition of the states where many maternity residences were located, ninety-four percent of the sample is white, and 6% is African-American. Four years post-birth, the vast majority of women (92%) have completed high school or received a GED; interestingly, however, small proportions have completed any degree beyond high school. Approximately half the sample (54%) are currently working for pay; 15% have received public assistance (AFDC/welfare) since they placed their child for adoption.

By design, only unmarried women were recruited into the study at Round 1. Four years later, 60% remain single, 30% are married, and a small proportion (10%) are separated, divorced, or widowed. Forty percent of the sample have been pregnant at some time since placing the referent child for adoption, and 32% have experienced one or more live births. Of those women who have had one or more live births since placing the referent child, only two women report having placed a subsequent child for adoption.

TABLE 1. Characteristics of Sample at Four-Year Follow-Up
(N = 171)

Characteristics	Percent
Age	
Under 21 years	16
21-23 years	55
24+ years	29
(Mean = 22.9)	
Race	
White	94
African-American	6
Education	
Less than high school	8
High school graduate/GED	79
Associates degree	9
Bachelors degree	4
Socioeconomic status	
Currently working for pay	54
Received AFDC/welfare since placement	15
Marital status	
Currently married	30
Separated/divorced/widowed	10
Never married	60
Pregnancy and birth history	
Pregnancy since placement	40
Live birth since referent date	32
Placed subsequent child for adoption since referent date	1
Lived in a residence	91

FINDINGS

Adoption Experiences. Table 2 summarizes the experiences of the sample with regard to six specific features of the adoption process and current arrangement. Overall, their experiences reflect the shift toward more openness in adoption. For example, more than two-thirds of the sample (69%) helped choose the couple who ultimately adopted their baby. Fre-

TABLE 2. Proportion of the Sample Experiencing Features of Openness in Adoption Process/Arrangement
(N = 171)

Characteristics	Percent
Helped choose adoptive couple	69
Met adoptive couple	28
Met adoptive couple pre-birth	14
Can obtain information through agency	52
Has received letters/pictures about child	62
Has received letters/pictures about child in the past year	28
Can contact adoptive family directly	15
Has phoned/visited since placement	12

quently, this was accomplished by the birth mother choosing from among several portfolios selected by the agency in accord with her stated preferences, e.g., the couple's religion or interests. Moreover, a smaller but non-trivial proportion of the sample (28%) have met the adoptive couple, and 14% met them prior to giving birth.

Similarly, 62% of the birth mothers report that they have received letters or pictures regarding the child since the adoption took place, and 28% have received letters or pictures during the past year. When asked if, currently, they could obtain information regarding the child and/or family through an agency or residence, about half, 52%, said that they could, 31% could not, and 18% didn't know if this is possible (not shown). Only 12% of the sample have actually visited or talked on the phone with the adoptive family since placement; 9% have visited or talked on the phone during the past year (not shown on table). Fifteen percent report that they could contact the adoptive family directly at this point in time.

One important aim of this study is to document the *desire* for these arrangements among birth mothers who have not experienced them. Overall, desire for moderately open adoption is more prevalent than desire for completely open terms. For example, three-quarters (75%) of birth mothers who have not received letters or pictures regarding the adopted child state that they would like to receive them. Similarly, the vast majority (85%) of those who are not currently able to obtain information through an agency, state that they would like to have that option. In contrast, less than half (45%) of those who cannot contact the adoptive family directly report that they would like to be able to do so for the adoptive *parents*, and a smaller group (19%) say that they would like to be able to have direct contact with the adopted *child*. About half (51%) of those who never met the adoptive couple wish that they had done so prior to the adoption.

Social Psychological Outcomes. We focused on six social psychological variables related to the birth mothers' feelings regarding placing the baby for adoption: grief, regret regarding the adoption decision, worry about the baby, sadness, relief, and the extent to which respondents feel "at peace" regarding the adoption decision. Measures were constructed to assess respondents' current level of feeling in each area using the Likert-type response categories of "a lot," "some," "a little," or "none." For each item a higher score indicates a higher level of feeling.

Table 3 summarizes the birth mothers' responses to these items. Overall, they are faring well at four years post-relinquishment. The majority of the sample report that they are currently experiencing low levels, i.e., "none" or "a little," grief, regret, worry, and sadness, and high levels, i.e., "a lot" or "some," relief and peace regarding the adoption decision. Conversely, relatively few birth mothers feel "a lot" of grief, regret, worry, and sadness, and report only minimal, i.e., "a little" or "no," relief and peace at this point in time.

Bivariate Analysis. Table 4 presents the mean scores on each outcome variable for those who have or not experienced each specific feature of

TABLE 3. Proportion of Sample Reporting Each Level of Six Social Psychological Outcomes

(N = 171)

	Grief	Regret	Worry	Sadness	Relief	Peace
A lot	9	11	9	6	59	74
Some	7	11	17	10	27	11
A little	29	13	25	28	10	6
None	55	65	49	56	4	9
Total Percent	100	100	100	100	100	100

TABLE 4. Mean Scores on Six Social Psychological Outcomes

	Grief	Regret	Worry	Sadness	Relief	Peace
Helped choose adoptive couple						
Yes	1.60*	1.52**	1.72**	1.55**	3.51**	3.63***
No	1.94	2.00	2.15	1.94	3.16	3.32
Met adoptive couple[a]						
Yes	1.65	1.72	1.61*	1.68	3.58***	3.48
No	1.73	1.66	1.98	1.68	3.32	3.54
Has received letters/pictures about child						
Yes	1.69	1.65	1.71*	1.68	3.48***	3.52
No	1.75	1.70	2.10	1.67	3.26	3.55
Can access information through agency						
Yes	1.69	1.70	1.81	1.74	3.47***	3.57
No	1.80	1.68	2.02	1.75	3.16	3.32
Can contact adoptive family directly						
Yes	1.72	1.72	1.52***	1.52	3.48	3.64
No	1.71	1.67	1.92	1.70	3.38	3.51
Has phoned/visited since placement						
Yes	1.42*	1.31*	1.36**	1.52	3.68*	3.88**
No	1.73	1.69	1.89	1.71	3.36	3.50
Has phoned/visited in past year						
Yes	1.40	1.26*	1.33**	1.60	3.60	3.86**
No	1.73	1.70	1.89	1.70	3.37	3.51

*p ≤ .05   **p ≤ .01   ***p = .06-.09

[a]Excludes four birth mothers who have visited baby in past year.

openness in the adoption process. The most notable pattern emerging from the data is the association between helping to choose the adoptive couple prior to relinquishment, and positive social psychological outcomes for birth mothers four years later. Without exception, those who had a role in choosing the couple report lower levels of grief, regret, worry, and sadness, and higher levels of relief and peace, than do their counterparts who did not have this opportunity.

Meeting the adoptive couple is the second process variable included in the analysis and is conceptualized as part of the adoption process if the birth mother meets them either prior to the baby's birth, or at some point between the birth and actual placement. Of those who reported ever meeting the adoptive couple, about half (48%) said that they did so prior to their baby's birth. Unfortunately, there are no data on what proportion met between the birth and actual placement, and what proportion got together subsequent to relinquishment. It is possible, however, that a minority of those who met the adoptive couple did so at some point after the actual placement. Because we intended this variable to represent simply meeting the couple, rather than establishing a relationship with them, we have excluded scores from the small number of women who have visited with the adoptive family during the past year.

Meeting the adoptive couple has a significant association with far fewer outcomes than the more moderate feature of choosing the couple. Nonetheless, those who have met the couple report lower levels of worry, and slightly more relief, than those who have not met them. Among respondents who have met the adoptive couple, there are no differences between those who did so prior to birth, and those who did so at a later point, on any of the social psychological outcomes (not shown).

Other moderately open characteristics of adoption arrangements are similarly associated with psychological outcomes. Those who have received letters and/or pictures report significantly lower levels of worry, and slightly higher levels of relief, than do birth mothers who have not received such updates. Again, there are no significant differences in mean outcome scores between those who have received letters or pictures during the past year, and those who received them at an earlier point post-relinquishment (not shown). Those who can currently get information through an agency also report slightly more relief than others, but do not score differently on the other outcomes than do their counterparts who cannot access information. Interestingly, this is true even among the subgroup of the sample who have never received letters or pictures (not shown). Overall, the associations between these two features of the adoption arrangement and the other social psychological outcomes are in the established direction, but do not reach statistical significance.

Finally, the most open features of adoption arrangements are associated with several positive outcomes for birth mothers. Because so few respondents have visited with the adoptive families since relinquishment (N = 12), and even fewer have done so within the past year (N = 4), we combined visiting and talking by phone into a single variable at each time period. Having ever visited or talked on the phone post-relinquishment is strongly associated with lower levels of grief, regret and worry, and greater feelings of relief and peace regarding the adoption. Having done so in the past year is similarly associated with lower levels of regret and worry, and greater feelings of peace. Interestingly, having the ability to contact the adoptive family directly (N = 25) approximates significance only for level of worry.

DISCUSSION

The experiences of the birth mothers in this study clearly reflect increased exposure to several features of more open adoption process and arrangement. As might be expected, a greater proportion have experienced moderately or semi-open features, e.g., helping to choose the adoptive couple, or receiving letters or pictures, than those which allow for direct contact with the adoptive family, i.e., meeting the couple, visiting or phoning the family. Nonetheless, the experiences of the birth mothers in this study stand in contrast, overall, to the completely closed arrangements experienced by young birth mothers even a generation ago (Chessler, 1988; Lifton, 1979; Sorosky et al., 1978).

Within the context of the current debate regarding open adoption, several policy-relevant findings emerge from the data. First, the vast majority of birth mothers desire moderately open adoption experiences, but this proportion decreases with movement toward the completely open end of the adoption spectrum. Three quarters of those who have never received letters or pictures would like to do so; about half of those who never met the adoptive couple report that they would have liked to do so before relinquishing the child, and only 19% of those who cannot do so would like to have direct contact with the adoptive child. In summary, most birth mothers do not necessarily desire a completely open arrangement, but rather some connection to or information about the child.

Second, moderately open features in both the adoption process and arrangement are associated with positive, long-term social psychological outcomes for birth mothers. This is most apparent in observing differences between those who did and did not play a role in choosing the adoptive couple. On virtually every outcome measure, birth mothers who did help to choose the couple have more positive scores than those who did not. A plausible reason for this is that in helping to choose the couple who will adopt her baby, a birth mother is given some measure of *control* over the baby's destiny. From a policy perspective, giving birth mothers this opportunity is a low cost, easily implemented strategy that does not mandate direct contact between birth mothers and adoptive parents. Much of the information relevant to birth mothers is collected as a matter of routine from potential adoptive couples by agencies, and can be made accessible to birth mothers on an unidentified basis.

The other moderately open features examined show limited associations with positive outcomes for birth mothers. Meeting the adoptive couple and receiving updates regarding the child are associated with reduced levels of worry and increased levels of relief. These conditions offer important "first-hand" information to birth mothers. In meeting the adoptive couple a birth mother can establish that the adoptive parents exist, and determine if they are loving/caring individuals, and want to be the parents of her child. In receiving letters and pictures, a birth mother has "proof" that the child is well and thriving. Both of these are likely to reduce worry, and increase positive feelings regarding having placed the baby. There are no other differences between those who have and have not had these moderately open experiences. Moreover, simply having the ability to access information through an agency is not particularly beneficial.

Finally, the bivariate data indicate that extremely open arrangements are associated with several positive social psychological outcomes for birth mothers. Those who have visited or talked on the phone with the adoptive family at any time post-relinquishment report lower levels of grief, regret, and worry, and higher levels of relief and peace with the adoption decision, than do other birth mothers. Since the proportion of the sample experiencing these arrangements is quite small (12%), these findings are viewed as preliminary, and generalizations are inappropriate. Additional empirical studies incorporating larger samples of birth mothers are essential. The ability to contact the adoptive family directly does not have similar associations with the outcome variables: the benefit is accrued through actual, rather than potential, contact. This pattern is similar to, but stronger than, that observed earlier for the more moderate feature of being able to access information through an agency. In each case, the benefit of actually having the experience is greater than simply having the ability to do so.

CONCLUSION

In conclusion, the experiences of the birth mothers in this study reflect a shift toward more openness in both adoption process and arrangement. In general, the majority of birth mothers report moderately open experiences, while a minority report experiences reflective of completely open adoption. Overall, the birth mothers report low levels of grief, regret, worry, and sadness, and high levels of relief and feelings of peace regarding the placement decision, at four years post-relinquishment.

The findings have implications for the development and evaluation of open adoption policies. First, the data clearly suggest that very open practices can and do benefit birth mothers across a variety of social psychological outcomes. As such, the data offer preliminary support for policies designed to encourage open adoption, at least from the perspective of birth mothers' well-being. Equally important, however, is the observation that moderately open features, particularly the easily implemented practice of allowing birth mothers to help choose the couple who will ultimately adopt their babies, are also associated with positive, long-term outcomes for birth mothers. Such features require minimal, if any, direct contact between adoptive families and birth mothers, and therefore represent a realistic "middle-ground" which can still offer direct benefit to birth mothers.

REFERENCES

Chessler, P. (1988). *Sacred Bond, The Legacy of Baby M* New York: Random House.

Cushman, L.F., Kalmuss, D., & Namerow, P.B. (1993). Placing an infant for adoption: The experiences of young birthmothers. *Social Work* 38(3):264-72.

Field, J. (1991). Views of New Zealand birth mothers on search and reunion. In Mullender A. (Ed.). *Open Adoption: The Philosophy and the Practice* London: BAAF.

Kalmuss, D. (1992). Adoption and Black teenagers: The viability of a pregnancy resolution strategy. *Journal of Marriage and the Family* 54:485-495.

Kalmuss D., Namerow, P.B., & Bauer, U. (1992). Short-term consequences of parenting versus adoption among young unmarried women. *Journal of Marriage and the Family* 54:80-90.

Kirk, D. (1964). *Shared Fate* New York: The Free Press.

Lifton, B.J. (1979). *Lost and Found* New York: The Dial Press.

Lindsay, J.W. (1987). *Open Adoption: A Caring Option* Buena Park, CA: Morning Glory Press.

McLaughlin, S.D., Manninen, D.L., & Winges, L.D. (1988). Do adolescents who relinquish their children fare better or worse than those who raise them? *Family Planning Perspectives* 20(1):25-32.

McLaughlin, S.D., Pearce, S.E., Manninen, D.L., & Winges. L.D. (1988). To parent or relinquish: Consequences for adolescent mothers. *Social Work* 33(4):320-324.

McRoy, R.G., Grotevant, H.D., & White, K.L. (1988). *Openness in Adoption: New Practices New Issues* New York: Praeger.

McWhinnie, A.M. (1967). *Adopted Children and How They Grow Up* London: Routledge & Kegan Paul.

Pannor, R., & Baran, A. (1984). Open adoption as standard practice. *Child Welfare* 63(3):245-250.

Richmond, J.B. (1957). Some psychological considerations in adoption practice. *American Academy of Pediatrics Proceedings* 20:377-382.

Ryburn, M. (1994). *Open Adoption: Research, Theory and Practice* Aldershot: Avebury/Ashgate.

Sachdev, P. (1991). Achieving openness in adoption: Some critical issues in policy formulation. *American Journal of Orthopsychiatry* 6(2):241-249.

Schechter, M.D., Carlson, P., Simmons, J., & Work, H. (1964). Emotional problems in the adoptee. *Archives of General Psychiatry* pp. 109-118.

Sorosky, A.D., Baran, A., & Pannor, R. (1978). *The Adoption Triangle* Garden City, New York: Anchor Press/Doubleday.

Variants of Open Adoptions: The Early Years

Harriet E. Gross

SUMMARY. This analysis begins with the argument that conceptual ambiguity and related measurement inconsistencies have surfaced in the growing number of studies about open adoption–because the term subsumes a range of possibilities of contact between birth and adoptive families, as well as other sources of variation which affect the developing post-placement relationship between members of these two families. It then turns to the first report from a longitudinal study of adoptive (n = 41) and associated birth parents (n = 26) based on initial face-to-face (within six months of the placement); subsequent follow-up (telephone) interviews (18 months to two years post-placement) with these families and observations from over three years of fieldwork in the private agency which arranged these adoptions. Three post-placement patterns are identified and distinguished: Rejecters, Acceptors and Embracers. The paper concludes with a discussion about enabling conditions for successful post-placement openness. *[Article copies available for a fee from The Haworth Document Delivery Service: 1-800-342-9678. E-mail address: getinfo@ haworth.com]*

Predictably, as the frequency of self-described "open adoption" becomes more commonplace, there is more popular familiarity with the

Harriet E. Gross is Professor of Sociology Emerita, Governors State University, University Park, IL.

The author thanks the staff of Open Arms of Lutheran Social Services of Illinois and the birth and adoptive families who have contributed to and continuously supported this research.

[Haworth co-indexing entry note]: "Variants of Open Adoptions: The Early Years." Gross, Harriet E. Co-published simultaneously in *Marriage & Family Review* (The Haworth Press, Inc.) Vol. 25, No. 1/2, 1997, pp. 19-42; and: *Families and Adoption* (ed: Harriet E. Gross and Marvin B. Sussman) The Haworth Press, Inc., 1997, pp. 19-42. Single or multiple copies of this article are available for a fee from The Haworth Document Delivery Service [1-800-342-9678, 9:00 a.m. - 5:00 p.m. (EST). E-mail address: getinfo@haworth.com].

term, if not complete comprehension of what it actually involves (Rompf, 1993; Soparkar, Demick, Levin, & Warner, 1988). Contributing to this greater awareness are the several films and television programs dealing with openness, and the media celebration of contested adoptions in the early nineties. Such focus makes it more likely that even those not personally affected, will learn more about adoption and the possibility of openness.

Yet this greater recognition of the term "open adoption" may actually obscure differentiation among, and the variety of arrangements between, birth and adoptive families so designated. As recently as a decade ago, and still to many lay persons and professionals alike, a typical open adoption implied the exchange of some non-identifying information between the birth and adoptive families and/or some direct contact before or at place-ment. But what has actually developed and come under the descriptor, "open adoption" is a continuum of degrees of relationship before and/or after the child's placement between the birth and adoptive families. Open-ness can mean minimal possibilities for a relationship at one end of this continuum, but can also designate frequent on-going contact and connec-tion at the other end.

Today, adoption professionals writing about adoption and its openness option are beginning to acknowledge this variation which modifiers such as "agency-mediated," "full disclosure" and "on-going contact" indi-cate. These modifiers reflect professionals' observation of the actual con-nections developing between the two families. Because, however, there have been few studies focused on distinctions in the defining dimensions, that is on the variation in those connections, much of the early nineties' discussion of openness (Bartholet, 1993; Smith-Pliner & Siegal, 1992; Reitz & Watson, 1992; Watkins & Fisher, 1993; Modell, 1994) could not use empirical results about openness variation as its basis.

The fast-moving developments among those participating in adoptions characterized as "open," in conjunction with non-comparable operation-alizations and inconsistencies found in early research, reported below, drive the need for the conceptual clarification which typically follows a construct's original invocation. In this paper I review research about open-ness variation and argue for the need to distinguish its defining dimensions and its logical status—as dependent or independent variable. Then I present results from my on-going longitudinal study that distinguishes some open-ness antecedents and consequences.

LITERATURE REVIEW

Despite the nearly two decade old debate among adoption professionals about the implications of open adoption, empirical research surfaced only recently and is still limited to fewer than a dozen studies, which focused mainly on post-placement satisfaction with the arrangement. Gross (1993) reviewed the earliest studies, before a discussion of her own results from a survey of adoptive parents from a private agency–all of whom had some degree of pre-placement openness and a smaller group who were in the early years of post-placement openness, mostly by phone or letter or through agency mediation. She also discussed early findings from another sample from the same agency of birth/adoptive parent counterparts which are the basis of her on-going, longitudinal study of openness. From the review and her own data she reported that most adoptive parents involved in infant adoptions with some degree of openness, express general satisfaction with openness–though they perceive some problems as well. Birth parents (mainly mothers) were also basically satisfied–even grateful for the openness, but were more likely, during the first few months after placement, to be still mindful of the pain of having placed their child. Since that review another pilot study (Demick, 1993) comparing 15 adoptive couples in closed and open infant adoptions also measured more positive feelings, "inner peace" and "empowerment," among adoptive parents in open adoptions.

Since the samples in all but one of these studies are small and most of these small-scale studies are limited to cross-sectional analysis, the corroborative results from the large-scale longitudinal study among them (Berry, 1993) add weight to this largely positive evaluation of openness. Among the frequently cited benefits mentioned are: biological parents' knowledge that their child is being loved and cared for; and adoptive parents' freedom from fear of the unknown and access to information important to their child.

Problems arise, however, in interpreting exactly what these positive outcomes (i.e., "satisfactions" and "advantages") indicate because of the lack of specificity in the definition and measurement of openness. Differing conceptual and operational definitions of openness make comparisons difficult among the few studies that have dealt with its variation.[1] Even when researchers acknowledge that the term "openness"–undifferentiated–obscures differences in the preconditions of, and subsequent contact between, birth and adoptive family members, they have not identified and catalogued the variation in ways conditions of contact have been operationalized. Operationalization consistency, from one study to another, has not been a research focus. In effect, these kinds of variation have not been analyzed, in contrast to having been identified, as variables in their own right. Among such variables are: availability of pre-placement counseling about openness to both sets of parents; type of adoptee (i.e., infant, older child, special needs, relative); private or agency assisted; time of contact relative to placement (i.e., pre/post/on-going); directness of contact (i.e., phone/mail/face-to-face); fully-identified vs. agency mediated; as well as incidence and frequency of post-placement contact among which members of each family.

So, for example, among the earlier studies, Belbas (1987) and McRoy, Grotevant, and White (1988) did distinguish directness and frequency of contact, presumably post-placement, but not so specified, while Demick (1993) defined openness in terms of pre-placement contact only. Demick's definition of openness, then, implies a significantly different referent from openness which includes the possibility of on-going, post-placement mediated or direct contact.[2] Again, Belbas (1987) and Berry's (1993) work suggests that greater and personal contact (presumably some pre- and some initial post-placement) between birth and adoptive families reduces adoptive families' fears. But McRoy et al. (1988) concluded that adoptive families fared better in "semi-open" relationships, i.e., less personal, post-placement contact. Belbas (1987) and Berry (1993) related openness consequences, e.g., comfort levels, to such antecedents as adoption auspices, e.g., private or public agencies; directness of contact (face-to-face vs. phone and mail); and Etter (1993) reported the positive effect of prior third-party, mediated agreements between birth and adoptive parents.[3] The different foci of these early studies, then, already suggested the need for distinguishing among the pre-conditions of, and the different operationalizations of, what was being studied under the rubric of "openness."

More recent publications have continued to differentiate specific aspects of openness, but they have not addressed ways in which their operationalizations compared to earlier work. Grotevant et al. (1994) found greater benefits for adoptive parents (they studied birth parents, too, but this report focuses on the former) in relationships with post-placement, on-going contact. Their analysis of several adoption-related measures confirms the importance of (a) recognizing post-placement openness as a process, usually begun in pre-placement; (b) which can develop into greater degrees of contact, including on-going, fully-disclosed openness, with (c) higher levels of positive consequences for adoptive parents in these compared to either confidential or on-going, mediated adoptions. In fact, they report the highest sense of "strong permanence" of the adoption and the lowest degree of fear that birth parents will want to reclaim among both adoptive parents in on-going, fully-disclosed adoptions (Grotevant, McRoy, Elde & Fravel, 1994:139-140).

An even more recent report highlights the value of distinctions among pre-placement antecedents and post-placement consequences. Cushman,

Kalmuss and Namerow (1997 in this volume) in a relatively rare discussion of birth mothers involved in varying pre- and post-placement arrangements distinguish antecedents, e.g., pre-placement opportunity to meet and/or choose adoptive parents, and post-placement consequences, e.g., desire for and frequency of post-placement contact. Though only a small proportion of these birthmothers (12%) had post-placement contact, the authors report over-all greater well-being among those with more rather than less pre-placement involvement, especially the ability to have chosen the adoptive family, and the possibility of, as well as, actual post-placement contact with them.

Despite the fact that these studies reflect sensitivity to the need to differentiate among the referents of pre- and post-placement openness, the variety of operationalizations among them make it difficult to compare results. Still, another source of non-comparability of openness measurement and consequences may complicate interpretations from Berry's large-scale, longitudinal study of all types of adoption in 1989 in the state of California. While this important analysis is likely to yield otherwise unattainable comparisons, conclusions about openness promise to be complicated. This is because openness here does not attend to its very possibly different meanings to different types of adoptees. The fact that openness in this study is defined so as to compare contact in older children adoptions, often with more problematic histories (e.g., previously foster placements, relative and/or special needs), with contact in infant adoptions means that "having had contact," or presumably pre-placement contact, but frequency unspecified, is what operationalizes openness in such comparisons.[4]

The ambiguity this definition and measurement variation produces is avoidable. Specifying and disaggregating (1) openness antecedents, what preceded the placement, from (2) openness outcomes, what happens in open relationships, and identifying effects, (3) on individual members of each family as these relationships endure over time will clarify analysis. We can anticipate that variation in the quality of the developing openness relationship (consequences) will reflect variation in such antecedent dimensions of openness, e.g., availability of counseling about openness, involvement of adoptive parents in the birthmother's pregnancy experience, their presence at the child's birth, and the opportunity to have met pre-placement with other members of the birth family. In turn, variation in post-placement, on-going openness (e.g., directness, frequency, etc.) will be both effect of, and contributor to the extension of the openness relationship, that is, its continuance and level of intensity.

As is often the case in human relationships what is "effect" from one perspective is "cause" from another. We expect interaction between effect and consequence—the operation of a feedback mechanism—in developmental or processual relationships. Researchers of openness will no doubt be well repaid for tuning into the various dimensions and logical status of contact between birth and adoptive family members. We must attend to the reality that the quality of the relationship between the two families will be situated in specific historical circumstance as the child grows and all involved contribute to the construction of their on-going relationship.

METHODOLOGY

This research continues an on-going longitudinal study of 41 families from the Chicago metropolitan region who adopted infants (mostly shortly after birth) through a private child welfare agency. In 1989 when I initiated this study, the agency was one of a handful nationally which in the mid-to-late eighties had begun to include as an option the possibility of contact between the two families. This sample includes all the domestic, infant (37 Caucasian; 3 bi-racial; 1 African-American) adoptions from the fall of 1989 to mid-year 1993, designated as "open." Such designation by the agency indicated that at a minimum there had been at least one pre-placement, face-to-face meeting of a birth parent and the adoptive parents and the exchange of non-identifying (at least) information and some level of post-placement contact had been agreed to as well. Those actually included in the sample all had some pre-placement and some post-placement contact. The data come from interviews of about one and a half hours (taped and transcribed) with the adoptive parents (Caucasian 37; bi-racial 4) in their homes, but sometimes in restaurants or other meeting places, before the child's first birthday. In addition, for two years I attended weekly staff and all scheduled support group meetings. My field notes from these observations of the staff's evolving position on openness and reactions of pre- and post-adoptive and birth parents are another data source. I also interviewed 26 of the associated birth mothers (one birth father, all Caucasian) for an equal amount of time, usually in their homes, but sometimes in restaurants or other meeting places. Data about how the relationship has been progressing comes from subsequent phone interviews with adoptive parents in their second or early third year post-placement (mean time elapsed between placement and second interview = 32 months, except for 5 families whose first interview was in 1993 and have not yet had their second).[5] Such information also comes from contacts I have with these families (including adoptive and birth parents' parents and siblings) at various gatherings (e.g., picnics and information meetings) sponsored by the agency. I have also learned of the nature of the relationship that has developed between these birth and adoptive families from discussions I have with birth parents at their monthly support meetings which I attend and from phone interviews I initiate with them from time-to-time. In addition, I have talked with other members of the birthmothers' families, usually their sisters or mothers, when I have met them at agency-initiated events.

VARIANTS OF POST-PLACEMENT OPENNESS

Among the 41 post-placement relationships between birth and adoptive families I am following, all had met at least once, but typically more often before placement. I find 3 types distinguishable by intensity and frequency of contact[6] as well as emotional significance of the developing relationship to the adoptive parents.[7] I made the assignment of families into each category on the basis of frequency of post-placement, face-to-face meetings and emotional tone and/or bond which I rated as "more" or "less." A research assistant made independent ratings. Differences between us (2) were negotiated to agreement.

I discuss these below as: Rejecters, Acceptors and Embracers. With respect to the concerns raised in the literature review about specifying referents of these "openness" consequences, the second and third patterns are fully-disclosed, on-going relationships. The third also involves a strong emotional bond between birth and adoptive family members. In terms of the openness range discussed earlier then, the first involved minimal openness (some pre- but then only immediate post-placement); the second, Acceptors, represent relatively advanced, and the third, Embracers, possibly end-points, of that continuum.

REJECTERS

At one end, are Rejecters, adoptive parents who have had none or very limited contact with the birth mother or any other birth family member since placement and do not want it or seek it. This is the smallest group, consisting of only 2 families.

It is understandable that this group is such a small proportion of the total. These two adoptive families have had minimal (one had initially exchanged letters through the agency) or no contact, which is consistent with the intentions they indicated in their first post-placement interview. Though each of these adoptive families had met their birthmothers (and birthfather in one case) before placement, they had not exchanged identifying information and seemed leery of doing so in my first post-placement interview with them. Openness meant to them, agreement to a pre-placement meeting, but with the expectation that afterward there would be letter exchange, through the agency.

That there are so few in this sample who are Rejecters of more contact, may reflect self-selection. Families who did not commit to some degree of post-placement openness would be less likely to adopt through this agency—known for its requirement of, by the late-eighties at least a pre-placement meeting, and by the early nineties, commitment to openness that was fully-disclosed, and allowed for on-going contact. Both of these were also private-identified and placements which occurred in the first few months of my coming to the agency, factors whose importance in limiting these parents' exposure to the openness advocacy later adopted by the staff (agency vs. private auspices and time in relation to staff's commitment to openness) will be discussed below.

OPENNESS ACCEPTORS

The second group (n = 26) are families who maintain contact with the birth family, mostly the birth mother but sometimes other birth family members as well, in the range of 0-5 face-to-face meetings. Typically, but not exclusively, connections (either contacts by mail or phone and/or face-to-face meetings which usually include the child) are largely communications between the birthmother or her own mother (i.e., the birth grandmother) and the adoptive mother. Face-to-face meetings were more concentrated in the months immediately following placement. By the time of the second interview, most of the contact was by phone or through letter and picture exchanges with face-to-face meetings leveling-off and centering around holidays and the child's birthday.[8]

All Acceptors view the instrumental value to their child–the promise of available information about his or her birth family–as the primary basis for maintaining the relationship.

> AF: We'll be able to answer his questions.[9]
> AM: It's to keep a connection. It's because of my experience as an adoptee, that I understand, so that when Mikey (child) grows up and wants the questions answered, he'll have someone to answer them.
>
> AM: It means he won't grow up with questions all his life, "Where did I come from?" And there are no secrets; he will always know his biological background.

The majority of the Acceptors continue to send letters or pictures and respond when they receive them from the birth mother (or a family member). But most, if they have not heard from her since the first year or so after placement, have not attempted to seek her out.

> AM: The first year we saw her three times, about every few months and had letters and pictures. Now we haven't heard anything since David (child) was two. We've been feeling guilty. Like should we call her? We don't want to intrude. She knows where we are and if she doesn't try to reach us, we don't want to pressure her.

> AF: We haven't seen her for almost a year. We will remain in contact because it's for Allen (child). We let her take the lead in determining how much contact we have.

This relatively limited contact in this group between the two families is consistent with the way they have shaped their definitions of openness. Accepting the instrumental value of information valuable to their child does not mean they, personally, feel a connection to the birth family. Nor do they have an emotional bond of their own to the birth mother or any member of her family—as distinct from one they may or not grant to her and their child. It is the relationship between their child and the birth mother that matters to them, not their own relationship with the birth mother or her family.

> AM: I don't see us getting together a lot. We don't want to share or have an extended family on holidays. They don't want that either. I am certainly not mommy number two stuff. For us, it's not to have contact with other members of her family. It is a private thing between her and us. He's not someone else's nephew or grandchild. Ours is a unique and special relationship with her and that is all. Also, I think it is to the child's mental well-being—that it not be too confusing—if he had other relatives around.

Several of these parents suggest that their fear of their child's possible confusion about the role of birth parents is what keeps them from pursuing more contact than they have.

> AF: We really have not had much contact with June (BM). It's good to know where they are (the birth mother and her parents). But I don't see June (BM) getting involved very much in Ruthie's (child's) life. I don't know what benefit it would have for Ruthie and it might just confuse her.

AM: I do wonder about the possible confusion of it all–that if it were a very open relationship he'll be confused. He'll have two moms, kind of thing. I worry about that kind of thing if it were too open.

Among this group then, having knowledge about, as distinct from a relationship with, their child's birth parents is their distinguishing feature. Yet, there is, as well, a sub-group within this category who actually do more to maintain the connection and, in this respect, lean more toward the third group, the Embracers to be discussed below. These Acceptors have made more of an effort to stay in contact with the birth mother or a member of her family and to initiate such contact. Among these five "initiators," it is the adoptive mother who calls or writes to the birth mother, if she has not heard from her or anyone in her family "for a while."

AM: I will be the one to call when I think it is time that we have some contact with her.

But, there is one adoptive father in this group who initiates, because, as he explains, he values the on-going contact for his child and he has more of an opportunity to contact the birth family.

AF: I know where a friend of hers lives. I'm going to go by and drop off pictures. After all that we have been through and openness training, now not to see her, it would be a let down. It's really Jean (BM) who doesn't want Tony (AC) to be confused. She thinks that. But we do want to keep it open; it's one less hurdle for Tony (AC) to have that information.

And later in the interview when I asked both parents what they thought would be the frequency of contact in the future, the adoptive father said:

AF: I sure hope the visits continue and I hope that she doesn't go off somewhere and get married and forget about us.

Yet, for all the importance these parents acknowledge about "having information," and even about maintaining the contact which initiators believe will insure such access, it is this focus on utility that distinguishes them from the next group.

EMBRACERS

This group (n = 13) is families in which there is frequent, on-going, face-to-face contact (more than 6, typically much more as expressed in phrases such as "A lot," "As often as we can" or "We get together often. We don't count.") The contrast between those in this category and Acceptors rests as much on a difference in emotional tone accorded to the relationship with the birth mother and/or her family members, as it does on the typically greater frequency of contact between the two families (at least six)—itself, as much effect as cause, of that more frequent and more emotionally-valued connection. Embracers define the birth mother and/or members of her family as emotionally significant to themselves as well as their child. And the birthmother counterparts I interviewed in this group confirm the same emotional bond to the adoptive family. To the adoptive parents, birth family members are seen as new and valued stars in their own (nuclear) family's constellation. They do not mention concern over their child's potential confusion of birth family members with adoptive family members, as do some Acceptors—possibly because these adoptive parents are so clear about the role they themselves accord to birth family members. The birth family is viewed as adding a distinct family heritage to their own.

The following two adoptive mothers used almost identical ways of phrasing how they take into account the birth family's impact on their nuclear families:

> AM: The way I see it is that we all bring a family to this relationship, I (AM) have a family and Sam (AF) has a family and Ellie (AC) brings a family to this relationship, too. Ellie (AC) calls Sally (BM) by her name and everyone else is called by their relationship, that is Aunt Tina and Aunt Maria (BM's sisters).

> AM: I'm a Sheridan (AM) and Len (AF) is a Cousins and Marty (older adopted child) is from Shelly's (this child's BM) family and now Allan (AC) is a Callamond (his birthfamily's name). That's who each of us is, and that's what each of us adds.

Both these adoptive mothers, then, view each member of their nuclear family as coming to it with a lineage that needs to be acknowledged. This heritage needs to be included in the identification of each member's distinctiveness within their nuclear family. The relationship with the birth mother or with her family members (usually her mother or sister) is valued for its own sake, not only for the utilitarian function it will play in their child's life.

In this group the adoptive parents account for the connection they feel to the birth family as pleasurable in its own right.

AF: They've become our good friends, probably even best friends around here.

AM: They're an extension of our family. We really like her father and step-mother and we enjoy being with them. In fact, this Saturday we're going to a cook-out with them. They've been here several times and we've been there, and I think that is a good part of it, that we have a relationship with them.

Surprisingly not having each other nearby—lack of physical proximity—does not preclude such feelings. The following adoptive mother has open relationships with two birth mothers, both of whom live out of state. Referring to the birth mother for the child included in this study, she says:

She (BM) stays with us for weekends and knows our other birth mother now too. They have talked several times and have actually presented at a meeting together and talked to birth mothers and others interested in open adoption. And we get members from all of the families together, just like with in-laws. We try to get together whenever we are in town. At Easter they were at my sister's and Bob's (second adopted child's) birth grandmother makes cakes and so we had a big party and she made the cake for it. She had both birth families there.

In three families in this group it is not a matter of greater emotional significance attached to birth family members other than the birth mother that qualifies them for inclusion in this category. Here, it is the strong, close bond between the adoptive mother and the birth mother that signals the greater emotional charge—relative to Acceptors—attributed to the openness of their relationship. In the following instance, the birth mother does not visit as frequently as is the case with the rest of these families in this category, and there is no contact with other members of her family. But the birth and adoptive mothers enjoy a strong emotional bond. The adoptive mother was the birth mother's Lamaze coach and, and as is true of the others with such a bond (mean age difference = 8 years), is closer in age to the birth mother than is typical for the difference between adoptive and birth members in the total sample (mean age difference = 15 years).

AM: We have a special relationship, the two of us. It's a bond and some people say to me 'How can you do this?' They don't understand the bond between us. She has never told her parents. I am someone she can talk to about it in a way she can't talk to other people. And she has other children, and Lynn (child) has a right to know her brothers and sisters.

Very similar in tone is the statement of this adoptive mother about her child's birth mother.

> AM: I consider Robin a very special person to me. She is my friend and we have a unique bond. It is good to talk and share ideas with her.

This bond is also affirmed in the corresponding birth mother's account of how it was the adoptive mother's warmth towards her that brought her into a relationship with the adoptive family she originally thought she did not want.

> BM: After the placement, I did not want to be with them. I really thought it would be better. But then Doris (AM), was so warm and we were so close—she just pulled me into a relationship with them.

So, these adoptive and birth families take each other quite literally as well as figuratively into "each other's arms" and in this sense "embrace" their counterparts more than do acceptors. They want to be together for the connection itself; its value to their child is assumed. Its benefit to themselves is celebrated.

ACCEPTORS AND EMBRACERS: DISTINGUISHING FACTORS

Likely factors that might distinguish these two groups are such background characteristics as: adoptive parents' age; education; income level; length of marriage; number of children already in the home; and birthmother's age. In fact, however there are no significant differences between these groups on any of these characteristics.[10]

Three pre-placement factors do distinguish the two groups: (1) whether the original connection between the birth and adoptive family occurred through the agency or privately; (2) whether the placement occurred before or after the agency's staff committed to full-disclosure openness; and (3) whether at least one of the pre-adoptive parents was not initially resistant to the idea of openness.

Agency vs. Private Adoption

An agency adoption means that the birth mother came to the agency and then chose the family with whom she ultimately placed her child.

Typically, she chose this family from among several on the agency's roster of approved families: a group waiting for placements who have fulfilled the agency's and legal requirements for adoption. The birth mother makes her initial selection after examining portfolios submitted by pre-adoptive couples which describe and picture them. A private or independent adoption means the birth and adoptive families have connected on their own, that is, without the birth mother first coming to the agency. The significance of the difference is that in an agency adoption both families are more likely to have had more contact with the agency's staff—particularly the social workers assigned to each family. Longer contact, in turn, increases these parents' exposure to the agency's philosophy about successful adoption; that is, openness. Families with agency adoptions are more likely to have had extensive conversations with their social workers, as a couple and in required pre-placement group meetings—exploring openness implications with a supportive and influential counselor. This exposure to a positive and beneficial view of openness was instrumental in getting these couples and birth family members to view openness more acceptingly than they originally did.

Table 1 (p . > 05, n.s.) shows the influence of this variable. Although not significant, the table shows as expected—given that this is an agency-based sample—more agency than private adoptions. It shows as well, that among Embracers only 15% (2 of the 13) were private, whereas about 80% (7 of 9) of the acceptors were. If, in fact a private adoption limits opportunity, or willingness, to listen to the agency's message about openness, this greater preponderance of private as compared to agency adoptions among those with less openness, is consistent with expectation. Origin of the connection between the two families then, appears to have some effect on the subsequent degree of openness they exhibit. But there is another factor

TABLE 1. Auspices of Adoption by Openness Orientation (N = 39)

AUSPICES OF ADOPTION

OPENNESS ORIENTATION	AGENCY		PRIVATE		Total	
	n	%	n	%	N	%
ACCEPTORS	19	63	7	78	26	67
EMBRACERS	11	37	2	22	13	33
TOTAL	30	100	9	100	39	100

X = .64, > .05, n.s.

related to exposure to the agency that appears to matter more. This has to do with the time of the placement: before or after February of 1990.

Pre vs. Post Agency Staff's Endorsement of Full Openness

The majority of couples who came to this agency knew little or nothing about openness when they began the adoption process. Only 10% (4 of 39, data not shown) had even heard of, or knew much about openness when they first considered adoption; and the majority was not receptive to it when they first understood what it might require. They almost uniformly describe coming to understand its benefits as an "evolutionary process" heavily influenced by what they learned about it from the staff: the birth and adoptive families they listened to from the agency who were in various kinds of openness relationships; and from the favorable description of openness in the readings suggested to them by the agency's staff.

> AM: In the beginning, we didn't know anything about 'open' period. We didn't even know what it was. Maybe, we had an idea of what it was, but didn't know the whole story.
> I: What was your first response to it?
> AF: I wasn't crazy about it.
> AM: Neither of us was.
> I: When you were going through the sessions and the workers were talking about open adoption, what were you thinking?
> AM: I thought it was good because I had read the book (the staff gave them to read). It was a book that had fourteen case studies. That's what sold us on the idea of it. Then they (social workers) brought up points that were very strong, that I will call selling points to open adoption. The whole thing just began to make a lot of sense.

The following couple, like most, had also not heard of open adoption, or did not have a clear idea of what it meant, until they came to the agency. Though "scared," they decided to listen to what the agency presented, because they did not want to foreclose any options.

> AM: The only reason we went along with it in the beginning was just to get our foot in the door.

They then (as often happened) talked about what this might mean to them on their drive home after the meeting and decided to consider it.

> AM: You know when you want a baby right off the bat you're willing to make exceptions: 'Well, yes I could live with that.' We

ended up fudging a little on part of the openness questionnaire. And that was fine, that got us in the door. But what we didn't expect was that once you go in the door, and you're actually educated, you just learn so much about the "other side."

I: And that's how you experienced it, that you were being drawn to something, educated to something?

AF: Yes, we did.

I: Okay, you felt yourselves being made aware of what openness meant—positively, at least.

AM: We learned pretty quick. We didn't agree with everything pretty quick. That came after time. I think we walked into it just like everybody else walks into it. We thought, 'We're going to adopt a baby and he's ours period.' Well, now we know, of course, he's ours, but we've come to know the other couple that's involved. You know she (BM) really does care. So we still say, "Yes he's ours," but we do realize somebody else is out there. It's almost like they taught us how to care for these other people. That's the big thing.

Though nearly all shared this initial unfamiliarity with openness, some came to the agency at an earlier time (in the late eighties) when the agency advocated a more restricted degree of openness than they later came to endorse. In February of 1990, the staff invited a consultant known to have been an early proponent of open adoption to come to the agency to address their staff's concerns about openness. Prior to this invitation there had been much staff discussion about the effect of their position on openness. The issue was their influence on the openness the couples coming to the agency were choosing—for the most part—openness without full-disclosure and on-going contact. They questioned whether their lack of endorsement of full-disclosure, on-going contact, led to the, in effect, semi-openness recently adopting families had been agreeing to—where pre-placement meetings and the promise of future exchange of letters and pictures was typical, but not much more. After the consultant's presentation, arguing that full disclosure and contact was desirable where possible, the staff decided to commit to full-disclosure and on-going contact as valued options.

Apparently, the staff's more unequivocal endorsement of full openness did have some influence. Table 2 (p. < .01, sig.) shows that all of the placements of Embracers (13) were subsequent to the consultant's visit—a clear indication of the effect of this variable. Among Acceptors, a goodly proportion, 38% (10 of 26), placed before the agency committed to full openness, that is, when their own choice of more limited openness reflected the staff's position at that time. Accounting for the seemingly

TABLE 2. Openness Orientation by Placement Date: Agency Transition to Full Openness Endorsement (N = 39)

PLACEMENT DATE:
AGENCY TRANSITION
TO FULL OPENNESS
ENDORSEMENT

OPENNESS ORIENTATION	Pre-		Post-		Total	
	n	%	n	%	N	%
ACCEPTORS	10	100	16	55	26	67
EMBRACERS	0	0	13	45	13	33
TOTAL	10	100	39	100	39	100

*February, 1990   X = 10, p < .01, sig.

anomalous (with this hypothesizing) remaining majority of Acceptors (62%)—because they have less openness, though their placements occurred when the staff had already committed to more—requires turning to another variable.

Initial Receptivity to Openness

As noted above, most of these families had no, or an unclear, idea of what openness entailed when they began the adoption process. Yet, not all were equally skeptical about its potential benefits. When at least one member of the pre-adoptive couple was initially-receptive to hearing more about openness, or recognized the merit of the positive claims presented about it, the couple was more likely to subsequently commit to full-disclosure and acceptance of more contact with the birth family.

Table 3 (p. < .05, sig.) shows that twice as many Embracers were couples where at least one member was initially responsive to the positive claims for it advanced by the agency (9 compared to 4 who were not), while among Acceptors more than three times as many (20 compared to 6) did not have this initial receptivity.

Table 4 (p < .01, sig.) shows the interaction among these variables, taking into account both the effect of time of placement and initial receptivity to openness. It indicates that the response of 9 of the 13 (70%) Embracers is related to (a) having shown initial receptivity to openness,

TABLE 3. Openness Orientation by Initial Receptivity to Openness
(N = 39)

INITIAL RECEPTIVITY TO OPENNESS

OPENNESS

ORIENTATION	Yes		No		Total	
	n	%	n	%	N	%
ACCEPTORS	6	40	20	83	26	67
EMBRACERS	9	60	4	17	13	33
TOTAL	15	100	24	100	39	100

$X = 5$, $p < .05$, sig.

TABLE 4. Agency's Transition to Full Openness by Type of Openness
(N = 39)

PLACEMENT DATE: AGENCY'S TRANSITION
TO FULL OPENNESS

OPENNESS	PRE*				POST*					
ORIENTATION	INITIAL RECEPTIVITY TO OPENNESS								Total	
	Yes		No		Yes		No			
	n	%	n	%	n	%	n	%	N	%
ACCEPTORS	0	0	10	100	6	40	10	71	26	67
EMBRACERS	0	0	0	0	9	60	4	29	13	33
TOTAL	0	0	10	100	15	100	14	100	39	100

*February, 1990 $X = 14.04$ p. $< .01$ sig.

and (b) having come to the agency after it endorsed the kind of openness these couples subsequently adopted. Among Acceptors, 77% (20 of 26) lacked one or the other of these facilitating factors. Only six cases, then, Acceptors who either placed after the agency's transition or had at least one initially receptive spouse, are inconsistent with the interpretations suggested here for the influence of these factors.

Interestingly, when I ask members of each family, birth and adoptive (both Acceptors and Embracers) what they believe contributes to the comfort level of their relationship, everybody accounts for this in terms of unique qualities of the particular people involved: "We could not do this with anybody else"; "We were meant to do this together" and "She's (if adoptive family, or "they're" if birth mother) the only one I could trust this way" are common responses. Whatever this says about the need to perceive such uniqueness for the bonds they have created, such perception does not preclude the impact of enabling preconditions.

Apparently, both structural factors (exposure to pro-openness philosophy) and attitudinal predisposition (willingness to learn about contact with birth family members) help construct the kind of openness in their relationships these families feel comfortable with and subsequently adopt. No doubt, the vagaries of interpersonal chemistry between members of each family contribute as well. Yet, these results do suggest that extra-relationship factors may shape such perceptions and contribute to them in ways these families, more accustomed to personalizing motivational sources, may not consider.

CONCLUSIONS

Though adoption professionals had already devoted more than a decade's discussion to possible implications of contact between birth and adoptive families, when I began this study in 1989, only a handful of agency-assisted adoptions had begun to allow for such "openness." Because there were so few actual adoptions involving even minimal degrees of openness, there was little empirical research about the conditions and consequences of these arrangements. In the intervening years more adoptions have included some degree of openness and, predictably, research has followed.

My review of existing research about openness, suggested that we need to refine our conceptualization and measurement as this research goes forward—distinguishing the variety of antecedent and consequent dimensions of openness arrangements. While the small scale of the study I presented here prevented me from being able to take into account all but a few of these dimensions, I think it is important for the continuing development of what gets subsumed under the heading "openness research" to enumerate and consider these sources of variation.

In the research discussed here, the common antecedent with which I began the analysis was at least one, but typically several, meeting(s) between birth and adoptive family members before placement with an understanding that there would be future post-placement contact as well. The analysis focused on patterns in the ways these adoptive and birth family members then continued to maintain contact and/or build relationships, that is, on post-placement consequences of this antecedent. Post-facto analysis also indicated the importance of another pre-placement condition: social workers' and other adoption professionals' formative role in defining openness possibilities and enabling their subsequent initiation. Without clear and unequivocal endorsement of openness by the professionals who orchestrated them, prospective parents were less likely to hear openness music.[11] Also, though initial receptivity to the potential value of openness may collude with the ability to listen for these themes as was the case here, what we have learned from these pioneer families is the importance of access and exposure to the necessary notes in the first place. At least at the beginning stages of a challenge to prevailing understandings, i.e., the traditional, closed adoption these parents accepted as normative, the facilitating effect of the professionals who guided these changes loomed large.[12] Ironically however, as important as their role appears to have been, the need for adoption professionals' defining and educating input to openness receptivity may turn out to have been historically specific to these early days of the transition to openness. In the future as cultural familiarity with the shift to openness grows, greater popular acceptance of its viability may lessen the need for the enabling influence the adoption professionals contributed to these early open adoptions.

The analysis of post-placement consequences yielded three patterns called here: Acceptors, Embracers and Rejecters. What do these patterns suggest about the future of openness? Most adoptions called "open," as the first two patterns in this study suggest, will actually be so in the sense that members of the birth and adoptive families will have met before or at placement and will continue to maintain contact, but with different meanings attaching to, and configurations of, the relationship that is developing among them.

Acceptors will most likely be the most prevalent type. These families value the future utility of information from each other as resources to be drawn upon to answer the child's future questions. Their post-placement openness relationship is more delimited and contained: it revolves around letter/phone/exchanges or meetings geared to pre-specified occasions (e.g., birthdays and holidays). A second, most likely smaller proportion of all self-described open adoptions, as with the Embracers discussed here, will involve more meetings and contacts between members of the two families and entail more emotionally significant bonds among several and different members (e.g., birth grandparents and adoptive parents) of each family. Embracers actively cultivate an on-going relationship with each other, acknowledging an emotional attachment, created by their mutual relationship to the child. Birth and adoptive family members view each other as part of their own family relationships. Embracers' relationships will be more inclusive, then, in terms of: times when they connect; members of each family who are included; and willingness to view themselves as incorporated into each other's respective families. On the basis of the admittedly meager number of the third type in this sample, Rejecters, I suggest this pattern will be the smallest proportion of those who initially commit to open adoptions, if–and this is an important, enabling pre-condition–they receive pre-placement counseling about openness and have prior understanding of its possibilities. I base this prediction of relatively few Rejecters on the suggestion here that it was just such a lack of preparation which contributed to these adoptive parents' failure to pursue further post-placement contact.

It is, of course, too early to yet know how long either of the two continuing relationships will last, or even remain at their current levels. Shifts from less to more involving relationships (or the reverse) will need to be assessed. More important, we do not yet know what the effect of either type of open adoption will be on the child–though anecdotal and clinical evidence with older children in adoptions with varying degrees of openness suggests the outlook is good (Silber & Dorner, 1990). Hopefully the longitudinal analysis projected here will enable us to address these and other related questions.

As ultimately consequential as these new connections are–so long believed to be detrimental–to the principals involved, they portend lasting significance, as well, for an even larger audience. This is because the existence of such family connections strikes at the very heart of what our culture uses to define family ties: to the primacy we accord to genetic basis, to "blood," as *sine qua non* of enduring family connection–without popular understanding or acknowledgment of the ambiguities this belief entails (Schneider, 1984, 1968; Gricar, 1990.) The viability of open relationship adoptions together with other non-biologically connected units who define themselves as "real" families (Humphrey & Humphrey, 1988; Marciano and Sussman, 1991) challenge anew the inconsistencies and ambiguities inherent in our culture's formal insistence on "blood" connection–with all its historical/contemporary political, legal and other policy undergirding (Gricar, 1990). Ironically, this challenge to the biological basis of family ties (with its implications for this undergirding) is surfacing just as reproductive possibilities previously unheard of are not only technologically available, but enjoying widespread demand and use (Ragonee, 1994; Pfeffer, 1993). Significantly, open relationship adoptions such as those of Embracers and Acceptors, like other non-traditional "families," challenge the necessity of biological connection, while these new reproductive possibilities appear to transcend barriers in order to maintain that connection. However different in intent, both developments have similar ultimate cultural import—forcing us to consider what defines family connection (Gross, 1992) and importantly this definition's ramification on competing policy issues.

NOTES

1. Understandably, initial research undertaken in a context in which closed adoption had been normative, focused mainly on participants' adjustment and satisfaction (the most salient issues) with the changes openness implied. Researchers, for the most part, defined openness globally as some form of pre-placement foreknowledge or contact—thereby obscuring variation in circumstances surrounding pre-placement openness as well as subsequent post-placement differentiation. While unintentional, this focus on early post-placement adjustment accompanied by the glossing of distinctions among the variety of pre- and post placement arrangements, with a few exceptions discussed below, both reflects and contributes to conceptual confusion.

2. Demick (1993) does refer to different degrees of openness, e.g., "restricted," "semi," and "full," but does not specify what distinguishes each. And, because there are so few cases in his sample, he disregards these differences in his analysis.

3. Both Belbas (1987) and Berry (1993) report that adoptive parents with high openness comfort had more direct contact. But see note 1 for the need to consider how pre-placement history may affect post-placement comfort.

4. Berry acknowledges the difference between older children adoptions (e.g., history of problematic past birth parent/child interactions) and infant adoptions. But her analysis does not indicate that the more problematic pre-placement history of older children adoptions may invalidate comparisons of post-placement contact consequences of these families with such consequences for families with infant adoptions. This likelihood is indeed supported by her finding that adopters of children with histories of unhappy childhood with their biological families have lower post-placement contact comfort levels (1993:247).

5. In two cases the adoptive parents did not respond to the request for a second interview. For these families it was a member of the birth family who gave the interview about how the relationship had been progressing.

6. To avoid excessive repetition I will no longer use the modifier "post-placement."

7. The basis for these characterizations comes mainly from material from first and second interviews and other contacts I have had with adoptive parents, although material from contacts and the first (and only to date) interview with birthmothers is also included. Birthmothers will be re-interviewed at a later date, as will adoptive parents, as this is a longitudinal study.

8. There could have been no post-placement meetings if the birthmother has, for example, moved to another country or as few as 1 if either family has moved away from the Chicago metropolitan area. But, these families still maintain contact.

9. I will use the following to designate source of each quote: AF adoptive father; AM adoptive mother; BM birth mother; BF birth father; AC adopted child. When the AM and the AF are from one family, the quotations will not be separated. A space separation, then, will indicate that another person is talking.

10. The data for Acceptors (A) n = 26 and Embracers (E) n = 13 are: Fathers' Mean Age, A = 37 yrs., 4 mos.; E = 38 yrs. Mothers' Mean Age, A = 35 yrs., 6 mos.; E = 36 yrs., 8 mos. Fathers' Mean Post-Secondary Education Years, A = 3.50, E = 3.54. Mothers' Mean Post-Secondary Education Years, A = 2.88, E = 3.23. Years Married, A = 10 yrs., 3 mos.; E = 10 yrs., 8 mos. Mean Family Income, A = \$75,689; E = 78,692. Mean number of children in home, A = .46; E = .54.

11. Saying this does not make the claim that adoptive and birth families cannot come to more open relationships on their own. They can and do as the many "Embracers" I have met at conferences and workshops indicate. Nevertheless, the conclusion here about adoption professionals' influence seems warranted.

12. The midwifery function the adoption professionals played in the relationship development between the two families reported here deserves underscoring. Too often, the adoption unit is described as a triangle, limiting its constituent elements to the child and her birth and adoptive families. This common metaphor obscures what this research highlights.

REFERENCES

Bartholet, E. (1993). *Family bonds: Adoption and the politics of parenting.* Boston: Houghton Mifflin.

Belbas, N.F. (1987). Staying in touch: Empathy in open adoptions. *Smith College Studies in Social Work,* 57:184-198.

Berry, M. (1993). Adoptive parents' perceptions of, and comfort with, open adoption. *Child Welfare,* 72(3):231-256.

Cushman, L.F., Kalmus, D. & Namerow, P.B. (1997). In H. Gross & M. Sussman (Eds.) *Marriage and Family Review.* 25(1/2).

Demick, J. (1993). Adaptation of marital couples to open versus closed adoption: A preliminary investigation. In J. Demick, Bursik, K., & DiBiase, C. (Eds.), *Parental Development* (pp. 175-201). Hillsdale, NJ: Lawrence Erlbaum Associates.

Etter, J. (1993). Levels of cooperation and satisfaction in 56 open adoptions. *Child Welfare,* 72:257-268.

Gricar, J.M. (1990). *How Thick is Blood?: The Social Construction and Cultural Configuration of Kinship.* Doctoral Dissertation. Columbia University.

Grotevant, H.D., McRoy, R.G., Elde, C.L. & Fravel D.L. (1994). Adoptive family system dynamics: variations by level of openness in the adaptation. *Family Process* 33:125-146.

Gross, H.E. (1993). Open adoption: A research-based literature review and new data. *Child Welfare* 72(3):269-284.

Gross, H.E. (1992). *Open adoption: Implications for definitions of family ties.* Paper presented at the Annual Meetings of the American Sociological Association, Pittsburgh, PA.

Humphrey, M. & H. (1988). *Families With a Difference.* New York: Routledge.

Marciano, T.D.& Sussman, M.B. Eds. (1991). *Wider Families: New Traditional Family Forms.* New York: The Haworth Press, Inc.

McRoy, R.G., Grotevant, H.D., & White, K.L. (1988). *Openness in adoption: New practices, new issues.* New York: Praeger.

Modell, J. (1994). *Kinship With Strangers.* Berkeley, CA: University of California.

Pfeffer, N. (1993). *The Stork and the Syringe: A Political History of Reproductive Medicine.* Cambridge, UK: Polity.

Ragonee, H. (1994). *Surrogate Motherhood: Conception in the Heart.* Boulder, CO: Westview.

Reitz, M., & Watson, K. (1992). *Adoption and the family system.* New York: Guilford.

Rompf, E.L. (1993). Open adoption: What does the 'average person' think? *Child Welfare,* 72(3); 219-229.

Schneider, D. (1968). *American Kinship: A Cultural Account.* Englewood Cliffs, NJ: Prentice-Hall.

_____ . (1984). *A Critique of the Study of Kinship.* Ann Arbor: University of Michigan.

Silber, K., & Dorner, K. (1990). *Children of open adoption and their families.* San Antonio TX: Corona.

Silverstein, D.R., & Demick, J. (1994). Toward an organizational-relational model of open adoption. *Family Process.* 33.

Smith-Plinner, D., & Siegel, D. (1992). Successful open adoption: Advice for parents. *OURS* (January/February): 15-17.

Soparkar, K., Demick, J., Levin, R., & Warner, S. (1988). *Community attitudes towards open and closed adoptions.* Paper presented at the Eastern Psychological Association Annual Meeting, Buffalo, NY.

Watkins, M., & Fisher, S. (1993). *Talking with young children about adoption.* New Haven: Yale University Press.

"Where Do We Go Next?"
Long-Term Reunion Relationships
Between Adoptees and Birth Parents

Judith Modell

INTRODUCTION

"And when I got off the plane we, neither of us had any problem recognizing each other. And she stood in the middle of the aisle, all the people are still trying to get–you know, the aisle just as you get out the gate. And people had to go around us. And we stood there and cried, for a long time. With our arms around each other. And it was the most wonderful tears I ever shed in my life. The most wonderful, unashamed . . . " With those words, a birth parent began the story of her reunion. She had made an adoption plan twenty years earlier and this was her first meeting with a child who was a virtual stranger to her.

More and more such reunions are occurring in the United States, reported in daily newspapers, displayed on television talk shows, and commented on in literature on adoption and on the family in American society. Individuals who have experienced reunions seem eager to report their feelings, their understandings of the meeting, and their reasons for having engaged in the behavior in the first place. Yet, in thinking about what is known about reunions–and what is reported in the media–one cannot help but notice the silence about what happens afterwards. That is, what is readily described and reported is the "thrill" of the first sight with

Judith Modell is Associate Professor of Anthropology, Department of History, Carnegie Mellon University, Pittsburgh, PA 15213-3890.

[Haworth co-indexing entry note]: " 'Where Do We Go Next?' Long-Term Reunion Relationships Between Adoptees and Birth Parents." Modell, Judith. Co-published simultaneously in *Marriage & Family Review* (The Haworth Press, Inc.) Vol. 25, No. 1/2, 1997, pp. 43-66; and: *Families and Adoption* (ed: Harriet E. Gross and Marvin B. Sussman) The Haworth Press, Inc., 1997, pp. 43-66. Single or multiple copies of this article are available for a fee from The Haworth Document Delivery Service [1-800-342-9678, 9:00 a.m. - 5:00 p.m. (EST). E-mail address: getinfo@haworth.com].

its accompanying tears and hugs. Alternatively, individuals confess to an initial awkward appraisal and lack of certainty about whether to touch, kiss, and hug. Next to nothing is available that tells about what happens weeks, months, and years after a birth parent and adoptee encounter each other for the first time. Do the birth parent and adoptee maintain a relationship after meeting? What are the terms of that relationship? How do a parent and child who are virtual strangers interact and interpret their feelings, as the years pass and the novelty gives way to routine?

This paper explores the issue of ongoing relationships between birth parents and their "found" children. It is about strangers who become kin, to borrow the title of my book on adoption, in the sense that birth parent and adoptee have not known each other, have not seen each other, do not know each other's patterns, behaviors, and beliefs.[1] It is also about the difficulties of establishing a relationship in a context of concern and of outright disapproval: the birth parent and adoptee who meet do so against the grain of the laws and norms surrounding adoption in America. Primarily, however, it is about what individuals do who enter such a situation: how, in essence, do birth parents and adoptees negotiate their ways through a new relationship? What are the models they use, the expectations they have, the chances of pursuing the connection beyond the aisles of an airport or the stage of a talk show?

WHAT IS REUNION AND WHY IS IT
A SUBJECT OF CONCERN?

Reunion can mean several things. Often, the word simply refers to an initial encounter: a birth parent and adoptee coming into contact after years of separation. More appropriately, the word can imply an ongoing relationship; contact made and then continued over time. This is the meaning the word has in other contexts, such as family reunions and school reunions. In those cases, reunions represent the recognition of enduring and essential ties between individuals. It is that meaning the adoptees and birth parents I am discussing here would accord to the word to characterize the phenomenon as it occurred in their lives. Yet when reunions are the subject of newspaper articles or television shows, the immediate encounter is emphasized and the aftermath usually not mentioned. The images are of two (or more) individuals ecstatic, tearful, confused—all in the flash of a moment. This sort of presentation underlines the awkwardness reunions still pose. They are fine if they only mean a meeting and not so fine if they suggest the beginning, or the acknowledgment, of long-term connections.

Despite the audience appeal, an evident taboo surrounds reunions between birth parents and adoptees. The event itself may be exciting but the consequences are not. A focus on the excitement, then, serves as a distraction from the real problem these meetings pose: are they the beginning of a parent-child relationship and what does that do to adoption as Americans have practiced and understood the institution for half a century? If the meeting between birth parent and adoptee is "only" an instant thrill of recognition, no one need pay much more attention. If the meeting leads to further contact, the event challenges our notions of adoption, parenthood, and kinship. Why and how that is so is the subject of my paper.

Since the 1940s, adoption in the United States has been closed, secret, and confidential. Once the child is transferred from birth parent to adoptive parent, the birth parent becomes (in the word I heard) *invisible,* no longer part of the child's life and completely anonymous for the adoptive parents. At the same time, the birth parent loses knowledge of and information about her child; the child has passed out of her life forever.[2] There were, and are, good reasons for this arrangement, given American cultural understandings of kinship and family. Adoption, in the United States, replicates the genealogical family; the child, in the well-known phrase, is "as if begotten." A new birth certificate is issued, in which the adoptive parents are listed "as if biological." The child achieves a new identity, her fate in the new family is sealed, and intrusion from an "outsider" (i.e., the biological parent) prevented. Adoption is a *fictive* (or made) kinship that upholds cultural interpretations of *real* kinship, which is presumed to be based on the centrality of birth and a blood connection.[3] The closer the adoptive family can come to the biological model, the more permanent, stable, and healthy it will be. Such an arrangement is presumed to be "in the best interests of the child." Or so adoption policy has held for the past half-century.

In this cultural context, reunions are threatening for several reasons. Clearly, meetings between a birth parent and an adoptee break down the notion that the child is "as if begotten" in the adoptive family: suddenly, the begetter is on the scene. Reunions also test the notion that every child ought to have one set of parents—a reigning idea in adoption circles despite the rising number of divorces, step families, and so forth. Reunions announce the presence of *two* real sets of parents in a child's life. There are other factors as well, less frequently discussed in literature on reunions. Reunions are regarded negatively because they announce dissatisfaction with one's choices or, more accurately, one's *circumstances,* and an inability to stick to a decision. According to this argument, the birth parent who begins to search for her child shows herself to be indecisive, inconsistent, and immature. Similarly, the adoptee who begins to search shows himself to be ungrateful, disrespectful, and immature. Reunions are also condemned, I think, because they represent *greed*. From this perspective, the birth parent is greedy to want back a child she has given to someone else; she is selfish and grasping. The adopted person is greedy for wanting more parents, more attention, and more kin in his life.

Overall, then, reunions are a concern because they deconstruct the institution of adoption as it has existed for decades in American society. They are also a concern because they challenge the core concepts of parenthood, family, and kinship in American culture. Prominent male politicians are not the only ones who despair at a (presumed) breakdown in the American family at the end of the twentieth century. I have argued elsewhere that adoption, with its emphasis on a unit composed of mother, father, and children, upholds what is seen as the "good" American family.[4] The *created* family represents and reaffirms the ideal family; or, in another way of putting it, the adoptive family *as if begotten* substantiates the cultural definition of a *real* (biological) family. Inasmuch as adoption policy replicates that family, reactions to changes in adoption suggest concern about "family" spreads beyond the Federal Government. Reunions thoroughly disrupt the carefully formed replication, throwing notions of and values attached to family to the winds.

Birth parents and adoptees are aware of the negative views of reunion. They are the first to admit that reunions are taboo and that those who search are stigmatized. Yet an increasing number of birth parents and adoptees are demanding contact and the instances of reunion (in some form) are growing, pushing adoption itself in the direction of openness.[5] Participants and professionals recognize that secrecy, lack of contact, and denial of information are not in the best interests of anyone; the pressure to "open" adoption initially corresponds with the pressure to "meet" in adulthood. Yet those who do meet remain at the vanguard of a movement which is surrounded by persistent controversy. What is titillating about reunions is also threatening—the questions they raise about relationships— yet such meetings show no sign of diminishing. How do the individuals who engage in such behaviors understand what they are doing, why, and where it leads over time?

THE WHY'S AND HOW'S OF MY STUDY

My analysis of reunions is part of a broader study of adoption as a form of kinship in American society. In that study, I reach several conclusions. One is that a fictive or *created* kinship compels individuals to consider what they "really" mean by being related. For a birth parent and an adoptive parent, this happens at the beginning of the transaction when a decision is made about who shall "have" a child. For the adoptee, it may happen when she or he is told about adoption, reaches adolescence, or has a child of her own. Another conclusion I reach is that in American culture a fictive kinship is perceived as lacking something, and this something is expressed in a vocabulary of blood, biology, genetics, roots, and other terms which have a similar rhetorical impact.

For the birth parent, what is missing is the tangible sign that she has given birth. Being a "childless mother" was the driving paradox for birth parents who decided to search: it made no emotional or cultural sense to have had a child who was non-existent.[6] For birth parents, the missing piece was flesh of their flesh, substance of the birth (or blood) bond. An adoptee also missed the tangible sign of a blood bond. "I did not know I was born," adoptees said to me, or, more frequently, "I looked in the mirror and saw a void." Like birth parents, adoptees drew on cultural conventions about genetic heritage and biological ancestry to define the "hole" in their own lives. Unlike birth parents, adoptees tended to insist on the fact of an incomplete identity; without a knowledge of birth, they were "no one." In essence, the search was for blood ties, biological connections, and an identity. But that can summarize the effort for birth parents as well. What was found, of course, was a living person with a biography of her (or his) own.

In this paper, I use the word reunion to refer to contacts that last beyond the initial encounter, for which I use simply the term "meeting." It is the problem of pursuing a relationship that I am interested in, not just the reasons for embarking on the quest or the feelings that arise when the quest results in an actual meeting. An exchange of letters or phone calls without personal contact is not part of my discussion here. In the case of reunions, a "parent" and a "child" come together without the usual components of a parental relationship. They lack the continual contact presumed to be part of such a relationship. They lack a shared set of expectations for the relationship. They often lack the age difference—the generational span—that is part of those relationships. At the same time, they share a cultural model for parent-child relationships and, as well, a cultural definition of adoptive kinship. How these conditions affect the creation of an ongoing relationship constitutes the gist of my argument. In my conclusion, I explore the impact on notions of kinship and of family an increasing occurrence of reunions will have.

Data come from extensive, open-ended interviews with adopted individuals and with birth parents. I met adoptees and birth parents in several ways: at support group meetings, through social workers, and through word of mouth. Of the adoptees and birth parents I met, not all wanted to pursue the possibility of a reunion. That all had critically considered the institution of adoption was evident from their willingness to discuss the subject with me. Interviews were taped and transcribed, and every individual was assured of confidentiality. In the following pages, names have been changed and identifying details disguised.

I interviewed sixteen adoptees who had made contact with a birth parent. Of these, fourteen had sustained a relationship for at least two years. I interviewed eleven birth parents who had had a reunion with a relinquished child; of these, eight developed long-term relationships. Only one of the birth parents was male. In one case, I spent a good deal of time with an adoptee and her birth mother and was able to observe their evolving relationship. Those observations influenced my analysis of interview materials.

The anthropologist David Schneider has provided a thorough account of American kinship and its juxtaposition of blood and law, biology and conduct, nature and culture (Schneider 1980, 1984). My research demonstrated the importance of these abstract concepts in the everyday experiences of individuals involved in adoptive kinship (Modell 1994). The sociologist H. David Kirk has written several excellent accounts of adoption as a form of kinship, setting forth its terms in a compassionate and comprehensive manner (Kirk 1981, 1984). Betty Jean Lifton's books have guided adoptees, adoptive parents, and birth parents through the rocky road of evolving adoptive family relationships and individual developmental cycles (Lifton 1977, 1979). Beginning with a plea for opening records, Sorosky, Baran, and Pannor have moved in the direction of arguing for a revision of American adoption in the direction of "blended families" (Sorosky, Baran, and Pannor 1979, Baran and Pannor 1990). Books like *Birth Bond,* by Gediman and Brown (1989), provide first-person testimonies about the importance of reunion in the lives of parents and of children. Edited collections like the one by Brodzinsky and Schechter (1990) demonstrate that adoption is a serious, complicated, and important subject for scholars, social workers, and lay people. My examination of post-encounter relationships carries these discussions further by showing that participants in an adoptive arrangement *actively* and *intentionally* construct definitions of kinship, family, love, and conduct.

My paper proceeds from a brief discussion of the reasons for searching, through an account of the significance of the first meeting, to an analysis of the ways in which a "real" relationship is established between birth parent and adoptee. I suggest that, lacking a script for this relationship, birth parents and adoptees borrow elements from the models for other lasting reciprocal relationships: patronage, friendship, courtship, and extended family ties—primarily those between aunt/uncle and niece/nephew. The adequacy of such models depends on the expectations a birth parent and an adoptee bring to a reunion, on the dent time makes in any relationship, and on the distinctive features of adoption in the United States.

The biggest challenge to adoptees and birth parents lies in establishing intimacy when neither daily interactions nor conventional generational distances control the expression of that intimacy. Adoptees and birth parents say they "want to be close," passionate, and loving, while noting the difficulties of containing such closeness in comfortable parameters or familiar patterns of behavior. Those for whom a decision to search is only the first step in a long process face this challenge with particular poignancy.

DECIDING TO SEARCH

Some (unknown) number of birth parents decide to search for a child relinquished to adoption. Exactly why and when that occurs is the subject of discussion in adoption literature, and few if any definite conclusions have been reached. What is known is that birth mothers are more likely than birth fathers to undertake the search for a relinquished child and that mothers who do search have often been prompted by the lively publicity surrounding meetings between "lost" kin. A birth parent is aware of the stigma that attaches to the desire to find a relinquished child and needs the support of others to embark on such a quest. Joining a group like Concerned United Birthparents (CUB), reading a newspaper article about a reunion, seeing a television show, are all cited as reasons for taking the first step.

Once embarked on the quest, birth parents elaborate on their reasons, borrowing the symbolism of birth, blood, and genetics to justify a proscribed behavior. The symbolism carries the argument that birth bonds are important, that "true" kinship rests on blood, and that all individuals have a right to their genetic heritage. Drawing on this argument gives a birth mother's search for her "own" child legitimacy in an American cultural context–or, at least, in her eyes. Descriptions of the first encounter may refer directly to birth, as in this statement: "I was filled with joy only equal to the day I gave birth to him" (Rillera 1982: 48). Others are less explicit, instead evoking the emotions the experience of birth is supposed to prompt: "I felt as if my body was turned inside out" (CUB Communicator 11-12/84: 4). Or, from my own interviews: "I went home, I was crying, I was laughing, I was screaming in the car. It was just too good to be true!" The significance of the genetic tie came out in remarks about instant recognition; there was no mistaking the "likeness" between the two people who were just meeting and no denying the absolute attachment.

Adoptees, too, were aware of the taboo surrounding the search for a birth family. Like birth parents, adoptees depended upon the publicity surrounding reunions to push them over the line into taking an action evidently stigmatized. If others had done it, it could be done. Like birth parents, too, adoptees went on to justify searching by using symbols that touched on core cultural assumptions about birth, identity, love, and rights. "I'm not looking for a family. I'm looking for roots. That's so important," said one adoptee, who added: "It's completing the circle to have it." In the adoptee case, the emphasis on identity and on finding oneself dominated, and references to birth and blood became significant primarily in that context. To "complete the circle" for an adoptee was to know "who I really am."

The biggest difference between the way adoptees and birth parents described the first encounter lay not in the content, or its symbolic representation, but in the emotional tone. Adoptees tended to be cooler in their language, less likely to claim they were overwhelmed or instantly attached, and more likely to refer to genetic heritage in medical than in mystical terms. Comments such as the following were characteristic of the adoptees I interviewed: "It wasn't, you know, hug and kiss and all this kind of stuff." Or: "Our reunion went very well and we talked for hours. She told me many personal things pertaining to my adoption." Acquiring knowledge was paramount for the adoptee as it was not for the birth parent. Adoptee searches had as a stated goal information and the acquisition of "vital statistics."

Ultimately, however, adoptees and birth parent searches shared fundamental elements, and these cast an especially sharp light on interpretations of kinship in American culture. Moreover, these elements are severely tested when a relationship continues over time. Whether from the perspective of birth and blood or from that of identity and wholeness, birth parents and adoptees equally relished the initial shock of recognition. One glance, and there was no mistaking the kinship. An adoptee told me: "I saw a face with genes like mine." A birth parent reported: "The most important discovery is that she is like me–looks like me! Personality and all" (Rillera 1982: 53). For a few adoptees and fewer birth parents, finding a "miraculous resemblance" was enough. For many, however, once met a long-lost relative should not be relinquished again.

But what kind of relative? Who was the stranger whose features were strikingly like one's own and whose similarities with oneself seemed to extend to "personality and all"? In American culture, "relative" is both a category and a role, a position in a system and a prescription for behaviors (Schneider 1980). The relatives who met during a reunion claimed the kinship proven by likeness but lacked the rules for interaction that would turn kinship into a script for continuing conduct. Here were two individuals, exactly alike, but could they act like parent and child? *Ought* they act like parent and child or was there another, better model if a reunion were to produce enduring solidarity?[7]

Ahead lay only perplexities. A plan for future contact was plagued with contradictions: a child too old and a mother too young for parenthood to seem "natural," yet whose every gesture asserted the naturalness of the bond; individuals who had never had a moment's conversation, yet knew each other instantly; individuals who were connected by blood yet forced to create a relationship, so that it was as *fictive* as were the links in an adoptive family. To walk forward after the first meeting and make a relationship was often so daunting that the individuals involved simply dropped the idea.

On the other hand, to meet a parent or a child and then let the contact go was not only a disturbing echo of the relinquishment but also a contradiction of cultural ideals about the permanency of parental attachment. One adoptee who had greeted his reunion with comparative calm, also insisted upon his birth mother's complete and permanent devotion to him: "she had this unconditional love for me." Birth mothers explicitly juxtaposed reunion to relinquishment and were even less willing to let the "child" go again.[8] "Nothing can ever erase 34 years of heartache over losing my baby. But I will not look back as I thank God I now have my child back again" (CUB Communicator 6/83: 9). Thus compelled by personal and cultural scripts, adoptees and birth parents turned to the next phase of the unfamiliar familial relationship.

The fact that adoptees and birth parents shared viewpoints about the first meeting while expressing different emotional responses influenced what came next. For both, the outstanding problem *was* the next step: where do you go after the ecstasy or, at least, the satisfaction of a first encounter? As one birth mother said to me: "It's like a virgin field, so I don't know what I'm supposed to expect and what I'm not supposed to expect. There's no map."

ROUTINIZING THE RELATIONSHIP

There might be no map, but there *were* cultural models for ongoing close encounters of a kinship sort. Birth parents and adoptees knew these models perfectly well, and tried them out time and again in the stories they told at support group meetings.[9] Even when an individual had not had a reunion, or was not certain about whether to take the next step after an initial encounter, the appeal of a long-term relationship with kin by birth was apparent. Eager as a birth parent might be for the "thrill" of seeing a once-lost baby or an adoptee to fill the gaps in her identity, neither of these experiences was finally enough. The pressure to turn the "first sight," whatever its emotional tone, into more than a one-time event influenced the accounts I heard at meetings and in interviews.

Separated by adoption in a culture that believes in the endurance of a genealogical connection, birth parents and adoptees yearned to prolong the relationship they had glimpsed initially. To make the kinship real, the "bond" had to be manifested in behaviors. And in order to determine the content of these behaviors, adoptees and birth parents borrowed from models of reciprocal relationships that existed in the culture, primarily, as I have said, patronage, friendship, courtship, and avuncular or, accurately, aunt-like kinship. For individuals who pursued the contact, each model had some elements to recommend it and some that made it inappropriate for interactions between a categorical parent and child.[10] An examination of these elements led me to two conclusions: one, the adoptive parent relationship always hovers in the background, probed and punctured as adoptee and birth parent create their "own" kinship. Second, reunions entail a critique of American kinship and, necessarily, of adoption policy that deserves serious attention.

In the initial encounter, two people come together with expectations about intimacy, love, permanence, obligation, and responsibility. Couched in abstract terms, these expectations did not always affect the immediate encounter, which was dominated by the feelings of joy, relief, and satisfaction adoptees and birth parents reported. Such expectations would, however, affect any prolonged relationship and in those instances participants drew on the models I mentioned to make abstract concepts concrete and useful for how they might *act*. In the process, the extent to which birth parent and adoptee agreed about the premises of a relationship became clear. Compelled to draw a map together, the participants had to negotiate both the territory and the way through it. As they struggled to establish a mutually satisfying map, adoptees and birth parents reflected on notions of parenthood, not always with consensus. These reflections, moreover, brought the adoptive parent into the center of the scene, the directional signal for both adoptee and birth parent.

When stated explicitly, patronage was the least appealing model for the relationship between a birth parent and child. In fact, given its political and commercial connotations, one might wonder why it came up at all. The answer lies in the references "patronage" has to notions of sponsorship and socially-sanctioned responsibility. "Patronage" implies a sense of duty that has roots in cultural values about concern and expressions of interest in another's well-being. The model accorded a pattern to the messy interchanges adoptees and birth parents engaged in to express interest in one another. In this situation, too, patronage was not rigid but allowed for different arrangements depending on individual circumstances. An adoptee was "patron" to her parent as reasonably as the other way around.

Adoptee demonstrations of patronage included behaviors that are familiar in a conventional family setting but that in a reunion setting lack supporting rules and customs. So, for example, adoptees invited birth parents for holidays, sent children to visit the "new" grandparent, and generally considered the parent's health and welfare. Lacking the usual textures of continual interaction, however, these behaviors could become tense. One adult adoptee complained to me about her mother's bad habits, behaviors she had nothing to do with and found strange: she "watches cartoons. For breakfast, a bowl of cereal and a cup of coffee, and I'm used to eating more." But the daughter continued to invite her birth mother for visits and to telephone her regularly. Birth parents, too, "patronized" an adoptee and, like adoptees, found the behaviors produced uncertainties about rights and duties. "It was hard, it's hard though, when she's telling me things like 'Yeah, I went over to this other frat house and we did this and we stayed up half the night.' I start feeling that I want to tell her like 'No, no, no!'"

Patronage served a purpose, insisting on responsibility and concern without locking these traits to love and affection. Yet as a concept patronage is discordant with a kin tie, and even the coolest adoptee rejected the notion when it became explicit—for instance, when a parent asked for favors. No one I interviewed associated patronage with god parenthood and with the sponsorship of a spiritual parent implied by that term. No one treated patron positively in this sense, as someone who provided that which the "raising" parent could not provide. That American kinship vocabulary is impoverished makes discussion of adoption occasionally awkward: we do not have a term for the parent who raises a child (see E. Goody 1982). Curiously, god parenthood never came up in the discussions I had with adoptees and birth parents, though it would seem a good model.

"I don't want to be her friend, though I told people I just wanted to be a friend, but that really wasn't true." This birth mother was resisting a model that was generally quite appealing in the context of reunions.

Friendship, as culturally defined, implies long-term obligation embedded in strong emotional ties. The duties friends owe one another are not "bloodless," as patron-client exchanges might be thought to be. Feelings fill out favors between friends. What friendship does *not* incorporate is a generational difference and a genealogical connection. Nor, in some understandings of the word, is friendship unconditional and unchanging. The birth mother quoted above recognized the inadequacy of "friend" when the subject of the relationship was a daughter. "I don't want to be your pal," were the words the birth mother repeated to me: "I want to be your mother.'"

Other birth parents liked the model of friendship, since it allowed ongoing, emotional contact without too much intensity. "Michael and I have established an affectionate bond between us that does not replace any previously existing ones. What has been replaced, he and I agree, is the pain and the fantasy." The position of friend seemed to require a certain amount of restraint or to be chosen by birth parents who had no experience of *acting like* a parent—and perhaps did not want that experience.

The problem with friendship was that it neglected the "birth" part of birth parenthood and also that it did not accord with what birth parents said about the first sight of the relinquished child. Birth parents who described "vomiting" in excitement or being "turned inside out" could not easily mesh that reaction with the calm of a friendship. Even less easily could birth parents who emphasized the "natural" gush of feeling upon encountering a child accept the "bloodlessness" of a friendship. "I believe in blood ties," a parent wrote to CUB, "but this is incredible" (CUB Communicator 1/83: 10). In one woman's terse statement, the whole issue came out: "I feel like I am her mom. I mean, I *know* I'm her mom. I mean, for God's sake I gave birth to her and I don't want to be called anything else."

Adoptees more readily accepted the model of friendship, and a birth parent had to deal with that definition of the relationship if she wanted to continue the relationship. In contrast to their found parents, a number of the adoptees I met were comfortable with the companionable quality of friendship as a way of handling the new parent-child relation. "When we'd go out to dinner alone, it would be more intimate discussions and learning more about each other," an adoptee told me about her repeated interactions with her birth father. They did not hug or kiss or acknowledge overweening intensity. Another adoptee said to me, and probably revealed to her parent: "I don't think that people have to establish *intimate* relationships with the people they find."

Another adoptee claimed he hoped for a good, solid friendship and not much more. "And we'll meet occasionally at the Black Stone [Tavern] and have a drink and we'll talk about our lunatic lives." But even for adoptees, this kind of drinking-together could come to seem inappropriate after the importance and the effort of searching for "genes like mine." Being pals and joking companions did not harmonize with the dominant tone of adoptee descriptions of the initial encounter. One man who had located his birth mother several years before I met him conveyed the sense of a friendship, but then quickly added: "she loved me without ever having seen me." The stirrings of a parent-child model are evident in this perception of love. Another adoptee placed his relationship smack-dab onto a parental model: "It is a special kind of love that neither time nor separation can diminish."

Love was a major problem with friendship, and especially the sudden rush of absolute unconditional love perceived by both birth parents and adoptees. Inasmuch as this notion of love was central to accounts of the first meeting, adoptees and birth parents almost inevitably inserted passion into the content of an ongoing relationship. And here the model used, and its implications, has only recently been confronted by participants—for the model is of courtship or romantic intimacy.

If in accord with descriptions of the first meeting, this model is discordant with conventions regulating the parent-child relationship in American culture. Yet birth parents who relished the love they felt for a child sound like lovers, borrowing a vocabulary from American clichés describing sexual passion. Images and metaphors extended feelings beyond the "thrill" attached to giving birth and brought them close to the ecstasy attached to falling in love. "My every thought was of him," said a birth mother, after having been in contact with her son for nearly a year. "I now knew what the term Magnificent Obsession meant."

Others talked about a constant yearning in between visits and the pleasures of being "in the arms" of this no-longer child. In an interesting fashion, talk of being in love mimicked adoptive parents' descriptions of their relationship with an adopted child; having fallen wildly in love at first sight, adoptive parents report, their feelings develop into a kind of passion. Manuals for parents repeat the message, accentuating the love that seals two people's fates forever, till death do us part. It is not surprising in a culture in which designated parenthood has to be sealed with passion that birth parents should borrow the same imagery for their own designed parenthood.

But for birth parents an emphasis on passion had a special meaning. Passionate feelings justified keeping in touch with the child, just as "blood" had justified finding her or him in the first place. Somewhat paradoxically, passion rationalized the contact between birth parent and adoptee, proving the relationship was "right" because it was beyond thought.[11] A passionate love also filled in for the script or map that no one had. It was as if by loving, a parent would be good and instinctively know how to act. Based on Spockian notions of love as the foundation for parental behaviors, this did not always work out for birth parents whose behaviors were with a grown-up child.[12] For Dr. Spock is reassuring parents of infants—their love will carry them through fits of crying and spitting—not the "new" parents of an adult. An assumption that love provides a chart of behaviors did not necessarily hold when, say, a 37-year-old mother found a 21-year-old son. Love, then, took on other connotations that occasionally bothered the individuals who noticed them.

In one example, a young birth mother told me about spending weekends in San Francisco with her found son. So troubled did she become about the strength of their love, and its intimacy, that she decided to go to parenting classes, where, sitting with the mothers and fathers of infants, she learned techniques of child rearing. She also learned to define herself as a mother and to separate herself generationally from her son; child rearing techniques drove a wedge into their too-erotic oneness. Yet, while diminishing the sexual nature of her link to her son, these techniques ran the risk of infantilizing the child who was the recipient of them. The choice to be a mother with a vengeance might come up against a child whose desire not to be babied was equally strong.

How did adoptees follow through on the strong feelings prompted by the first sight of a birth parent? The adoptees I met who maintained a relationship with a birth parent did not use a vocabulary of passion, longing, or obsession. These words did not suit the calm rationality adoptees tended to affect when the meeting turned into a long-term relationship and which, as well, fit the cultural model for how grown children interact with parents. Emotional restraint also fit the original stated reasons for making contact: to complete one's identity, find one's roots, know a person with similar features. The driving energy was not the idea of unbreakable bonds and overwhelming love, as it (presumably) was for birth parents, but the need for facts and figures.

One birth parent I interviewed understood the adoptee viewpoint so well that I will quote her words: "That's what my mom said to me. She said, 'OK, just think if you or I, or if I raised you all these years and even if you knew you were adopted and all of a sudden this strange woman comes up and says, 'Hi, I'm your mom.' She says, 'Do you think that you would feel this instant love for this woman or. . . . ?' And I, you know, *no*. And you know, even if it's curiosity or an interest, I don't think I could fall in love with somebody that easy. So I imagine it is totally different from that [adoptee] point of view."

It *was* different. The closest adoptees came to expressing passion was when they referred to "miraculous resemblances" between themselves and a birth parent. Descriptions of "exact-sameness" conveyed the sense of intimacy and oneness that in birth parent accounts were couched in a language that evoked romantic passion. One adoptee distinguished her birth mother from her adoptive mother, accentuating her identification with the birth mother. "My [adoptive] mom is real outgoing," she began, "and she loves to drive and she would get in the car and go anywhere. Like she would drive to Florida. I would go up to the store, but I don't really—. And Joan [birth mother], she's the same way." As she warmed to the story, the domestic details one learns over time also emerged: "And I can't sew worth a darn and my mother is a really good seamstress and she made all of our clothes when we were kids. And I can't even sew buttons on. And Joan said she's not good at that. She said she can sew but she's not good and she's not mechanical, which I'm not either."

Even here the birth mother is distanced, called by her first name while the adoptive parent is simply "mother." Still, in the adoptee's narrative, discovery of the multiple ways in which she and her birth mother resembled one another set the foundation for a bond that would last forever. Any two people who were so much alike belonged together—and in this assumption the adoptees *were* just like the birth parents.

In the longest-lasting reunions I knew, adoptee and birth parent tried out the conventional model for a parent-child relationship. But this model turned out to be perplexing and misleading, despite the fact that it incorporated the love, intimacy, obligation, and responsibility each participant wanted. The model did not fit the life stages of the "child" and the "parent," or (often) their generational closeness, or their pasts, which were empty of each other. Another model entered the picture that represented generational difference and interactional distance while acknowledging the "natural" bonds between the individuals. A model of parenthood was modified by a model of extended-family kinship, specifically uncle/aunt and niece/nephew relationships. That Americans have the word avuncular but no analogous term for aunt-like behavior may contribute to the difficulty adoptees and birth parents have making maps for their interactions.[13] Two examples will indicate how the model of parenthood was negotiated in ongoing reunions.

Encouraged by his adoptive mother, Ned located his birth mother when he was in his mid-thirties. The first encounter was marked by a lack of physical contact: no hugging and no kissing. But the relationship soon settled into a long-term one, with visits exchanged between Ned and the birth family, as well as between birth and adoptive families. Ned described a wedding to me, at which there was a conglomeration of relatives, including: "my two brothers named Jim." His wife added, "and I have two mothers-in-law!" All this contact and communication made the reunion relationship smoother. In fact, Ned's case demonstrated something adoptees had told me all along, which was the importance of embedding a parent-child relationship into a wider network of relationships. It was as if the *created*–either adoptive or new birth–parent-child link could be better formulated in the context of other family links. That made sense to me, and evidently made sense to adoptees like Ned who had to work out complicated interactions.

Yet even Ned did not fall into complete ease about his four parents, and what he was to them and they to each other. He put the difficulties this way: "You know, see it's hard for me to call them [birth parents] Mom and Dad in front of Mom and Dad. . . . But as far as I'm concerned, they're [adoptive parents] Mom and Dad. Because they are. What am I going to call them? Mr. and Mrs. Blackman? You know, I mean, that's not, to me that's not respectful." Behind the uncertainty about terms lay a deeper confusion about what to feel and how to act with each of these four parents. "And then you think about all of them," he said to me. "Both sides of the family, all the time. So you don't want to neglect one for the other and it's, you know, it ain't as easy as it sounds." I met Ned's adoptive mother, who told me Ned had become "much more talkative" since his reunion, possibly (though she did not offer this explanation) because he had become self-consciously alert to the terms of his relationships.

In general, Ned was pleased with his large extended family. "I'm telling you," he concluded, "all of everything worked out real good." He had added numerous kin to his world. At the same time, in a sense he had lost four parents, each of whom was falling into another kind of relationship with the "child." The birth mother, at a distance, resembled a loving older, female relative, as did the adoptive mother, now distanced by the presence of a genealogical parent. The terms of Ned's relationships with the women closest to him but a generation older did sound like those between a nephew and an aunt. Gift exchanges, telephone calls, visits on holidays bore the imprint of non-nuclear family ties. Ned's adoptive mother and his birth mother fit American cultural definitions of a *relative in general* rather than of a *parent in particular*: love and obligation were expressed under certain circumstances, not unconditionally; contact obeyed rules of conduct not waves of emotion; interactions were controlled by position in a kinship system rather than by an experience of "oneness."

. One more example before I come to my conclusion. The other adoptee I knew who had a long relationship with her birth family was Carey. Her case was somewhat exceptional in that, in her mid-twenties, she had a number of medical problems which prompted continual intervention by her birth mother. Happy to take on a responsible and loving role, this birth mother also revealed ambivalence about becoming a "real" mother to the child she had just met. First she told me it bothered her that Carey wanted to use the terms Mom and Dad in the birth family: "She calls him Dad. All the other kids call him Chuck. But Carey calls him Dad. She asked if it was all right if I call you Dad. She calls me Mom." Second, she admitted she resisted the pressure Carey put on her to be fully incorporated into the birth family. Carey did this in one interesting way: "Well, she even said to me," the birth mother reported, "'Can you re-adopt me?' I said no." I spent a good deal of time with Carey and with her birth mother. It was perfectly clear that Linda wanted to be completely involved with Carey but, simultaneously, that she did not want to be another mother or a mother to another child. With five children (all adult) in her family, Carey best came in as a beloved and well-attended niece. A different birth mother confessed to me: "I never miss her [found birth child] at Christmas the way I miss my sons."

I met adoptees and birth parents who, after the excitement of the first encounter, did not want to pursue a relationship at all. I also met adoptees and birth parents who constructed a polite and formal contact with the "found" relative, fearful of repeating a relinquishment experience traumatic to both but not wanting anything more. And then I met the adoptees and birth parents who are the subject of this section--the individuals who worked to construct a relationship that would last over time, be comfortably interactive, and be satisfyingly emotional.[14] I have suggested that, lacking maps for this fictive (made) relationship, adoptees and birth parents turn to the models for reliable reciprocal relationships that are available in American culture, primarily patronage, friendship, courtship, and non-nuclear intergenerational kinship ties. In doing so, and in talking about what they did, birth parents and adoptees expose contradictory elements in American cultural interpretations of parenthood and of kinship. In this regard, and in my conclusion, adoptive parents take a central place.

A VANISHING PARENTHOOD?

Reunions that lead to a long-term relationship can be interpreted by outsiders in two ways: one, as an affirmation of parenthood, both as a concept and as a prescription for conduct; two, what seems to be exactly the opposite, as an indicator of the vanishing of parenthood in the United States. The affirmation aspect is very much part of the public rhetoric surrounding reunions, especially when that rhetoric has a source in birth parent statements. From this point of view, reunions demonstrate the true (and traditional) meaning of parenthood: a bond based on birth and enacted in performance. The second interpretation of reunions, that they prefigure the disappearance of parenthood, is less easily supported with "hard" data since neither observers nor participants are likely to make such a claim. That interpretation of reunions is also not as threatening as may appear at first sight.

The second interpretation is not exactly the opposite of the first, inasmuch as both imply a confrontation with the concept of parenthood. I argue here that anyone who is involved in a reunion, from whatever position, ends up reconsidering the meaning of parenthood; I have suggested some of the dimensions of that reconsideration in the previous section. And though at first such revision seems to wipe away the concept of parenthood, in the end "parenthood" will be reconstructed in ways that better suit the experiences of those involved in parental relations—which is, of course, everyone. For decades, those who are responsible for adoptive placements have been concerned about defining a parent in the best interests of a child. Reunions between a "lost" child and a "found" parent (especially those that endure with solidarity) can provide a definition that is faithful to experience. Then parenthood as it has been handed down to a late twentieth century society will vanish—transformed into something else.

My interviews and observations show that individuals who know adoptive kinship in particular are quite bold about revising kinship in general. For the adoptee and the birth parent who search, the notion of a *real* parent lies at the core of this revision. Given that, the adoptive parent is never completely out of the picture in a search, affecting assessments of the first meeting and, equally, the creation of a new relationship. And for both the birth parent and the adoptee, "adoptive parent" is at once an image presented by agencies, the media, and popular culture and an actual living, breathing, annoying, loving, present person. In each of these capacities, the adoptive parent constitutes a stronger part of the missing map than either the adoptee or the birth parent is likely to admit.

The map offered by the adoptive parent *is* a funny one for participants in a reunion, and it is greeted with suspicion, hostility, and attempts at subversion by those who use it. Still, as a map, adoptive parenthood points a way from here to there. The signposts taken from this map by adoptees and birth parents appear in descriptions of ongoing reunion relationships:

absolute and unconditional love; love that arises instantly and not after long acquaintance; reciprocal obligation and demonstrations of concern; shared traits tempered by a marked generational span. These elements are inscribed in placement policy and in conceptualizations of a good parent-child relationship in American culture.

Adoptees and birth parents find much to resist in a conventional model of parenthood precisely because that model is supposedly embodied in the adoptive parent. Adoptees who search take a measure of their adoptive parents, concluding either that they do not meet the criteria for a good parent or, if they do, that they remain distant from the adoptee in profound respects.[15] The bond, from this perspective, was never sealed but always permeable. The view of an adoptive parent constructed before a search becomes part of the relation with a birth parent after a reunion—if not immediately, then certainly over time. To pursue my analogy, the map exists even if just to show what detours are possible.

The birth parent also brings her or, less commonly, his idea of the adoptive parent into the reunion, where it plays a part in what happens next. Like the adoptee, too, the birth parent regards the map attached to adoptive parenthood with critical distance, creating her parenthood in the face of the parenthood social workers, lawyers, and judges created for her child. The presence of the adoptive parent in the background facilitates and complicates the map-making an adoptee and a birth parent embark on together and, lacking guidelines, on their own. Adoptive parents represent chosen parents, but not necessarily the parenthood a birth parent any more than an adoptee would have chosen.

Adoptee and birth parent react to the adoptive parents by emphasizing the *non-chosen* aspect of their bond. As I have pointed out, they do not do this in the same way. The adoptees I met tended to downplay the symbols of birth and blood—flesh of my flesh—and to accentuate similarities that lay beyond shared experiences or time spent together. But at core the purposes were the same: to underline the oneness that exists between a *real* parent and child, beyond the law or, at least, the decision of a social worker. In addition, both adoptees and birth parents were convinced that "likeness" justified and prepared the groundwork for a solid, continuing relationship.

In this, they sound like social workers who claim that matching an infant to adoptive parents establishes the basis for an enduring attachment. Adoptees detailed for me the ways they resembled a birth parent as frequently as a birth parent told me that "birth" bonded her to the relinquished child. One might argue that the adoptee emphasis on resemblance is just another way of talking about blood and birth, and it partly is, but I think the differences are important as well. For an adoptee, visible and superficial (on-the-surface) likenesses—red hair, a love of sweets, mechanical ability—prompted a feeling of relatedness and of ongoing commitment. And though birth parents also pointed to this kind of visible trait, they were more likely to let "blood" be the seal of a permanent attachment—the closeness one *naturally* felt to the child of one's body.

Underlining the significance of the resemblances discovered in a reunion, adoptees often went on to deny any resemblance to the adoptive parents. By this light, the chosen parents were not real parents—though probably the adoptee had been matched and did resemble at least one member of the family. Birth parents, too, emphasized the source of their real parenthood by denying it to adoptive parents in assumptions about their physical and emotional frigidity.

Looking alike was so significant a part of the reunion that it determined an adoptee's assessment of a birth parent's behaviors. One adoptee expressed amazement that her birth mother pretended the resemblances were not there for all to see. "My mother is still in the closet," she said to me (with an interesting choice of words). "When I go to Chicago, if she meets someone she knows down the street, she'll introduce me as her friend from Colorado because she's not able to face it. Now if any, if you were to walk up to us on a street corner even without knowing you would automatically assume that we were mother and daughter. I mean, it's, you know, pale complexion and same eyes, same nose." The physical features social workers looked for in placing a baby turn out to be significant for the very people who accuse social workers of being heartless and calculating.

Resemblances might be evident, joining adoptee to birth parent, but they also were embedded in a generational distance. The woman quoted above insisted: we were mother and daughter. Adoptees did not want to find a twin or a sibling, unless an unmistakably older sibling. The parent was a twin only in an old photograph, showing the birth parent at the age the adoptee currently was. Adoptees, then, created the proper parental relation by keeping generations separate and by stressing that traits were handed *down,* parent to child. For birth parents, the symbolism of birth itself implied both oneness and the natural distance between "begetter" and "begotten."

Was love, and the expression of love, missing from the map adoptees and birth parents drew for an ongoing relationship? For adoptees, the answer might well be yes. Love was not what they seemed to be searching for or hoping for when the relationship continued. This fit the life stage of most adoptees who searched, and the cultural assumption that "grown" children do not require unconditional, abundant love from a parent. After experiencing the force of an attachment at the first meeting, adoptees did not insert love into their accounts of what happened next. Nor, consequently, did adoptees say much to me about how birth parents should act—not even Carey who so badly wanted to be part of her birth family. And not Ned, who worried about his own performance as a child in his blended family but not about the love or actions of his parents.

Birth parents were more likely to talk about love, but mainly linked to the notion that giving birth creates a feeling of permanent bonding. They did not use love as the prescription for particular conduct, any more than their "children" did. The mysterious tie of blood existed, but action and expressions of affection did not automatically stem from these feelings. I have argued here and elsewhere that the assertion of undying love frames birth parent discussions of searching, but the assertion fades when a birth parent actually engages in interactions with the found child. Ongoing reunions, then, reveal just how far love can carry a parent and a child when habit and custom are not there to solidify the ties.

One birth mother I interviewed openly admitted that the feeling of love attached to giving birth was inappropriate to the reunion relationship. "And I realized afterwards that what I wanted to find was this cute, cuddly, needing little baby who was going to say 'Mother,' you know, after all these years. Because that's what I wanted and that need, although I had two sons, was never filled. I still had this baby somewhere that was taken from me and so when I saw her I wanted to hold her and cuddle her and buy her things and take her shopping and shower her with my love and attention and move in and 'Anything, anything you want, I'll lay down and die, anything.'" But the response from the college-aged daughter did not permit this scenario. The birth mother continued: "I write her very emotional, loving letters and tell her what the relationship means to me or what she means to me. . . . And she writes back and says, you know, 'The weather's nice and we're real busy and we went to the football game.'" As this relationship evolved (I have known it for nearly ten years), the two accommodated to one another, creating a kinship tie appropriate to adults who had more than the usual intensity of connection—but not, as the birth mother noted, a bond based on birth.

My analysis of ongoing reunions suggests that love does not play a central part in the enduring solidarity between adoptee and birth parent. A less radical statement of the idea would be that love is created in a form appropriate to the origin of the relationship. To assume one kind of parental love, in other words, does a disservice to individuals who are constructing emotional ties that recognize the *circumstantiality* of all relationships between parent and child. Like adoption itself, then, reunions display the creativity of individuals in making kinship and in determining the behaviors that seal the bonds between them.

I am not arguing against reunions but rather for a consideration of their meanings and consequences. Reunions, like an adoptive family arrangement, show how flexible the content of "parenthood" can be. Furthermore, reunions go beyond adoption in indicating how much *fictionalizing* occurs in any parent-child relationship. I think this is good, if we remember the roots of the word "fiction" (to make) and the faith we put in adoptive families to sort out their feelings for one another. The point is that just as for years a biological model has been applied to the adoptive family (through a matching policy and an "as-if-begotten" principle), perhaps now it is time to think about how the social model drawn from adoption can be applied to the biological family. Support for that point lies in the material I have presented on reunions, in which child and parent reassert biological bonds in terms of socially-constructed kinship.

At the same time there is no denying that, as Ned put it, a reunion "ain't as easy as it sounds." Reunions are not easy for the participants or for the observers. As a culture, we have worked hard to write the script for adoptive arrangements and not as hard to write a script for making biologically related individuals into "real" kin–despite Dr. Spock and many parent-training manuals.[16] That reunions remain both stigmatized and titillating confirms both the threat they pose and the attraction they have: it may be that every parent and every child desires the moment to "find" a relative and to "build" a link. Or, perhaps, there must be more than one such moment.

As adoptive policy leans toward openness and an acknowledgment that adoptive families are composed of several parent-child dyads, one may hope not simply that reunions will become more acceptable but that they will vanish altogether from the adoption scene–a no longer necessary form of contact for people who have known each other all along.

NOTES

1. Modell, *Kinship with Strangers*, University of California, 1994.

2. In this paper, I am using the convention of referring to the birth parent as "she." There are, of course, male birth parents, but the reunion scene seems to be dominated by birth mothers.

3. This assumption has implications for adoption practice, including the choice of a two-parent family as the ideal adoptive family, the policy of matching (a child should look like her parents), and the requirement of a generational age difference between adopting couple and adopted child.

4. See Modell 1994.

5. As in much concerning adoption, numbers of reunions are not available—and, as I have pointed out, even the meaning of the term is not unambiguous. The topic of openness is beyond the scope of this paper. See Modell 1994; McRoy, Grotevant, and White 1988.

6. See Modell 1986.

7. Several of my phrases, including this last one, refer to Schneider's analysis of American kinship; 1980.

8. Modell 1986.

9. I also joined a local adoptee search group; the group did not have formal connections with any of the national adoption search groups.

10. I use the word "categorical" as a reminder that the persons fit into a category; the *implications* of being in a category caused the perplexities in ongoing reunions.

11. As I show below, some of this is directly juxtaposed to views of the adoptive parent.

12. I mean here, of course, Benjamin Spock, whose many editions of *Baby and Child Care* all claim that a parent who acts natural is naturally a good parent. See Modell 1988.

13. The fact that most birth parents who are contacted are female not male makes "avuncular" the wrong term. In addition, I think that avuncular carries connotations of a joking relationship that are inappropriate to the seriousness with which everyone takes a prolonged reunion relationship.

14. These versions of contact bear a strong resemblance to the degrees of "openness" now becoming part of adoptive placement policy. Openness ranges from letters conveying information, through phone calls or supervised face-to-face contacts, to ongoing interactions between birth and adoptive families.

15. See Modell 1994; Schechter and Bertocci 1990.

16. Modell 1988.

REFERENCES

Baran, A. and R. Pannor. "Open Adoption." In *The Psychology of Adoption,* edited by D. Brodzinsky and M. Schechter, pp. 316-331. New York: Oxford University Press, 1990.

Brodzinsky, D., and M. Schechter (eds.). *The Psychology of Adoption.* New York: Oxford University Press, 1990.

CUB Communicator. Newsletter. CUB Headquarters, 1979-1986 (Dover, N. H.) and 1986-1990 (Des Moines, Iowa).

Gediman, J. and L. P. Brown. *Birth Bond.* Far Hills, New Jersey: New Horizon, 1989.

Goody, Esther. *Parenthood and Social Reproduction.* New York: Cambridge University Press, 1982.

Kirk, H. David. *Adoptive Kinship.* Toronto: Butterworths, 1981.

Kirk, H. David. *Shared Fate.* Port Angeles, WA: Ben-Simon, 1984.

Lifton, Betty Jean. *Twice-Born.* New York: Penguin, 1977.

Lifton, Betty Jean. *Lost and Found*. New York: Dial, 1979.

McRoy, R., and H. D. Grotevant, and K. L. White. *Openness in Adoption*. New York: Praeger, 1988.

Modell, Judith. "In Search: The Purported Biological Basis of Parenthood." *American Ethnologist*, v.13 (1986): pp. 646-661.

Modell, Judith. "The Meanings of Love." In *The Social Construction of Emotion*, edited by C. Z. Stearns and P. Stearns, pp. 48-61, New York: Holmes and Meier, 1988.

Modell, Judith. *Kinship with Strangers*. Berkeley, CA: University of California, 1994.

Rillera, M. J. (ed.). *Searching for Minors*. Huntington Beach, CA: Triadoption Library, 1982.

Schneider, David. *American Kinship*. Chicago: University of Chicago, 1980.

Schneider, David. *A Critique of the Study of Kinship*. Ann Arbor, MI: University of Michigan, 1984.

Schechter, M. D. and D. Bertocci. "The Meaning of the Search." In *The Psychology of Adoption*, edited by D. Brodzinsky and M. Schechter, pp. 62-90. New York: Oxford University Press, 1990.

Developing Definitions
of an Adoptee-Birthmother
Reunion Relationship

James Fraser

SUMMARY. The phenomena of adoptee-birthparent reunion has recently become of interest to psychologists, social workers, and sociologists. This paper looks at one adoptee-birthmother reunion through a symbolic interactionist lens in order to understand the developmental phases that the participants experience. The direction of such reunion relationships is affected by the lack of pre-existing definitions, such as "friendship" or "family," to guide these interactions. Adoptee-birthparent relationships also provide a situation whereby the past, present, and future are highly interrelated. Participants in these relationships negotiate meanings of what was, what is, and what will be. This paper demonstrates that a central determinant of successful negotiation of an adoptee-birthparent reunion relationship is to develop and convey a similar definition of the situation from which future interactions can be based. *[Article copies available for a fee from The Haworth Document Delivery Service: 1-800-342-9678. E-mail address: getinfo@haworth.com]*

It was like any other Saturday morning during my time as a student at the university, marked by the impending load of reading I had so judi-

James Fraser is a PhD candidate in the Department of Sociology at Georgia State University.

The author would like to thank Lara Foley, Denise Donnelly, and Michael Hodge for their helpful comments and suggestions on earlier drafts of this paper.

[Haworth co-indexing entry note]: "Developing Definitions of an Adoptee-Birthmother Reunion Relationship." Fraser, James. Co-published simultaneously in *Marriage & Family Review* (The Haworth Press, Inc.) Vol. 25, No. 1/2, 1997, pp. 67-78; and: *Families and Adoption* (ed: Harriet E. Gross and Marvin B. Sussman) The Haworth Press, Inc., 1997, pp. 67-78. Single or multiple copies of this article are available for a fee from The Haworth Document Delivery Service [1-800-342-9678, 9:00 a.m. - 5:00 p.m. (EST). E-mail address: getinfo@haworth.com].

ciously put off until the weekend. As I sat down in my favorite soft-cushioned chair with a scalding hot cup of coffee, I peered out of my front room window and saw a Federal Express truck screech to a halt in front of my apartment. To my surprise the driver appeared to be walking, or rather one pace faster, towards my front door. After I signed the invoice I took the letter and peered on the neatly printed label to figure out who could have been sending me an overnight parcel that cost $9.95. The label marked Denver, Colorado, baffled me for I knew of no one in that region of the country. As I opened the letter and read with anticipation my mind went blank. All I could feel was a buzzing sensation that jolted through my being like a soft electric shock. From that moment on my life was changed forever. The "lost moments" that I had never consciously considered were starting to fill my being like a river bed that had not seen water for ages. My walls were not able to hold all of the thoughts and feelings. So, I sat stunned.

I am an adult adoptee. In this essay I analyze the events that occurred as I became re-united with my birthmother. I examine some of the features of such a reunion which should be understood, not as a singular event, but as an on-going process with its own developmental stages and characteristic history. The reunion between an adoptee who is now an adult and the birthparent who did not raise him poses interesting constraints on a key process involved in "taking the role of the other"–the hallmark of social relationships (Mead, 1934).

Sociological insight alerts us to how even the most ephemeral and least emotionally significant interactions rely on pre-existing definitions (Goffman, 1959). However, because the re-united parent and child are unable to define the developing connection between them within standardized notions (e.g., of "friendship" or "family")–to enter such a relationship is to face unknown and potentially injurious consequences (McColm, 1993). Each must engage with an "ill-defined" other without much in the way of advance cues about each other's perspectives. Ambiguity about the implications of their biological connection and the circumstances which separated them hovers over each move toward the other, threatening to undermine even the possibility of initiating a reunion meeting, let alone stabilizing a reunion relationship.

The microsociological forces that affect reunion relationships between adult adoptees and birthparents are a relatively new area of interest. At least two questions should guide the study of these forces. First, how do the participants come to orient themselves to each other? Secondly, what are the consequences when the participants have incongruent expectations and orientations? A corollary concern of the second question focuses on the potential for problems which can derail progress towards a lasting and mutually satisfying relationship.

An analysis of my reunion with my birthmother will address these questions as it reveals the developmental processes involved. Some issues that arise from an adoptive reunion relationship center on the initial defini- tion of the relationship and on the subsequent expectations that each participant brings to social interactions (McColm, 1993). I will recount from my personal experience how my effort to come to terms with such constraints has re-shaped my own sense of "self."

ROLE ORIENTATIONS, EXPECTATIONS, AND REUNIONS

Thornton and Nardi (1975) offer a four stage model in which actors orient themselves to their role incumbency. Each of these stages involves more information about the role in question as well as greater identification with it by the potential role occupant. Not surprisingly these authors attend to the handicap of inadequate prior preparation to subsequent successful role performance. But as noted above, in the case of reunions there is characteristically little anticipatory socialization, or even awareness of available parameters and expectations for successful role performance. Since one is unlikely to try to learn about a future role one does not expect to assume, advance preparation has rarely been available, let alone sought out by the party who has not initiated the search. Some peer support groups such as Concerned United Birthparents (CUB) do enable those who come to them to listen to, and learn from, others who are involved in various stages of searching and reuniting. But very often neither party—"searcher" nor "searchee" has much opportunity to learn about what it may mean to be "found" and to become enmeshed in a reunion relationship. Participants to reunion initiation cannot count on any but the vaguest (and at this point largely media driven) preliminary structuring of what is to follow.

This indeterminacy of role relations provides fertile ground for exploring how participants compensate for missing relationship guideposts. That is, how do people construct the framework for appropriate communication when there are no significant shared meanings through which to communicate. Do they attempt to appropriate possible parallel relationships (e.g., that of friend, family member, stranger) to guide relationship constitution? How do pre-existing differentials in the social status (e.g., prestige, position and power) of each participant color their first and then subsequent encounters? Other characteristics of the relationship that emerge may also influence how this reunion relationship develops.

The potential of such factors to influence the reunion relationship suggests we should move beyond our current singular focus with the original re-connection period (as media accounts have framed these) to a discussion of the processes involved in developing and maintaining reunion relationships. Absorption with the finding process, its legal and other obstacles, has eclipsed the relationship's ultimate meaning to its participants, its development and stabilization. My experience will show that significant as the initial connection may be, it is just the beginning of a series of stages, albeit unpredictable in specific circumstances, which need to be distinguished and attended to as well. This analysis of my personal biography highlights the process of defining and maintaining a reunion relationship.

ESTABLISHING CONTEXT OF MY REUNION RELATIONSHIP

I entered the reunion relationship without any prior preparation because I had never considered my identity as an adoptee salient. I had never given serious thought to associating with my birthmother or biological father. That day when the Federal Express truck pulled up to my apartment marked the point at which I became self-conscious of my being an adoptee. Opening that letter has lived with me as a turning point in my conception of self.

I remember questioning almost everything about the form and substance of my birthmother's first letter to me. I dissected it over and over for clues as to how she wanted to represent herself to me. For example, the handwriting was on a banking investment firm's letterhead that read ". . . . . , Vice-President." I wondered if she was consciously presenting a self as a "Vice-President" of a corporation. Was she communicating success, prestige, power, or was it "only" that she was at work when she authored the letter?

Although she requested contact from me, she communicated that no further interaction between us would occur unless I initiated it. This interpersonal ritual (Goffman, 1967) could be viewed as an act of deference allowing for my wishes to define the relationship. While this may have been considered an act of respect or acknowledgment of the yet to be defined boundaries of a relationship, I argue it was also a gesture that symbolized her relative power to me. Since she had no information to establish the level of motivation I might have towards constructing a relationship with her, her presentation of self seemed to serve a double function. The first was to express her various identities as successful business woman, wife, and mother. The second message seemed to imply that she would not pose a threat to my well-being, and would not forcibly disturb the family relationships I had already constructed, as son of two adoptive parents. There was no other available information in her letter offering any cues for the type of relationship she wanted to build with me.

It became evident through our conversations that my birthmother had acquired information about me prior to our meeting (e.g., my identity as a college student, marital status), and she had even constructed an image of what I was like. While I knew nothing about her she had contemplated how she would interact with me through this previously acquired knowledge. An empirical analysis of initial presentations of self between potential reunion participants should attend, not only to the processes involved in symbolically constructing a relationship, but also to the ways in which information and power are not equivalent between the two participants. The person initiating a search has more initial power to define the relationship because he or she may have already procured knowledge about the other party. According to Thornton and Nardi (1975), prior information may produce two possible outcomes. The ability to get correct information about a potential role partner may forestall some obstacles to successful role performance. However, prior knowledge can also create a problematic situation between newly acquainted participants by creating a power imbalance. My birthmother's prior knowledge about me allowed her to prepare for meeting me. I did not have any preparation time or knowledge about the person she might be.

DEVELOPING A RELATIONSHIP

Useful clues about the person with whom one is attempting to form a reunion relationship are not the only factors which shape its subsequent development. While neither participant may have much by the way of pre-existing definitions for what a reunion participant is supposed to feel or do, each has some conception of what it means to be an adoptee and a birthparent. How such pre-conceptions figure into the subsequent behavior of reunion participants needs to be studied.

For me, contact with my birthmother presented a conflict with my feelings about being an adoptee. I felt that my obligations to my adoptive parents, my "real parents" who had raised me, would be compromised if I allowed the contact with my birthmother to occur. It was somehow "not right" to enter into a relationship with a person who had relinquished me at birth. At the same time, I was extremely drawn to the possibility of creating a positive relationship with my birthmother. My birthmother also had unsettling prior definitions which affected how she viewed her desire to know me. She had images of a relationship between us for many years. She shared with me that the "imagined possibilities" (Lancette and McClure, 1992) of having a relationship with me were accompanied by guilt and sadness for relinquishing me.

We each approached the possibility of meeting with misgivings based on what we accepted about being an "adoptee" and a "birthmother." I think that my early forebodings about the relationship were only the beginning of on-going tensions that seemed to stalk the relationship as it developed. A significant part of our difficulties derived from our inability to create an acceptable "routine" or basis for our contacts. Not being able to draw on recognized guidelines or ratifying family relationships to help us define how we were to relate to each other, our relationship lacked the support it needed.

After initial contact, we had to decide between developing a "closed" relationship characterized by secrecy and lack of regard for our other role relationships with family members and friends; or acknowledging the parameters of our relationship based upon our pre-existing lives and people in them. As we attempted to establish a relationship we suffered from the constraints of role conflict. Instead of integrating our reunion relationship within her pre-existing family structure, my birthmother separated me from her family and continued to promote the secretive quality that surrounds the adoption process for many people. This was illustrated by her uneasiness with me interacting with her family. This aspect of our relationship was difficult for me because I desired to be part of her extended family, I did not want to be kept in a separate world for her to escape to when she felt like being close to me.

March (1990) found that some adoptees who were involved in reunion experiences had similar concerns about remaining stigmatization as an adoptee.

> These reunited adoptees found, however, that their search and reunion experience set them further apart from others because they no longer carried the stigma trait that was expected of adoptees. They encountered a new process of stigmatization as a result of their search and reunion activities. (p. 281)

The stigmatization process that I experienced was two-fold. First, I became estranged from her family as my birthmother and I began to argue about our differing relationship expectations. The process typically involved: (1) a fight between my birthmother and me over our relationship; (2) her subsequent acts of separating me from her family; (3) her accounts to her family of my "personal problems"; and, (4) subsequent arguments between myself and my birthmother over the separation I felt from her family. Our dissimilar ways of handling the "secrecy" factor in our relationship created a rift between us. The most damaging aspect of this process, according to my birthmother, was the anger I directed toward her. The most damaging aspect of this process to me was the devaluation I experienced when she told her family that our relationship problems were really my personal problems.

The second source of stigma occurred when my friends and associates questioned the basis of the reunion relationship. I was constantly asked, "What does she want?" People who knew me prior to my reunion experience thought that I would "get over" the infatuation of knowing my birthmother. Why did they expect that we would just have a chance meeting and forget about one another? I sensed that these people believed it was acceptable for me to entertain my reunion relationship for awhile, but ultimately, they expected me to "let it go."

Giving up my relationship with my birthmother was the last thought I had at the beginning of our relationship. At that time I asked myself, "Where did we fit-in?" After a year had passed I was asking, "How could we continue?" The euphoria of initial contact between my birthmother and me had diminished, and we continued to struggle with the definition of who we would be for one another.

INSTITUTIONALIZED POWER
AND SECRETIVE RELATIONSHIPS

> Even in the most successful situations, birthmothers reunited with their relinquished children confronted confusion about their roles. They both *were* and were *not* mothers, since their children already had adoptive mothers. Neither, however, did they consider themselves merely "friends" to the people whom they had given birth. Their children, moreover, were not children; they'd grown up and had independent identities, relationships, and histories that did not involve their biological relatives. Having found each other, birthmothers, and their children were usually left to search further: this time, for places in each others' lives. (Jones, 1993:201-202)

The reunion relationship that my birthmother and I developed was affected by at least two different power relationships. The first power relationship was between her, as a pregnant seventeen year old teenager, and her friends and family. Soon after we had met I asked her about the circumstances that led to my birth and subsequent adoption. I was not prepared to hear the account of that period of time in her life.

What follows relies, of course, on my interpretation of what she told me. Although I had several discussions with her about this period of time, my account is at least once removed from her actual experience. She told me that she felt a lack of support from her family when they found out she was pregnant. She did not want to get married, and she also did not want to deal with being a student and a parent. Her mother decided that the best solution to her pregnancy, as practicing Catholics, was to send her away from their home to live across the country with a brother.

Her mother made the decision in order to keep the fact of her pregnancy a secret. It was her mother's home, and I perceived that my birthmother felt like an unwanted guest there. The 1960s were a period of time when being a pregnant, single teenager of a middle-class family was definitely considered shameful as Jones (1993) describes.

> In 1964, Cathy was fifteen and pregnant. 'My parents shipped me off to a home for unwed mothers. I never saw the father of the child until it was all over. Nobody was allowed to visit me except my mom and dad. No one even knew where I was, except for my parents and one aunt. I was just put in the home and told that I was going to give up my child. I didn't want to give up my baby, though. I tried to keep her–I ran away from the home twice but was found and taken back both times.' (p. 23)

Even though my birthmother and I have discussed this time of her life, I still wonder what effect her early experiences have had on the way we relate.

I do know that when she contacted me by letter she was involved in a support group. I also know that her search was expedited by a friend who illegally obtained records about me. Her experience of birthing me and finding me was enveloped in secrecy; and again her letter to me was "secretly" sent with the proviso that if I did respond she would not continue her attempts to meet me.

This secrecy was not just her personal desire, but reflected an institutionalized reality that defined her search process. Our relationship was initiated and formed in such a clandestine atmosphere. The effect of having to operate with the knowledge that what she was doing, by searching and contacting me, was subject to disapproval carried over to our relations. Secrecy meant we were not honored as legitimate. In addition, as a result of this condition, we created a private world which others could not fully access. The process, in which we both participated, separated us from other relationships we had. Thus, when our reunion relationship was dissolving I found that my birthmother and I had no common family members or friends to help mediate our problems.

Our family statuses also conditioned our reunion relationship. I was single and living alone, and she was a wife and mother. She had significant others with whom to share her hardships and concerns. I could only bend the ear of friends. She had a family to return to after deciding I was not part of that unit; but, I was not a parent or spouse with all of the recognition those positions confer in our society. While I spent many nights alone thinking about our relationship difficulties, she had the opportunity to focus attention on her husband and children. Even though my parents were both extremely supportive, I did not want to hurt them by constantly discussing my birthmother. Yet it was also possible that my birthmother might have been similarly burdened with a loneliness she could not outwardly acknowledge to others.

The second power relationship was between her and me. When she found me I was not prepared to respond for I had not anticipated our reunion. I was just about to finish undergraduate school and did not know exactly what my next step would be. Interestingly, research shows that most adoptees are in their twenties when they are searched out by their birthmothers (Campbell, Silverman, and Patty, 1991). This was a time of uncertainty for me, and her arrival in my life seemed to offer the possibility of a safe haven from other decisions that were impending. She was more powerful than I was because of her societally defined success, and I was not in a position to relate to her as an equal.

The most important distinction that emerged during the beginning of our relationship was that she presented herself as my biological mother who wanted to somehow reclaim me. I was her son, and that in itself added to the uncertainty of a twenty-two year old person who was unsure of his future. Further, while she may have felt the need to fend off negative imputations for being a birthmother who broke her original bargain to stay away from me, I was also vulnerable as an adoptee who was not supposed to have knowledge of her.

I believe that the vulnerabilities in both of our positions have played off of each other. As our relationship continued I became less secure I was a steering force that could direct what we would be for one another. This culminated in anger towards her because I perceived that she was the sole participant who made decisions about when, where, and how often we would interact. The "union" in reunion had begun to recede from our everyday interactions.

While doubts about her right to find me, as a birthmother, probably weighed on her, my sense of aloneness was accentuated by the fact that I was never supposed to expect anything from her. Society did not honor our relationship, so she was not held accountable for coming in and out of my life. I wanted to continue interacting as a part of her family, but she did not want me to play that role. I wanted to know that she would be available to me as would a relative even though our relationship was thought of by others as a passing phase. The tension surrounding such feelings in me increased so that ultimately we chose not to interact with one another.

SEARCHING FOR A UNION

Some of the widely reported benefits of reunions are "the unique experience of being able to connect themselves for the first time with their generational line" (Sachdev, 1992), and acquiring a "power over self because it completed their biography" (March, 1990). Research has determined that most reunion experiences bring a certain satisfaction for both the adoptees and birthmothers involved, but problems can still stem from these couplings (Sachdev, 1992; March, 1990). Many of the problems in reunion relationships may stem from the expectations of adoptees over role obligations.

> The difficulty over mutual role obligations and birthmother-adoptee interaction patterns stems from the motherhood myth that our society promotes. The myth proclaims that the predominance of the indestructible blood bond permanently connects biological mother and child. These reunited adoptees possessed a latent expectation that a parent-child bond would exist between themselves and their birth mothers. They were shocked and disillusioned to discover what appeared as a 'stranger' to them. This factor let some adoptees effortlessly disengage from the reunion contact. (March, 1990:284)

Cultural messages about the "proper" mother-child relationship inevitably shape the contours of a reunion relationship. While both parties may "understand" that they do not possess the history or experiences that define a traditional parent-child relationship, one or the other or both yet cast themselves or each other in such roles.

I have not seen my birthmother in five years, but we have had conversations on the phone this last year. Now, after this lack of contact we speak of developing a different type of relationship. But I don't know what she desires to get out of it, and I am not sure that I want to take another risk in meeting her again. Is this situation due to our personal histories? Is it because of a fear of the effects of continued secrecy? What would it take for us to relate more as equals? Would this reunion attempt be honored by others? Unfortunately, I still do not think that currently a relationship is possible. Not much has changed in five years.

My friends would look down on me for attempting a reunion. Perhaps another meeting is viewed in the same light as people who get divorced and then decide to re-unite. Most people wonder how a failed relationship could ever produce a positive result in either of our lives. I share that same concern, but the fact remains she is my only birthmother. We are not lovers who can find other people with whom to have a unique relationship. I am the only son she relinquished and she is the only birthmother I have to acknowledge. Although our reunion relationship may not find much social support I want to continue to try to develop a relationship we can each feel good about.

Preparation for the effects of this type of relationship upon other role relationships might ease the transition into these unique couplings. A theoretical model for addressing reunion relationships should recognize the social forces that direct them (Haimes and Timmes, 1985). Knowledge about the potential consequences of engaging in a reunion relationship ought to be available to all adoptees and birthparents to help them navigate the stages of reunion. I hope that this personal account suggests research questions that will provide insights to adoptees and birthmothers.

REFERENCES

Campbell, L.H., Silverman, P.R., & Patty, P.B. (1991). Reunions Between Adoptees and Birthparents: The Adoptees Experience. *Social Work,* 36(4),329-335.

Gediman, J.S. & Brown, L.P. (1989). *Birthbonds.* New Jersey, New Horizons Press.

Goffman, E. (1959). *Presentation of Self in Everyday Life.* Garden City, New York, Doubleday.

Goffman, E. (1967). *Interaction Rituals.* New York, Random House.

Haimes, E., & Timms, J. (1985). *Adoption, Identity, and Social Policy.* Brookfield, Gower Publishing Company.

Jones, M.B. (1993). *Birthmothers: Women Who Have Relinquished Babies For Adoption Tell Their Stories.* Chicago, Chicago Review Press.

Lancette, J., & McClure, B.A. (1992). Birthmothers: Grieving the Loss of a Dream. *Journal of Mental Health Counseling,* 14(1), 84-96.

March, K.R.A. (1990). *The Stranger Who Bore Me.* Unpublished Dissertation, McMaster University.

Mead, G.H. (1934). *Mind, Self, and Society.* Chicago, University of Chicago Press.

McColm, M. (1993). *Adoption Reunions.* Toronto, Second Story Press.

Richardson, L. (1988). Secrecy and Status: The Social Construction of Forbidden Relationships. *American Sociological Review,* 53, 209-219.

Sachdev, P. (1992). Adoption Reunion and After: A Study of the Process and Experience of Adoptees. *Child Welfare,* 71(1), 53-68.

Thornton, R., & Nardi, P.M. (1975). The Dynamics of Role Acquisition. *American Sociological Review,* 80(4), 870-885.

Adopting Romanian Children:
Making Choices, Taking Risks

Roberta Goldberg

SUMMARY. This paper is a preliminary investigation into the experiences of adoptive mothers of Romanian children. As a case study of international adoption, this research focuses on the following questions: What were the important choices over which families wanted control? What risks were they willing to take to complete an adoption? How did the specific circumstances in Romania and the respondents' own efforts influence their ability to maximize choices and minimize risks? This paper is primarily descriptive, linking economic, demographic, and political factors to the very private experience of people creating families through international adoption.

The respondents adopted children from Romania in 1990 and 1991. Eight married mothers were interviewed in depth. They were selected through their participation in a "mother's group," an informal association established initially by the adoption agency through which most adopted their children. In the "group" they socialize and discuss issues relevant to adoption in general and Romania in partic-

Roberta Goldberg is Associate Professor of Sociology at Trinity College, Washington, DC.

The author is indebted to the following people for their time, their ideas, their skills and their support in the preparation of this paper: Ioana Ieronim, Sylvia Steed, and the members of the mother's group whose names must remain anonymous. Heartfelt thanks to all of you.

An earlier version of this paper was presented at the XXX Seminar of the Committee on Family Research of the International Sociological Association, *Gender and Families: Choices, Challenges and Changing Policy*, Annapolis, MD, November 1993.

[Haworth co-indexing entry note]: "Adopting Romanian Children: Making Choices, Taking Risks." Goldberg, Roberta. Co-published simultaneously in *Marriage & Family Review* (The Haworth Press, Inc.) Vol. 25, No. 1/2, 1997, pp. 79-98; and: *Families and Adoption* (ed: Harriet E. Gross and Marvin B. Sussman) The Haworth Press, Inc., 1997, pp. 79-98. Single or multiple copies of this article are available for a fee from The Haworth Document Delivery Service [1-800-342-9678, 9:00 a.m. - 5:00 p.m. (EST). E-mail address: getinfo@haworth.com].

79

ular. The group also serves as a play group for children who share a Romanian heritage. One respondent had a peripheral relationship to the group, while the rest were active participants. Their experiences are not intended to represent Romanian adoption on the whole. The semi-structured interviews were tape recorded with the consent of the respondents, and lasted about two hours each. To protect confidentiality, no names of respondents or their family members have been used. Where direct quotations are used, there has been some editing for clarity, but no change to content. As an adoptive mother of a Romanian child and a participant-observer in the "mother's group," I come to this study with some information gathered through my own experience in the adoption process, but mostly with a great deal of curiosity about what is shared among those who adopt. *[Article copies available for a fee from The Haworth Document Delivery Service: 1-800-342-9678. E-mail address: getinfo@haworth.com]*

BACKGROUND

As is well documented, many American families adopt children internationally for reasons tied to patterns of infertility and the availability of adoptable children in the U.S. (National Council for Adoption, 1993, Taylor, 1992, Bachrach et al., 1988, Serrill, 1991, Daly, 1988, Feigelman and Silverman, 1983). As was the case with Romania, children are typically adopted from politically and economically unstable countries where families face extreme poverty and unwed mothers face stigmatization. In 1990 and 1991 with the Romanian Revolution and the fall of Ceausescu, one legacy of the former ruler was an orphanage system that had been built and sustained by his plan for population growth, which began in 1966 with a policy banning abortions and contraception for most women. This policy created a significant burden for families and indeed, for the state itself, as many children who could not be cared for at home were turned over to state-run orphanages called "children homes." These institutions were not able to provide healthful environments, either physically or emotionally for the numerous children in them. It is estimated that as many as 100,000 children lived in more than 250 institutions of various sorts at the peak of this period (Quinn, 1990).

The American mass media aired stories on the conditions in Romanian orphanages, setting off an avalanche of interest on the part of families seeking to adopt, and a massive relief effort to bring much needed medical and other supplies to institutions. At the same time, Romanian law enabled adoptions to be completed rather quickly compared to U.S. domestic adoptions, and even other countries. Changes in procedure making even faster adoption possible after August 1990 resulted in 2,552 adoptions in the peak year of 1991, compared to 121 in 1990 (DCI/ISS 1991, p. 8). During this period, Romania was experiencing a public relations nightmare. It did not have adequate economic resources for its orphanages, nor could it control the image of black market babyselling spreading through Western media, which, indeed, was flourishing (DCI/ISS, 1991, p. 9). Due in part to the publicity, foreign adoptions were suspended in the summer of 1991, and later resumed under much greater restrictions. By 1992, only 145 Romanian children were adopted by Americans (National Council for Adoption, Inc., 1993, p. 11).

For adoptive parents there were significant risks and many choices to be made. Following, I examine why adoptive mothers selected Romania for their adoptions, what they expected in their children, what their experiences through the adoption process were like, and the meaning Romania has to them in their families.

WHY ROMANIA?

Several respondents had explored or attempted domestic adoption. Others had been planning to adopt internationally, in Colombia and Chile. Because of lengthy waiting periods for other adoptions, their ages, and the publicity about Romanian orphanages, these families turned to Romania as the country of choice, though few knew anything about Romania at the outset, or had any personal connection to it. A few mothers expressed a personal connection to Europe in a general way, while one respondent described a familial tie to Eastern Europe. Most respondents indicated that their interest grew as a result of media exposure, and their subsequent exploration through the adoption education network. As one respondent explained:

> . . . it seemed there were a lot of children that needed homes and that the process appeared to be relatively short. We were on the desperate end of wanting a baby so bad that we decided to look into it for basically that reason.

Another mother who had pursued adoption elsewhere but was over the age limit, found herself upset by the media images of the orphanages, and saw the situation in Romania as a way of creating a family while also helping people in need:

> These kids were so in need of homes. It was so clear that there was just a crisis going on with the children in this country . . . I really feel very strongly that you've got to do things to help children . . .

Thus, most families initially considered Romania because of the lack of restrictions, concern for the plight of the children, and the relative speed of getting the process completed in comparison to other adoption programs. Ironically, these very characteristics increased the risks to families seeking children. In the following sections, I examine the choices made by families and the inherent risks in more detail.

MATCHING CHILDREN'S ATTRIBUTES
WITH PARENTS' DESIRES

Characteristics such as sex, race and ethnicity, age, health status, and developmental issues are significant factors for families making decisions about adoption. Among respondents, the child's sex was reported as unimportant, and in fact, almost an equal number of boys and girls were adopted. Concerns about race were expressed by several mothers. With one exception respondents consistently reported that race was important because they wished to minimize their public appearance as an adoptive family. As one mother put it, "raising an adoptive family has its own issues without maximizing them by having strangers know there is an adoption in your family." Some respondents expressed guilt about the preference for a child of the same race, but as this respondent explains, "I want my adopted family to imitate a birth family to the degree it can."

Romania was one of the first countries since World War II with many adoptable children who were predominantly white and of European appearance. The major exception to this are Gypsies whose appearance differs from other Romanians. None of the respondents in this study adopted Gypsies, though a number have been adopted in the U.S. Race clearly played a role in the attractiveness of Romania as an adoption source, given the certainty families had about the racial backgrounds of the children and the importance they gave to same-race adoption.

Age at adoption is significant in several respects. Institutionalized children and those who have experienced continual changes in foster families, as have many American children, reportedly have problems with attachment as they grow older and may experience developmental delays. In the case of Romania, many of the children were not only institutionalized, but deprived of basic health care, nutrition and nurturance. As such they represented a considerable risk to adoptive parents.

Among the respondents, all but one of the children were under one year of age at the time of adoption, thus minimizing age as a risk factor. Several mothers expressed a preference for newborns or infants as they were concerned primarily about attachment issues with an older child. For a few, the desire for an infant also involved their love of babies. Age alone was not significant for most respondents, but rather the related problems of long-term neglect, health and development.

Other studies have shown that institutionalized children in Romania experienced widespread health problems, among them Hepatitis B, Hepatitis A, AIDS, tuberculosis, and psychic disorders (Rovner, 1992, DCI/ISS, 1991). These conditions are consistent with those found in other countries from which children are adopted and pose some of the greatest risks for adoptive families.

Most respondents in this study openly preferred a child with few or no health problems, despite the fact that they knew these children were deprived of basic health care and that medical information was sketchy. Concerns about health were tied to family status. For example, one mother with her own chronic health problem coupled with financial constraints, explained that it would be impossible for the family to cope with an unhealthy child. Another mother related more general concerns about the ability to manage a child with health problems:

> We just felt that as first time parents we had to worry about parenting and we thought a child with a questionable health status would be something that on top of being first time older parents, we weren't sure how well we could handle it.

Health concerns posed the greatest risk to the respondents both because of the conditions in Romanian orphanages and the limited information available on the health of individual children. Families attempted to minimize those risks and to increase their options in several ways.

Most families had basic information such as birth date, name, hair color, and general assurances about health. Only a few parents had pictures of the child prior to the adoption. Many went to Romania with advice about what to observe in the children, but little concrete information. As one mother explained:

> I knew what I was willing to accept. And up to and including the minute we saw the child, neither I nor my husband were necessarily going to accept the placement.

Upon return to the U.S., respondents reported that their children had a range of unanticipated health problems including parasites, malnourishment, hernias, bronchitis, ear infections, Hepatitis B, and failure to thrive. Some children were remarkably healthy, and there appeared to be few long-term health problems.

Along with health risks, developmental delays are common among internationally adopted children, and Romanian children were no exception. Lack of adequate nutrition and health care, limited physical mobility and minimal contact with care givers set the stage for a range of problems. Low weight and significant developmental delays were common among the children of the respondents. Most of these children had been in the U.S. about two years at the time of the interviews, and had caught up to age appropriate behavior either through the normal course of events, or with intervention. Anecdotal information in the wider adoption community indicates that some children are still experiencing delays of varying degrees, some of which may be permanent.

In addition to concerns about the children, there were considerations involving uncertainty in a region undergoing rapid political and economic transformation. Prospective parents had to consider the difficulty of transportation, communication and sparse living conditions. While discussion of the actual travel to and around Romania isn't directly relevant to this paper, it should be noted that it enhanced the sense of risk for those involved, particularly for those who had lengthy stays, multiple trips and fall-throughs in the placement of their children. While all reported feeling enriched by their experience in Romania, for none of them was the experience easy.

THE ADOPTION PROCESS

Some of the difficulties faced by adoptive parents were tied to the adoption process. Those who adopted in late 1990 or early 1991 faced the fewest obstacles and had the shortest stays, usually just a few days. Those who adopted in the summer of 1991 as adoptions were curtailed, had fall-throughs, longer stays or multiple delays. Another factor affecting the process was whether the formal adoption took place prior to or after traveling to pick up the child. For those who adopted prior to travel, generally the only official business necessary upon arrival was getting Romanian passports and visas for entry into the U.S. and other transit countries. While this arrangement saved time and assured a completed adoption, there was some risk in not seeing the child prior to the finalization of the adoption. This required a great deal of trust in the screening processes of the Romanian sources and the adoption agency. Those who travelled prior to the adoption had the choice of refusing a specific child before the adoption was finalized, but they risked losing the chance to adopt.

Several families experienced fall-throughs after children were identified for them, prior to leaving for Romania. In one case, a birth mother initially changed her mind though later decided to go through with the adoption. The adoptive mother learned that the child's grandmother balked for "fear of selling body parts or slavery," a persistent rumor in Romania. In another case, a child was found to have an undefined health problem, and the source in Romania discouraged the adoption. In an extreme case, a family experienced five fall-throughs in the spring and summer of 1991 before finally succeeding in adopting a child.

Those who traveled to Romania in the summer of 1991, when adoptions were coming to a halt, felt enormous pressure to take any child offered to them. One family, who had arrived in Romania to adopt a child they found to be seriously ill, chose not to adopt despite warnings that she might be their only chance. They also turned down another ill child who was offered to them on the spot in the local courthouse. Ultimately, they were able to complete an adoption. Even for those whose adoptions went smoothly, there were often delays prior to traveling. One mother described six postponements before they left, due to the child's illness and delays in the court proceedings. Each postponement removed a degree of choice and increased the sense of risk to this family.

Whether parents met children prior to or after the formal adoption, the first meeting was unforgettable and reflected their understanding of the role sheer chance played in the adoption. One mother who adopted in the fall of 1990 describes meeting her child for the first time at a maternity hospital after the adoption was completed. It was a relief to her that even institutionalized children had people who cared about them:

> ... A lot of the nurses or staff came out to see us off. They were very nice and gave us a bottle and told us when the next time she needed to eat was ... When we were leaving they all were gathered around near the elevator or stairs ... They all seemed to really have enjoyed her and seemed happy for her.

By contrast, another mother adopting in the summer of 1991 described first meeting her child when it was handed to her through a car window on a side street near the courthouse where the adoption was to take place. She and her husband waited in the car while the birth mother relinquished the child in court.

Even when there is the appearance of choice, the respondents understood the limitations. For one family that adopted independently, the husband travelled directly to an orphanage to find a child. The adoptive mother describes the experience:

They only bring you out children who the orphanage says can be adopted. So, it's not like you get a whole tour of the place. You're in a waiting room and they bring the children in to you and they're swaddled and wrapped up and with numbers on them . . . I think seventy-something was [our daughter]. So when you say yes . . . you just see this little bundled tag.

For families whose adoptions were completed prior to arrival in Romania, children were brought to their adoptive parents shortly after their arrival. One mother met her crying son at 11 p.m.:

And they said, "here's your kid, here's a bottle. Feed him and go to bed." And there we slept that first night on this bed that was the size of a cot. [My husband] slept one way, I slept the other way and [our son] was next to me . . . And that's our first experience with our son.

Regardless of where in the process parents were when first meeting their children, that meeting was overwhelming for them in several ways. They were finally meeting their children, but they were also exhausted from long journeys, dependent on strangers, and unsure of themselves as parents. None felt they had control over their situations. One mother describes it this way:

It was funny when I first saw him because all I could think of is, wow! That shock of seeing the baby that's going to be your baby. There you are in Romania and it was night and we're in this . . . sort of project-looking building and it was pitch dark and being led down this hallway, [thinking] this could really be bad, and, we'll have to deal with it . . . The door opened up to this cozy apartment of the woman who was taking care of him and I think our concerns were more about our own adequacy as parents . . . I mean we felt totally inadequate.

Once in Romania, those whose adoptions were not yet complete went to court for the proceedings. One respondent found the court hearing significant in understanding the scope of the issues surrounding adoption and was impressed with the seriousness with which the judge took the proceedings:

It was so moving . . . They talked about our infertility and. . . the attorney for [the birth mother] talked about how things were in Romania and you had a sense of their pain about giving up their

children. And that felt quite real to us and very sad . . . We took that
very seriously. And we felt like we knew that we were lucky to be in
this situation and how sad it was that they couldn't take care of their
own children.

Another commented on the judge's discussion with the birth mother:

When you go to court and stand in front of the judges, they ask
directly to the birth mother, "Do you understand what this means
and why can't you take care of your child?" And to me, if I were in
that position, it would be very painful. But they clearly knew what
[they were doing] . . . They'd made up their mind long ago.

The formal steps of the adoption coupled with the respondents' positive
interactions with sources, judges, orphanage staff and birth families
pointed to a process which, while flawed, was clearly concerned about the
fate of the children, and took seriously the need to legitimize the adoption
process.

The next formal steps after the adoption were to acquire a Romanian
passport for the child and a visa from the American Embassy. Those
adopting in 1990 and early 1991 and those who adopted children from
institutions had few problems. Later, with large numbers of Americans in
various stages of adoption or with questionable adoptions flooding the
Embassy, respondents described the experience of obtaining visas as
chaotic. Widespread publicity about the black market in adoption exacer-
bated the problems. Even though adoptions may have been legally completed, there was increased risk that a visa to enter the U.S. could be
denied. Even as early as February 1991, difficulties were apparent as one
respondent recounts:

There were several people who were very upset because they found
out that their children were not legally adoptable orphans by American Embassy standards . . . And, once you adopt a child in Romania,
that's your child by Romanian law. It's up to you to figure out how to
get the child out.

The experience at the Embassy was particularly difficult once it was
known that adoptions were about to stop in the summer of 1991. The fear
of illegal adoptions fueled the greater scrutiny, though only one respondent observed irregularities that had the appearance of baby-selling. None
of the respondents had difficulty obtaining visas, though they were aware
of the problems other families experienced.

CONTACT WITH THE BIRTH MOTHER

A central issue in adoption pertains to the circumstances in which birth mothers agree to the adoption of their children. Little is written about birth mothers in international adoption, and almost none of it from their perspective. Extreme poverty, dismal job prospects, high infant mortality rates and sanctions against unwed mothers prevail in countries where international adoptions take place. In Romania, these conditions existed first amidst years of totalitarian rule and later with the instability of the post-revolutionary period. Choices for birth mothers under such conditions are obviously limited. Yet some opted for adoption, while others either struggled to raise their children or abandoned them to institutions without formal relinquishment.

Adoptive mothers had several ways to obtain information about birth mothers, primarily official documents and meeting face to face in court. Several respondents indicated that they were unsure of the accuracy of the official information they received; however, meetings with birth mothers generally confirmed the reports. Little was known about the birth fathers. At best, the name, age or marital status was recorded in official documents. There were no face to face meetings with birth fathers, though one adoptive mother thinks he was present when she first met her child. The birth mothers ranged in age from 14 to mid-thirties, most being in their 20's. They were all reported to be poor and either working in factories, on farms or unemployed. Several birth mothers were described as illiterate. Most were unmarried, though some had men in their lives, including some birth fathers, and a number had older children living with them. It was not always clear what the living circumstances of the children were prior to their adoptions. About half the children appeared to live with their birth mothers up to the adoption. The rest lived in institutions, mostly maternity hospitals, or in some combination of a hospital and the birth mother's home. Only one family adopted directly from an orphanage, and this was done independently without using an adoption agency. It should be noted that the living arrangements of the children in this study were not typical of many other adoptions, where long periods of living in orphanages were more characteristic. The effects of these various living conditions are not the subject of the study, but should be part of ongoing research on Romanian adoptions.

Those adoptive families who met birth mothers in court were afforded an opportunity for some contact, though the language barrier and the circumstances of the meeting were not conducive to a great deal of interaction. Often, translators and other assistants frowned on any attempts at substantive communication. Nonetheless, adoptive mothers came away with information and distinct feelings about the importance of meeting birth mothers. Some birth mothers seemed equally interested in the families adopting their children. One adoptive mother brought pictures of the extended adoptive family and their home for the birth mother to keep, but she found the language barrier coupled with disdain exhibited by the translator created a frustrating situation:

> We attempted to speak to her through the lawyer as an interpreter, but he of course had nothing but disgust for her . . . He felt that we were a different class, he and us included, and she was just peripheral to the situation. . . . and she and her sister sort of smiled . . . when we persisted in wanting communication.

Another adoptive mother found the birth mother quite willing to give information, but again the translator was uncomfortable:

> We did a little social history. We did it like a family tree . . . So we had generations and we have all the names of his siblings. And [the translator] was uncomfortable with that. At one point he said, "Why are you asking this?" I asked about the health issues and his birth father's family . . . I just wanted to get information. But he was uncomfortable with that, and I think that's more European. In fact he said to us, and this was almost humorous, it was so extreme. He said, "You know when you get back to America you really don't have to tell anybody that [your son] is adopted."

One adoptive mother was anxious for more detailed information about the family background and was met with silence, believing the birth mother was fearful that the information would be used against her. Yet another adoptive mother had an opportunity for some exchange with the birth mothers of the two children she adopted:

> They both wanted to know if I was healthy also . . . I basically thanked them and said I appreciated what they were doing and that I'd love and cherish their children . . . Each one of them gave me a little slip of paper with something written on it for their children, with their address and just a few notes.

Aside from seeking practical information, meeting the birth mother gave the adoptive mother an opportunity to try to understand what the birth mother was feeling about the adoption. One mother reports:

> I think she was saddened appropriately, that this was the situation that she was in, but there were no signs that she was doing anything under duress . . . She was really young, very quiet, very shy . . . There wasn't any breakdown or anything that made it seem as if she had been forced into doing this.

The mother who had adopted two children had an opportunity to sense the birth mothers' emotions and concerns for their children, indicating that while they had concerns there was no doubt they wanted the children adopted:

> They were definitely teary-eyed. And in [my son's] case, the uncle was present and the uncle was more stern about it. I think he was trying to get this over with and I think she would have liked to have asked me more questions . . . They knew very little about America, what part of the country we were going to, so we gave them our address. But there was more a sense of finality about it. She'd heard that America had food and a better way of life. She asked if I had yards and places for the children to play, and would they go to school.

She adds, "They had made up their minds at birth . . . They'd never seen the children except to take them out of the orphanage [for the adoption]. They'd never visited them."

In contrast, another adoptive mother reported that the birth mother who was 21 and unemployed, with two other children, "wasn't happy. I think she was pretty much being told that she had to give the baby up . . . She would try and look at us, try and stare at us. But when we would look up, she would look down." Perhaps it is significant that in the first two cases, the children had lived at a hospital or orphanage since birth, while in the third case, the child had lived with her birth mother.

Another adoptive mother found that meeting the birth mother was quite positive. In this case, the birth mother was a "warm and lively" 36-year old widow with other children by her husband prior to his death. This child was fathered by another man after her husband died.

> She was basically telling us about her life, telling us about her husband's death and how hard life had been for her and some of her hopes for [our son] . . . This was the part of her that was going to get this opportunity that she wished she had. And I think that allowed her to give him up really . . . I think she was still grieving for her husband because he had only died not much more than a year before

> . . . and then [our son's] birth father didn't want to marry her . . . It felt like there was something about giving him up for adoption that sort of completed this time in her life and then she was going to be able to move on . . .

Several respondents discussed the importance of contact with the birth mother to their own relationships in their families. For example, one adoptive mother who did not meet the birth mother but had pictures of her said

> Seeing her birth mother, where she comes from. It was very comforting to see these [pictures]. These people have had incredibly hard lives and look at how healthy [she looks] . . . She looks happy, healthy, and she was posing . . . for the purpose of communicating with the future adoptive parents of her daughter.

Another respondent commented more generally on the importance of the contact:

> Some people say they don't want to meet the birth mother and they don't want to know anything about her because . . . it takes away from the fact that they feel the child is theirs, solely theirs. And I don't think that's the case. I think that you can love a child and know that it came from another person without diminishing the love you have or the connection you have to that child.

In every case where birth mothers were met, the adoptive family took pictures to preserve for their children. Several families who did not meet the birth mother also have pictures provided by the Romanian source. While some families currently share the pictures with other family and friends, others have chosen to put them away until the child is old enough to decide if he or she wants to share them. Several adoptive mothers expressed interest in the birth mother's motivation to go through with the adoption. Some information was found in the official documents, but the families looked for more. They worked with what little information they could get. One mother speculated about the circumstances of a 14-year old birth mother who still lived with her mother, citing both her age and poverty as significant in her decision to have the baby adopted. Another respondent was convinced of the economic motivation in the context of trying to support families in dire poverty, and felt it was important not to judge the birth mother:

I think they view this as a one-time opportunity to make their lives, the lives of their entire family better . . . most of them are getting an opportunity to greatly improve their lives. So, perhaps they saw that better than we did . . . I think Americans come here and judge people on moral values based on American morals. Well, it just isn't correct.

Another mother agrees:

I felt like a lot of the criticism around Romanian adoptions is really Western values about what we have. I mean she couldn't even take care of her own kids. She really couldn't. Her family really fell apart when her husband died . . . It's not like there's any social support in that system . . . There's no foster care . . . no safety net.

To see the birth mother's decision in a larger economic and political context is crucial to understanding her motives. It is also important to understand that not only was this seen as the best opportunity for the child, the birth mother and her remaining family; it is also a systemic failure. A society that forces such choices on large numbers of families fails those families, particularly because many children remain institutionalized.

Whether or not adoptive mothers met birth mothers, they were keenly aware of the importance of the adoption to the birth mother. When asked what they would say to birth mothers if they met them now, all wanted to assure the birth mother that the child was well and happy and loved, and to express gratitude for their sacrifice. They wanted to show appreciation for the pain the birth mother suffered at relinquishing her child. At least part of the purpose of the communication would be in hopes that the birth mother would feel some relief or comfort in the information they provide. As one mother put it, "I just want you to rest easy." The love they feel toward their children and gratitude toward the birth mother is evident in the following remark tying the child to both families:

I would just say I wanted to come tell you personally how much I love [my daughter] and how much she means to me, and how beautiful and happy and loving she is and I can't help but think a lot of that is due to you.

Adoptive mothers understood that the choices made by birth mothers were painful and difficult. Communicating that the children are well and happy are attempts at telling birth mothers that for the children, the choice was a good one.

TELLING THE ADOPTION STORY

Many adoptive families are keenly aware of the importance of giving their children knowledge about their origins, so that they too can make choices in their lives. Respondents were asked how information about Romania and the adoption experience would be conveyed to children, and how such information would impact the choices and risks their children would face in the future. Some parents were reluctant to share the details about the birth mother and the circumstances of the adoption as they know it from official documents. A number of respondents were not sure of the validity of the descriptions provided to them, either because of questionable translations, or attempts to facilitate the adoption through exaggeration of circumstances. Additionally, the circumstances of the adoption were likely to be hurtful to the child. Despite their concerns, all the adoptive mothers plan to tell their children about their adoptions, and some have already begun the conversation. Since the children are still young, their comprehension is limited, but the parents agree that it is important to raise the issues early.

The adoption discussion is very much intertwined with conditions in Romania. Respondents were especially sensitive to the negative images of Romania regarding institutionalization of its children and questionable adoption practices. They felt they had a legitimate right to disassociate themselves from the public image of black market adoptions, since this was not their own experience, having gone through legitimate channels.

> I do feel protective of the issue of how Romanian adoptions are perceived. I feel sort of defensive about it because I feel good about how things went for us . . . I think people have complicated feelings about adoption anyway. You can just tell that by the questions people ask. Sometimes people say to us, "Well, did you buy him?" . . . maybe not in that crude way, but sort of . . .

Parents also wanted to convey their own positive experience in Romania as a place where they observed loving families and caring officials. They saw Romania as having a unique history and culture that tends to get lost in the public image portrayed in American media. This mother contemplated the public image of Romania in contrast to her own experience:

> Romania has a bad name right now for some of the stuff that's gone on there. But, you know, everybody I met there was kind, and they do have a lot to be proud of . . . There are people who are proud to be Romanian. That's what [our daughter] is going to be is a Romanian.

There was a concern that children need to know the political and economic conditions under which so many children were abandoned, but to be proud to come from a country with a rich culture and decent people.

> I like being aware of the country. I'll talk about the country in positive terms because I only have really positive things to say. But, as he grows older, he'll have to understand, and I think it's important that there were things going on . . . That it was a very turbulent time . . . But in terms of the people–they're warm, they're wonderful people, and I hope to continue to keep in contact . . .

Finally, another mother notes the importance of family to Romanians, despite the circumstances of their experience there:

> . . . Even though this country was poor and desperate there was a sense of family and strong bonds . . . it's unlike poor families in our country where the family gets torn apart . . . We weren't used to families that on one hand didn't have much but were very connected in other ways . . . We were very admiring of different parts of their culture.

RETURNING TO ROMANIA: "PART OF YOU IS THERE"

Most mothers expressed an interest in returning to Romania "one day" with their children, primarily to learn more about the country and its culture and to connect on a more personal level. One mother commented, "I want to go back . . . It's just profound . . . It's really like a part of you is there." Parents try to keep up with current issues in Romania, particularly as they pertain to adoption, but also the broader political and economic concerns. One family plans to visit in the near future.

Respondents were asked if they want their children to meet their birth mothers upon visiting Romania. There were mixed reactions, but most believed it was their children's decision whether to try to make contact and would help them do so. One mother admitting feelings of guilt toward the birth mother, was hesitant about contact, but would like to see her child's birthplace. Another mother has corresponded with the birth mother and sent pictures of her child. Yet another mother plans to send pictures of her child to the birth mother, but does not plan to have her daughter meet her birth mother: "I don't think we'd try to . . . reunite them because their lives are so different now." Another mother was reluctant about contact, explaining that, "I think at this point it would be too painful on both sides."

Several mothers eloquently argued for the importance of the connection to the birth mother. One who regrets not meeting the birth mother had this to say:

> Before all this happened, one of the thoughts that went through our heads was, well, at least we won't ever have to worry about this birth mother coming back to find you. And that was comforting at first. But the more you read about and get into understand the whole process, birth mothers aren't out there to do that anyway . . . . We're very committed to the fact that if [our daughter], when she gets older, has a desire to find [her birth mother], we'll help her all we can.

Another who acknowledges the importance of the child's connection to its birth mother, said:

> I hope he goes . . . I wouldn't mind as an adult if he did go back and try to find his birth family . . . I don't think that's wrong. I think . . . for as long as these kids are ours, they have other roots and you have to let people explore that. It's different for adoptees than it is for other kids . . . [I'll do] whatever I can to help him get through that.

The circumstances of these adoptions are forever linked to Romania, and the families seem intent on making sure their children understand the relationship. To do so affirms the choices made and acknowledges the risks that were taken. To pass on that affirmation to their children, families committed themselves to a permanent tie to their children's origins.

CONCLUSION

The conditions in Romania that encouraged families to adopt there were complicated by the significant risks involved in pursuing and completing adoption, the lack of certainty about their children's health, and the lack of knowledge about their children's backgrounds. Set against an extremely negative image portrayed in the media these mothers along with their spouses and children had successful outcomes by all accounts. It is commonly known that not all those seeking to adopt in Romania were as successful. Many families who pursued adoption without the sponsorship of an adoption agency or other organization were disappointed either because they did not succeed in adopting or fell prey to the underground black market economy fueled by the desperation of those seeking children. Some families came home with children with serious illnesses or who are profoundly affected by the experiences of institutionalization.

This study shows that the families who adopted through a legitimate process and who understood the risks were successful in part by virtue of their efforts to exercise choice among the possibilities presented to them. They have positive feelings about Romania, and have an ongoing interest in the culture and politics of the country. They care about the birth mothers of their children, and they want their children to be proud of their origins.

The experience of this small group of adoptive families must be understood in a global context. The recent increase in adoptions from Russia and China indicates that families continue to seek children abroad while policy reform allows institutionalized children in these countries to become available for adoption. Though there are important differences unique to each country, these families have experiences similar to those found in this study. They make choices regarding sex, age, race and ethnic origin. At the same time they face risks associated with institutionalization, a child's health and development status and changes in adoption laws. What is shared in these circumstances is the need for children to find loving families and for those considering adoption to understand both their choices and the inherent risks in such changeable circumstances as prevail in international adoption. Our understanding of this experience would be greatly enhanced by comparative research. The future of international adoption in general will be affected by how children come to be adopted under a variety of economic and political conditions. The Hague Convention on International Adoption is currently addressing a widespread concern that adoptions are poorly regulated at a cost to all parties involved, but especially the children. How widely this convention will be accepted and by whom, and how it will be enforced, will impact adoptions throughout the world. Romania was one of the first signers of the Hague Convention. Research on international adoption not only increases our understanding of family formation, but can help direct the many policy options future global changes undoubtedly portend.

REFERENCES

Altstein, H. and Simon, R. (Eds.). (1990). *Intercountry adoption: A multinational perspective.* NY: Praeger Publishers.

Amadio, C. M. (1991). Doing the right thing: Some ethical considerations in current adoption practice. *Social Thought,* 17 (3), 25-33.

Bachrach, C. A. (1986, May). Adoption plans, adopted children, and adoptive mothers. *Journal of Marriage and the Family, 48,* 243-253.

Bachrach, C. A., London, K. A., Maza, P. L. (1991, August). On the path to adoption: Adoption seeking in the United States, 1988, *Journal of Marriage and the Family 53,* 705-718.

Bak, K. (1988, October). A tale of two mothers. *Ms, XVII,* (4), 22-23.

Bartholet, E. (1993). *Family bonds: Adoption and the politics of parenting.* Boston: Houghton Mifflin Co.

Czech, J. M. (1991, Winter). Romania's waiting children: Where is the greater need? Financial support . . . Or adoption? *Roots and Wings,* 33-34.

Daly, K. (1988, April). Reshaped parenthood identity: The transition to adoptive parenthood. *Journal of Contemporary Ethnography, 17* (1), 40-66.

Defence for Children International and International Social Service (DCI/ISS). (1991, April). *The adoption of Romanian children by foreigners.* Geneva, Switzerland.

Defence for Children International and International Social Service Briefing Paper. (1991). *Romania: Why the international adoptions have to stop.* Geneva, Switzerland.

The Economist. (1988, Jan. 18). Boom in the baby trade. *306* (7533), 44.

Feigelman, W. and Silverman, A. (1983). *Chosen children: New patterns of adoptive relationships.* NY: Praeger.

Goldberg, R. (1992). Defining parenthood and the adoptive family: Adoption agency criteria and family realities. Unpublished raw data.

Gruner, G. (1991, August). Romania's lost children. *World Press Review, 38,* 54.

Gubernick, L. (1991, October 14). How much is that baby in the window? *Forbes,* 90-98.

Johnson, H. J. (1993, April). *Intercountry adoption: Procedures are reasonable, but sometimes inefficiently administered.* Washington, DC: U.S. GAO, National Security and International Affairs Division.

Johnson, S. (1992, Nov./Dec.). Girls: Easier to give up–and adopt. *Ms, III* (3), 91.

Kamen, A. (1991, May 23). Adoption laws trap Americans in Romania," *The Washington Post,* p. A1 and A16.

Levy-Shiff, R., Bar, O., and Har-Even, D. (1990, April). Psychological adjustment of adoptive parents-to-be. *American Journal of Orthopsychiatry, 60* (2), 258-267.

National Council for Adoption. (1993). *Adoption today: A report produced for NCFA members excerpted from the adoption factbook.* Washington, DC.

National Council for Adoption. (1993). *National Adoption Reports.* Washington, DC.

Neely, A. (1991, Jan/Feb.). Adopting from Romania. *OURS, 24* (1), 13-17.

Pfund, P. H. (1993, April). *Draft Hague Convention on Intercountry Adoption.* Washington, DC: U.S. Department of State.

Pierotti, D. (1991, Nov.-Dec.). From abortion to contraception in Romania. *World Health,* 22.

Quest: The official Newsletter of KinQuest, Inc. (1991, Sept.). New Romanian adoption law enacted in July. III (2), 1.

Quinn, H. (1990, Aug. 20). A cruel legacy: Canadians fight to adopt Romanian orphans. *Maclean's, 103* (34), 48.

Ramos, J. D. (1991, Mar-Apr). Adopting from Romania. *Families United for Adoption, 4* (2), 4-6.

Register, C. (1991). *"Are those kids yours?" American families with children adopted from other countries.* New York: The Free Press.

Rovner, S. (1992, Feb. 4). Adopting from abroad. *The Washington Post, Health,* 12-16.

Serrill, M. S. (1991, Oct. 21). Going abroad to find a baby. *Time, 138* (15), 86-88.

Simon, R. (1992). *Adoption, race, & identity.* NY: Praeger Publishers.

Smith, L. M. (1988, March). Babies From Abroad. *American Demographics, 10* (3), 38-56.

Taylor, P. (1992, March 1). Unwed white mothers seen much less likely now to offer babies for adoption. *The Washington Post,* p. A 11.

Tizard, B. (1991). Intercountry adoption: A review of the evidence. *Journal of Child Psychology and Psychiatry, 32* (5), 743-756.

Viguers, S. T. (1986). *With child: One couple's journey to their adopted child.* Carbondale: Southern Illinois University Press.

Vitillo, R. J. (1991). International adoption: The solution or the problem? *Social Thought, 17* (3), 16-24.

Effect of Transracial/Transethnic Adoption on Children's Racial and Ethnic Identity and Self-Esteem: A Meta-Analytic Review

Leslie Doty Hollingsworth

SUMMARY. This paper reports the results of a meta-analytic review of comparative studies of racial identity and self-esteem in transracially/transethnically-adopted, inracially-adopted/same ethnic group, and biologic African-American and Mexican-American children. Six studies, including one longitudinal study with four phases, met the established criteria. Study level effect sizes were calculated. Twenty-nine dependent measure effect sizes were also calculated. There was an overall effect, in the negative direction, of transracial adoption on a combined variable of racial/ethnic identity and self-esteem (d = −0.3775, p = .001). The effect size increased when racial identity was considered separately (d = −0.5220, p < .01). Effect size associated with self-esteem was not statistically significant, although a positive direction was noted. Tests failed to achieve homogeneity

Leslie Doty Hollingsworth is Assistant Professor, The University of Michigan School of Social Work, 1065 Frieze Building, Ann Arbor, MI.

Grateful appreciation is expressed to Professors Alice Eagly and Gail Melson for their assistance.

This review was conducted while the author was a graduate student at Purdue University Department of Child Development and Family Studies. An earlier version was presented at the Biennial Conference of the Society for Research on Child Development, April 2, 1995, Indianapolis, IN.

99

among included studies. Age of study participant was a moderating variable. Several other potential moderators were also identified. Results are discussed in terms of implications for future research. *[Article copies available for a fee from The Haworth Document Delivery Service: 1-800-342-9678. E-mail address: getinfo@haworth.com]*

The question of whether Caucasian parents should adopt children of ethnic minority groups has been surrounded in controversy since the practice increased substantially in popularity in the 1960s and 1970s. Most of the controversy has centered around whether transracially- or transethnically-adopted children are able to develop the racial or ethnic identity which is characteristic of the identity of members of their racial and ethnic groups. Meta-analytic reviews can be useful in deriving additional information about a controversial subject from separate studies which have been conducted (Halvorsen, 1994). The purpose of this paper is to report the results of such a review.

The paper begins with an historical summary of the transracial adoption controversy, including effects of the controversy on public and private child welfare policy and on research. This is followed by a presentation of the meta-analysis itself which includes eligibility criteria for inclusion of studies in the review, hypotheses, analyses, and results. The paper ends with a discussion of the results and direction for future research.

HISTORICAL BACKGROUND AND RELATED RESEARCH

The 1960s and 1970s witnessed a substantial increase in the numbers of children of ethnic minority groups who were adopted by Caucasian couples. McRoy (1989) reports that in 1968, 23% of all African-American children adopted were placed with Caucasian families, while by 1971, the figure had increased to 35%. A frequent reason was the small number of healthy Caucasian infants who were available for adoption by Caucasian couples desiring to adopt them (McRoy & Zurcher, 1983). A second reason was an altruistic desire by Caucasian couples, whether childless or with one or more biological children, to offer a permanent home and family to children who might otherwise grow up in foster homes or institutions (Feigelman & Silverman, 1983). A third reason was a desire by Caucasian families to intervene to reduce racism and prejudice through the integration of their own families. Organizations were established, such as the Open Door Society in Canada and the Council on Adoptable Children in the United States, to particularly facilitate adoptions of children with "special needs" (Simon & Alstein, 1992, pp. 6-7).

Development of the Controversy

Accompanying the increase in transracial adoptions, however, was criticism against the practice, initiated by the National Association of Black Social Workers. The basis of this criticism was the organization's emphasis on the development of racial identity as crucial for African-American children and the complaint that non-African-American parents were not capable of providing the necessary racial socialization. In its now historical resolution, NABSW stated:

> Black children belong physically and psychologically and culturally in black families where they can receive the total sense of themselves and develop a sound projection of their future. Only a black family can transmit the emotional and sensitive subtleties of perceptions and reactions essential for a black child's survival in a racist society. Human beings are products of their environment and develop their sense of values, attitudes, and self-concept within their own family structures. Black children in white homes are cut off from the healthy development of themselves as black people. (NABSW, 1972, cited in McRoy, 1989, p. 150)

Additionally, NABSW asserted that there were many available potential African American adoptive parents for African-American children and that public and private agencies had not actively sought them out and had used adoption qualification standards which often resulted in disqualification for African-American adoptive parents (McRoy, 1989). The practice of informal adoption in the history of the African-American community, children without available parents being reared by relatives or friends without involvement of public or private agencies, was cited as evidence that openness to adoption was much more prevalent among African-American people than was apparent from formal and public adoption statistics. Robert Hill (1977) subsequently confirmed this in a comprehensive study of informal adoption patterns of African-Americans.

The criticism of transracial adoption was met with the response from advocates that such children benefit more from being in homes with families who love them than they do in foster homes or institutions where they are not part of a permanent, intact family. In fact, advocates accused agencies of discriminating, when such agencies held out for same-race adoption of African-American children (McRoy, 1989). Used as evidence of such discrimination are the statistics indicating that on a single day, an estimated 464,000 children are being cared for in foster family homes, group homes, and residential treatment centers (Children's Defense Fund,

1995). Depending on the particular state of residence, as many as 51% of such children may be African-American (Children's Defense Fund, 1995). Of the original number cited, it is considered likely that about 100,000 will never return to their biological families and are available for adoption (McRoy, 1994a). However, McRoy has also indicated that a substantial number of these are children who have other difficulties which may affect their adoption (McRoy, 1994, November).

Policy Response to the Controversy

In response to the controversy, and especially to the criticism brought by NABSW, a number of public and private agencies modified their policies and procedures. Incentive for these modifications was strengthened by the passage of the Indian Child Welfare Act (1980). Whereas most adoption legislation, at that time, was at the state level, this law established federal standards for removal of Native American children from their families, including the return of control over social service and child welfare programs to tribal governments (Wares, Wedel, Rosenthal, & Dobrec, 1994). During the same period, separate programs, and in some cases, separate agencies were established to encourage adoptions by African-American families. Moreover, assessment criteria for potential transracially-adopting parents were modified to include capabilities to parent cross-racially and cross-culturally. For instance, the 1991 Manual of the Indiana Children and Family Services division (Revised April, 1992) included, as one of many criteria for assessing an adoptive applicant's ability to parent cross-racially/culturally, "capacity and commitment to provide the child with positive racial and cultural experiences and information and knowledge of their care and culture" (Appendix WWW, p. 2).

Changes in procedures and policies of public and private agencies, while in some cases making transracial adoption more difficult, at the same time facilitated adoptions of children of ethnic minority groups by same-race parents. An example of this was the passage of the Adoption Assistance and Child Welfare Act of 1980 (1981) which provided subsidies in the form of direct income, medical insurance, or special education allowances to families who adopt 'children with special needs' (Karger & Stoetz, 1990), with ethnic and racial minority groups included. Some Caucasian parents, especially those who had been foster parents for African-American children but who were restricted by public or private policies in seeking to adopt them, filed legal action to reverse such restrictions (McRoy, 1989). Ultimately, the Multi-ethnic Placement Act of 1994 (1995) was passed by Congress. This act [prohibits] an agency, or entity, that receives Federal assistance and is involved in adoption or foster care programs from delaying or denying the placement of a child based on the race, color, or national origin of the child or adoptive or foster parent or parents involved, and for other purposes. (Multiethnic Placement Act, 1995)

The law does go on to designate that "an agency or entity to which [the above] applies may consider the race, color, or national origin of a child as a factor in making a placement decision if such factor is relevant to the best interest of the child involved and is considered in conjunction with other factors" (p. 5). Undoubtedly, experience with the law will determine how it is applied from a practical standpoint and what the results are for children.

Problems with Empirical Studies

The theoretical and pragmatic controversy surrounding transracial adoption should be apparent from the above historical discussion. Potential problems have also presented themselves in some of the empirical work surrounding this area. Several of these will be discussed.

First, data about the adoption experience, in some instances, were gathered only from the adoptive parents. There were several reasons for this. In the earliest studies, researchers were interested in what there was about couples who adopted transracially, or what there was about the transracial experience, that could be used to encourage other transracial adoptions (Bayerl, 1977; Harris & Wyrsch, 1974; Krebbs, 1972; Priddy & Kirgan, 1970; St. Denis, 1969). At times, the children were too young to participate in the study or there were not appropriate measures available to collect data from them. In these instances, data which were collected represented the parents' interpretations or observations of the child's experience. The potential for respondent reactivity, given such a controversial topic, may have increased in such instances.

Second, comparison groups in some studies included only transracial adoptees, Caucasian adoptees, and Caucasian biological children (Bayerl, 1977; Falk, 1970; Feigelman & Silverman, 1983; Simon & Alstein, 1977; 1981; 1987; 1992; 1994). While data from such studies were apt to provide information about uniformity of experience regardless of race, the question underlying the controversy was whether transracial adoptees who were members of racial or ethnic minority groups, would be able to develop the racial or ethnic identity and corresponding self-concept comparable to ethnic minority group adoptees of same race parents, while controlling for adoptive status itself.

Finally, some researchers summarized their data and made conclusions which omitted important outcomes. For instance, McRoy notes that in one instance the researchers "reported that they did not discern any significant racial identity problems occurring for African-American children in their longitudinal study of transracial adoptive families" (1994, p. 68). McRoy observes that this was in spite of figures from the third wave of that study which "indicated that 11% of their transracially adopted adolescents stated they would prefer to be white (p. 114) and that 27% of the transracial adoptive parents believed that their adopted children self-identified as white (p. 47)" (McRoy, 1994, p. 68). Moreover, in the concluding remarks to a 20-year longitudinal study, the authors of the study wrote "but we found that, both during adolescence and later as adults, the [transracial adoptees] clearly were aware of and comfortable with their racial identity" (Simon & Alstein, 1994, p. 115). A consideration which must be made in such a summary statement is that this was in the context of an attrition of 128 families (from an original 204 in 1971-72 to 76 in 1991). There is the possibility that the families who dropped out experienced greater difficulty with their transracial status.

Needed Conceptual Definitions and Distinctions

Racial/Ethnic Identity

Racial identity and ethnic identity have tended to be used synonymously. Potential difficulties with that will be discussed further in the paper. In the meantime, the same tradition of treating the two terms synonymously will be followed in discussing this phenomenon conceptually.

Rotheram and Phinney (1987) define ethnic identity as "one's sense of belonging to an ethnic group and the part of one's thinking, perceptions, feelings, and behavior that is due to ethnic group membership" (p. 13). They distinguish this from 'ethnicity,' taking the position that "ethnicity refers to group patterns" while 'ethnic identity' "refers to the individual's acquisition of group patterns" (p. 13).

Rotheram and Phinney (1987) point out that ethnic identity is conceptually and functionally different from one's personal identity as an individual, even though the two may reciprocally influence one another (p. 13). The question of interest in this paper, however, surrounds 'race dissonance,' that is, the extent of expressed preference, by children of ethnic minority groups, for items, such as dolls, which are of a different color from themselves. Is race dissonance greater for transracially-adopted children and does the difference vary with age? To answer that question, theorists have found it necessary to discuss ethnic identity within the context of self-identity development (Aboud, 1987). That conceptualization will be presented briefly here. Although cognitive considerations have also been presented (Ramsey, 1987), those will not be included except as they relate to self-development theories.

Between the ages of 15- and 18-months, infants begin to differentiate images of themselves from others, indicating a beginning physical self-other distinction (Berk, 1991). At around three-years-old, a 'categorical self' begins to develop, in which children make concrete descriptions of salient dimensions on which people differ. Spencer (1985) points out that during this age period, race dissonance may occur. For instance, African-American children may express preferences for, and assign desirable qualities to items, such as dolls, which are white, without holding any negative self-concept or low self-esteem. In fact, Spencer cites results from her research in which forty-seven percent of Southern black children (63% of Northern black children) showed simultaneous positive self concepts and race-dissonance (1985, p. 223).

Early in the preschool years, children begin to develop an "inner self," in which they think more deeply or internally about themselves and describe themselves in terms of at least momentary internal states (Berk, 1991). In the late preschool and early school-age years, "constancy" develops in children. They begin to understand characteristics of themselves and others as permanent and unchanging. It is at this point that a child would recognize the finer distinctions on which racial color is based. Spencer also points out that the child's evolving object capacity requires "an attempt to fit social experiences with existing knowledge" (p. 224). The African-American child, for example, may begin to relate societal attitudes and depictions of black people with the recognition that she, herself, is black.

Self-Esteem

By eight- to eleven-years-old, the period of development of the "psychological self," children hold evaluative judgments about themselves, utilizing social evaluations as the framework from which such judgments are found. Self-esteem, defined as *the judgments we make about the worth of ourselves,* is believed to coincide with this stage of the child's development (Berk, 1991). It would be expected that this would be the time that the reciprocal influence between ethnic identity and self-esteem would occur. Spencer points out that "without intervention on the personal/psychological or extrinsic/sociocultural level, the expected course of identity evolution for African-American children is toward identity imbalance" (1985, p. 224). She goes on to say that what is implied by the concept of identity imbalance is "a nonfit, or imbalance between personal identity (i.e., the self-concept) and group identity (i.e., cultural values, beliefs)" (1985, p. 224). Her research indicated that 46 percent of the variance for children's "white-choice" behavior was predicted, in a stepwise regression, by parental intervention associated with socializing their children, using accurate and ongoing information about ethnicity (1985, p. 228).

This discussion, then, formed the backdrop for the dialogue regarding transracial adoption—that being, whether Caucasian parents were able to socialize their adoptees of ethnic minority backgrounds sufficiently to offset identity imbalance and to instill self-pride and ethnic awareness. Also, it was for reasons associated with this framework that Caucasian parents who adopted transracially and transethnically began to be encouraged, by adoption agencies, to rear their children in thoroughly integrated neighborhoods, schools, and social groups, so that the child could establish the appropriate racial and ethnic identification and identity. The reality was that although many transracially- and transethnically-adopting parents started off in such circumstances, they gradually tended to associate with predominantly Caucasian neighborhoods, and schools and social groups. For instance, in her study of transethnic adoptive families of Mexican-American adolescents, Andujo reports that seventy-seven percent "resided in primarily Anglo-American neighborhoods and their children attended schools that had predominantly Anglo-American populations" (1988, p. 532). In another comparative study, of transracially-adopted and inracially-adopted African-American children, 87% of the transracial families lived in communities of less than 10% African Americans and 73% of the children attended schools with less than 30% African-Americans (McRoy, Zurcher, Lauderdale, & Anderson, 1984). The latter authors point out that "children whose families were residing in integrated areas, who attended racially integrated schools, and who had parents who acknowledged their children's racial identity, tended to perceive themselves as black persons and to feel positively about it" (pp. 38-39).

In summary, the literature noted suggests that during the early, preschool years, children of ethnic and racial minority groups may ascribe values to color without making evaluative judgments of their own worth on that basis (race dissonance). However, as children move into the school-age years, the threat of identity imbalance increases. The extent to which identity imbalance occurs seems to depend on whether their socialization allows them to develop accurate ethnic identification and ethnic identity. The assumption is that these will be practically automatic when children are raised by parents of the same ethnic group, but may not occur as spontaneously in transracial and transethnic adoptions.

Resulting Research Questions and Hypotheses
for the Meta-Analysis

The criticism of transracial or transethnic adoption has been that it prevents, or substantially interferes with, the development of positive racial or ethnic identity which children and adults of ethnic minority groups need in order to recognize and cope with the racism with which they will eventually be confronted. Given the perceived close relationship between self-esteem and racial and ethnic identity, noted in the conceptual definitions above, it seems safe to assume that transracial or transethnic adoption would simultaneously interfere with the development of self-esteem in adoptees.

The research questions addressed by this synthesis are: first, whether there is such an effect of transracial/transethnic adoption on racial/ethnic identity and self-esteem of children of ethnic minority groups across multiple studies; second, what is the direction of such an effect; and, third, how strong is it. A fourth, and related question is whether racial identity and self-esteem are associated. Finally, age differences are noted which coincide with the theoretical conceptualizations of racial and ethnic identity development discussed above.

The present author offered the following hypotheses: (1) A moderate effect size of transracial/transethnic adoption on racial or ethnic identity and self-esteem of children of U.S. racial and ethnic minority groups will be noted; (2) such an effect will be in the negative direction; that is, indicators of racial identity and self-esteem will be lower in transracially/transethnically-adopted compared to same race/same ethnic group-adopted children; (3) these outcomes will be maintained when racial/ethnic identity and self-esteem are analyzed separately; and, (4) racial/ethnic identity and self-esteem will decrease with increasing age in transracially/transethnically-adopted children.

THE META-ANALYSIS

Literature Search

The following computerized data-bases were used to access information on studies of transracial adoption: Academic and Magazine Index; Books in Print; Dissertation Abstracts; Educational Resources Information Center (ERIC); PsycLit; Social Work Abstracts; and Sociological Abstracts (Sociofile). In addition, the following were accessed through First Search: Periodical Abstracts, Social Sciences Index, and WorldCat. Numerous Master's Theses, which had not been located previously, were

accessed through WorldCat. Key words and phrases used in the search
were: transracial adoption, interracial adoption, black adoption, and interracial families. The first two proved the most productive. Family
Resources Database was also used, although it was not available to this
writer on CD-ROM. Reference lists of empirical studies and theoretical
papers were scanned for additional studies.

Sources of, and Eligibility Criteria for Included Studies

Six criteria were observed for the inclusion of studies in this review.

1. *Use of comparison groups.* Studies which involve contrasts between
   two situations are considered a necessary characteristic of meta-analytic synthesis (Hall, Rosenthal, Tickle-Degnen, & Mosteller, 1994).
   This criterion was followed in the present review. For this reason,
   several studies of worth, which did not use comparison groups,
   could not be included (Allen, 1976; Brown, 1974; DeBerry, 1991;
   Feigelman & Silverman, 1983; Grow & Shapiro, 1974; Moore,
   1978; Thompson-Issacs, 1988).
2. *Comparison groups are Caucasian families who adopted non-white
   children (transracial/transethnic adoptions) and non-white families
   who adopted same-race children (same race/same ethnic group-
   adoptions) and/or non-white biological children.* In those studies
   which included non-white biological children as an additional comparison group (Baker, 1992; Womack & Fulton, 1981), effect size
   was calculated with and excluding these groups. Some studies used
   Caucasian adoptees and Caucasian biological children as comparison groups to transracial adoptees (Simon & Alstein, 1977; 1981;
   1987; 1992; Zastrow, 1977). However, the primary controversy is
   whether children of ethnic minority groups, reared in Caucasian
   families, can receive the racial and ethnic socialization and orientation which is necessary for them to be able to maintain adequate
   racial/ethnic identity and self-esteem. While the issue of how the
   experience of transracially-adopted children compares with the
   experience of Caucasian children who are adopted by, or born to
   Caucasian parents, is an important one, it is not the issue of focus
   here. Thus, those studies were not included.
3. *Racial/ethnic identity and self-esteem as dependent variables.*
   Again, since the controversy surrounding transracial adoption specifically surrounds these variables, it was appropriate that they be
   used as outcome measures. Other research has looked at other
   dependent variables in studying effect of transracial adoption. These

include: intellectual functioning (Scarr & Weinberg, 1976; Weinberg, Scarr, & Waldman, 1992); characteristics of transracial adoptive parents (Bayerl, 1977; Falk, 1970; Harris & Wyrsch, 1974;
Krebbs, 1972; and Priddy & Kirgan, 1970; Womack & Fulton, 1981);
and presence of behavior problems (Baker, 1992; Rosenthal &
Groze, 1992). These were either not appropriate to the specific
research questions being addressed or were beyond the scope of this
particular review.

4. *Studies which collect data directly from adoptees.* While information from parents regarding the child's experience may be relevant
and useful, the possibility of greater subjectivity and social desir-
ability bias may increase in moving from child to adult subjects.
Thus, this review only utilized data obtained from children.

5. *Bi-racial children were categorized according to the biological parents whose race or ethnic group was considered an ethnic minority
in this country.* In this country, children with distinguishing and permanent characteristics, especially physical characteristics, which are
associated with a particular racial or ethnic group, tend to be considered members of that group. That assumption was adhered to in this
review. It was recognized that in some cases both biological parents
of a child may have been members of different ethnic minority
groups. However, it is believed that that number would have been
small enough not to influence the results substantially.

6. *U. S. studies.* The issue of transracial adoption is not exclusive to the
United States. However, the experience of members of ethnic and
racial minority groups in this country has a specific history and climate. This is considered a separate variable and one which is being
controlled in this review.

Although adhering to these criteria only permitted six eligible studies,
to have softened the criteria more would have further affected any generalization from the data.

Six studies, including one longitudinal study with four phases, met
these criteria. (See Table 1 for included studies and characteristics
associated with each.)

Analysis

Operational Definitions

In this review, racial and ethnic identity were defined, as was self-esteem, according to the interpretation given by, or suggested in the mea-

TABLE 1. Characteristics of Included Studies

Author	Publication Source	Year of Publication	Design	Recruitment Source	Recruitment Region	Mean Age (Years)
Andujo	Journal	1988	Cross-sectional	Private adoption agency	West	14.1 years transracial 13.9 years inracial
Baker	Master's Thesis	1992	Cross-sectional	Adoption advocacy group	Misc. combination	13.5 transrac. 13.5 inracial 13.5 biological
Black	Master's Thesis	1985	Cross-sectional	Adoption Advocacy group and public adoption agency	Misc. combination	3.5 all classes (Modal class: 1-7)
McRoy and Zurcher	Book	1983	Cross-sectional	Adoption advocacy group	Midwest	13.5 transracial 14.1 inracial

Comparison Groups	Dependent Variable	Number of Subjects	Measure	Statistic Used	Neighborhood Racial Make-up
Transracial; Inracial	Racial Identity Self-esteem[a]	30 transracial 30 inracial	Twenty-Statements Test: Use of ethnicity in self-description; use of color; (Kuhn & McPartland, 1954) Mexican American Value Attitude Scale (Lopez, 1970)	Frequencies and Proportions	"Primarily Anglo": 77% transracial 30% inracial
Transracial, Inracial, Biological	Self-esteem	15 transrac. 15 inracial 15 biological	Harter Self-Perception Profile (Harter, 1985)	Means and Standard Deviations	"White or Mostly White": 66% transracial 0% inracial 53% biol.
Transracial; Inracial	Racial Identity	20 transracial 12 inracial	Levine Scale (Modified) (Levine 1976)	Means and Standard Deviations	Transracial and inracial adoptees were not separated.
Transracial, Inracial	Racial Identity; Self-esteem	30 transracial 30 inracial	Twenty-Statements Test (Use of racial self-description; Use of adopted) (Spitzer, Couch, & Stratton, 1966); Tennessee Self-concept Scale (Fitts, 1965)	Frequencies and Proportions	"Less than 10% Black": 87% transracial; 10% inracial

TABLE 1 (continued)

Author	Publication Source	Year of Publication	Design	Recruitment Source	Recruitment Region	Mean Age (Years)
Shireman and Johnson	Book	1980	Longitu-dinal	Private adoption agency	Midwest	3.5 transracial 3.5 inracial
Shireman and Johnson	Journal	1986	Longitu-dinal	Private adoption agency	Midwest	8 transracial 8 inracial
Shireman	Unpublished document	1988	Longitu-dinal	Private adoption agency	Midwest	13 transracial 13 inracial
Vroegh	Meeting Proceedings	1992				17 transracial 17 inracial
Womack and Fulton	Journal	1981	Cross-sectional	Comb. adoption advocacy group and adoption agency	West	5.28 transracial 5.66 inracial

Comparison Groups	Dependent Variable	Number of Subjects	Measure	Statistic Used	Neighborhood Racial Make-up
Transracial, Inracial[b]	Racial Identity	34 trans-racial 34 inracial	Clark: Which doll looks like you? Doll puzzle test; Clark doll preference test (Clark & Clark, 1958)	Frequencies and Proportions	Two-thirds of transracial adoptees lived in white neighbor-hoods
Transracial, Inracial	Racial Identity[c]	25 trans-racial 24 inracial	Clark: Which doll looks like you? Clark: Overall doll pref. test	Frequencies and Proportions	Three-fourths of transracial adoptees lived in white, suburban neighborhoods
Transracial; Inracial	Racial Identity	21 transracial 17 inracial	Morland Social Distance from Black Americans Scale; Morland Semantic Differential of Black Preference Scale (Williams & Morland, 1976)	Means and Standard Deviations	1/2 of transracial adoptees are in schools where less than 1/2 the school population is white
		35 transracial 20 inracial	Interview: How identifies own race; dating choices by race	Frequencies and Proportions	In predomi-nantly white communities: 73% transracial; 5% inracial
Transracial; Biologic	Racial Identity	28 transracial 13 Biologic	PRAM II (Preschool Racial Attitude Measure), (Williams, 1971)	Means and Standard Deviations	15 transracial adoptees lived in neighborhoods with 1-5 Black families

[a]Although self-esteem was a dependent variable, statistics were not sufficiently available to allow its inclusion in this review.

[b]Single-parent adoptions made up a third comparison group; however, it was not included because the race of the parents was unclear.

[c]A measurement of self-concept was included in this phase but was not included in the present review.

sure(s) used in the particular study. These definitions were used accordingly in the calculation of effect sizes. A negative direction (sign) of an effect indicates that transracial or transethnic adoption was associated with lowered racial/ethnic identity or self-esteem compared to inracial or same ethnic group adoption. Alternately, a positive sign indicates high racial identity among transracial/transethnic adoptees compared to the same-race group. This is based on the formula for calculating effect size which is written as the difference between the mean of the racial or ethnic identity scores of the transracial/transethnic adoptee group (the experimental group) and the mean of the scores of the same-ethnic adoptee group (the control group), divided by the pooled standard deviation. In some cases signs were transformed so that a negative sign would mean the same in all cases and a positive sign would mean the same in all cases. For example, in the McRoy and Zurcher (1983) study, use of racial self-descriptors among transracial adoptees was perceived by the authors as indication of the transracial adoptee's constant awareness of color differences between herself and the rest of her family, and therefore was interpreted, in the present review, as a negative effect. Results showed that the transracial adoptee group used racial self-descriptors more frequently than did the inracial adoptee group. In applying the formula for the calculation of the effect size, d, the resulting effect size would carry a positive sign, meaning a negative effect. So that a negative effect would carry the same meaning in all cases, and thus could be used in the same way in calculating an overall or summary-level effect size, the sign was transformed in such cases as the above. See Table 2 for a description of the operational definition of each measure.

In summary, throughout this review, a negative effect size means that transracial or transethnic adoption had the effect of lowering racial/ethnic identity or self-esteem of the adoptee in relation to that of the same-race adoptee and a positive effect size means that transracial or transethnic adoption had the effect of increasing racial/ethnic identity or self-esteem.

Data Collection

A coding form was developed on which were coded the following variables: (1) authors; (2) source of data; (3) year of publication; (4) type of study; (5) source by which subjects were located and recruited; (6) geographical area from which subjects were recruited; (7) mean age of adoptees; (8) comparison groups; (9) dependent variable; (10) number of subjects providing effect size information; and (11) statistics used in reporting study results. An attempt was made to code and analyze attrition rates in longitudinal studies and racial make-up of the community in which the majority of transracial families in a study lived. Effect of racial make-up of the community could not be analyzed because a single level characterized studies for which such data were available or because the primary study failed to quantify these data or to clearly define integrated neighborhood. Attrition rate was relevant only for samples in the one longitudinal study, and therefore could not be compared. Although it may have been possible to develop levels within the category of attrition rate for those particular study phases, the last phase of that study combined single-parent inracial adoptions with two-parent inracial adoptions so that the n for that comparison group was inflated. Analysis outcomes of all other study variables will be discussed in the results section.

Statistical Procedures

In most studies, including the four phases of the longitudinal study, multiple measures were used to study the same constructs. Separate effect sizes were calculated for each measure and on each set of comparison groups. Thus, twenty-nine dependent measure effect sizes were analyzed, sixteen associated with racial identity and thirteen with self-esteem. However, the thirteen effect sizes associated with self-esteem included one study (Baker, 1992) in which the same transracial adoptees were compared first to inracial adoptees, then to biologic children on the same six measures of self-esteem, resulting in twelve effect sizes. The thirteenth dependent measure effect size was from the measure of self-esteem in the McRoy and Zurcher (1983) study. Because of the assumption of independence of meta-analytic reviews, summary effect sizes were calculated for each study. These were accomplished by calculating a simple mean of the effect sizes (g) of the dependent measures within each study, entering them manually, and calculating an overall effect size (d) of transracial/transethnic adoption on racial/ethnic identity and self-esteem.

The DSTAT software package (Johnson, 1989) was used to analyze data in this review. Statistical data from the studies which were included in the review were presented in frequencies and proportions or in means and standard deviations. Therefore, these statistics were used to compute effect sizes. Effect sizes were arrived at by calculating the difference between the experimental group (transracially/transethnically-adopted) and the control group (inracially/same race-adopted), divided by the pooled standard deviation.

In a meta-analysis, the calculation of a homogeneity statistic (Q) determines whether an effect size which has been obtained is consistent across all included studies (Halvorsen, 1994, p. 432). A statistically-significant Q indicates that heterogeneity, or variation, exists among the studies, which

TABLE 2. Operational Definition of Racial/Ethnic Identity or Self-Esteem with Effect Size, by Measure and by Study[a]

Racial Identity

1. Twenty-Statements Test: Use of Racial Self-Referents (used by McRoy and Zurcher, 1983). Negative effect size means transracial adoptees were more likely to use racial self-descriptors than inracial adoptees ($d = -0.6305$).

2. Twenty-Statements Test: Use of the Term 'Adopted' (used by McRoy and Zurcher, 1983). Negative effect size means transracial adoptees were more likely to use the term adopted than inracial adoptees ($d = -0.6557$).

3. Doll Puzzle Test (used by Shireman and Johnson, 1980). Negative effect size means transracial adoptees were less likely to correctly identify the doll which looked more like them (color) ($d = -0.3651$).

4. Clark Doll Study (used by Shireman and Johnson, 1980). Negative effect size means transracial adoptees were less likely to correctly identify the race of their adoptive parents ($d = 0.0283$).

5. Twenty Statements Test: Use of Ethnicity as a Self-Descriptor (used by Andujo, 1988). Negative effect size means transethnic adoptees were less likely to use ethnicity as a self-descriptor ($d = -1.6543$).

6. Andujo: Twenty-Statements Test: Use of Color as a Descriptor (used by Andujo, 1988). Negative effect size means transethnic adoptees were more likely to use color as a self-descriptor ($d = -1.1614$).

7. Mexican-American Value Attitude Scale (used by Andujo, 1988). Negative effect size means transethnic adoptees were less likely to have low scores on the acculturation scale (low scores = low levels of acculturation) ($d = -1.2446$).

8. Morland Semantic Differential Black Preference Scale (used by Shireman, 1988). Negative effect size means transracial adoptees were less likely to have low scores on this scale (low scores = high black preference ($d = 0.0579$).

9. Morland Social Distance from Black Americans Scale (used by Shireman, 1988). Negative effect size means transracial adoptees were less likely to have low scores on this scale (low scores = high comfort with Black Americans ($d = 0.6814$).

10. Correct Identification with Own Race on Interview (used by Vroegh, 1992). Negative effect size means transracial adoptees were less likely to correctly identify their own race (presumably according to the way the larger society would label their race) ($d = -1.1961$).

11. Clark Doll Study (used by Shireman and Johnson, 1986). Negative effect size means transracial adoptees were less likely to correctly identify the doll which was of the same race as themselves ($d = 0.0214$).

12. Clark Doll Study: Overall Preference Test (used by Shireman and Johnson, 1980). Negative effect size means transracial adoptees were less likely to have low scores on a overall "preference for the white doll" test (low scores = low white preference) (d = 0.4147).

13. Clark Doll Study: Overall Preference Test (used by Shireman and Johnson, 1986). Negative effect size means transracial adoptees were less likely to have low scores on an overall "preference for the white doll" test (low scores = low white preference) (d = − 0.1979).

14. Frequency of Dating Blacks (used by Vroegh, 1992). Negative effect size means transracial adoptees were more likely to select white dates (d = −1.1961).

15. Preschool Racial Attitudes Measure (PRAM II) (used by Womack and Fulton, 1981). Negative effect size means transracial adoptees were more likely to have high scores (high scores = high bias in favor of whites) (d = − 0.3411).

16. Levine Scale: Choices of the Black Child's Picture (used by Black, 1985). Negative effect size means transracial adoptees were less likely to have high scores (high scores = strong racial identity) (d = 0.2644).

Self-Esteem

---

17. Tennessee Self-Concept Scale (used by McRoy and Zurcher, 1983). Negative direction indicates that transracially adopted children are less likely to get high scores, with high scores indicating high self-esteem (d = 0.0851).

18. Harter Self-Perception Profile (used by Baker, 1992). Negative direction indicates that transracially adopted children are less likely to get high perceived competence scores on a measure of global self-worth and on measures of scholastic competence, social acceptance, athletic competence, physical appearance, and behavioral conduct compared to same race adoptees (d = − 0.4813, 0.5861, − 0.2642, 0.8006, 0.0000[b] and 0.2527 respectively) and compared to biological, non-adoptees (d = − 0.5638, 0.1638, 0.1235, 0.2156, 0.0000, and 0.0328 respectively).

---

[a]In instances of negative effect size, the transracially/transethnically-adopted group is perceived as having lower racial/ethnic identity than the inracially/same ethnic-adopted group; where effect size has a positive sign, the transracially/transethnically-adopted group is perceived as having stronger racial/ethnic identity.

[b]There was no difference between transracial adoptees and inracial adoptees or between transracial adoptees or between transracial adoptees and biological children on perceived physical appearance.

potentially influences the effect size and which cannot be attributed to sampling variation alone. If the Q statistic is not significant, homogeneity is said to exist among the studies.

A categorical model can be calculated to determine the influence of particular study qualities on the obtained effect size [Q(B)]. It is also possible to perform contrasts within categories, to determine the potential sources of variation [Q(W)]. Additionally, outliers can be studied for their possible influence on the homogeneity of the effect size.

All of these calculations were carried out in this review and will be reported in the Results section.

Finally, the DSTAT program uses a fixed effects (conditional) model in calculating effect sizes and in testing their homogeneity. This model was therefore followed in the present review. The (fixed-effects) model allows the researcher to generalize the results of the review only to that ensemble of studies which is similar to those included in the review (Hedges, 1994).

Results

Hypotheses

Four hypotheses were set forth with regard to a synthesis of studies of effect of transracial and transethnic adoption on racial or ethnic identity or self-esteem. They will be presented below and followed by a discussion of the results of each. A summary of study level effect sizes, for the combined racial/ethnic identity and self-esteem variable and for racial identity separately is found in Table 3. Results provided represent effect sizes when the four phases of the Shireman/Johnson/Vroegh longitudinal study were treated as a single study.

Support for the first three hypotheses was determined in three ways: first, by a negative mean effect size, with negative meaning that transracial/transethnic adoption had the effect of lowering racial/ethnic identity or self-esteem compared to that of same race/same ethnic group adoption; second, by a mean effect size which differs significantly from zero, that is, by a mean effect size whose confidence interval does not include zero; third, by an effect size of .20 or greater.

Hypothesis 1. There is a moderate effect of transracial/transethnic adoption on racial/ethnic identity and self-esteem of children of U. S. racial and ethnic minority groups.

This hypothesis was partially supported in the case of the composite racial/ethnic identity and self-esteem variable. Cohen's (1988) guidelines set .20 as a small magnitude of d, .50 as a medium or moderate magnitude,

TABLE 3. Study Level Effect Sales

Criteria	Value: Racial/Ethnic Identity and Self-Esteem	Value: Racial/Ethnic Identity Only
n	6	5
Unweighted effect size (d+)	− 0.3775	− 0.5220
Mean weighted effect size (d)	− 0.3221	− 0.4526
95% Confidence Interval for d+	− 0.62/ − 0.14	− 0.78/ − 0.26
Homogeneity (Q) of effect sizes comprising d+Note	17.343**	15.012**
Mean effect size (mean d)	− 0.3221	− 0.4526
Median effect size	− 0.2650	−.341 1
Differences favoring inracially/same ethnic adopted children	4/6 (67%)	4/5 (80%)

Note Significance indicates rejection of the hypothesis of homogeneity.
** p < .01

and .80 as a large effect. In the case of the combined racial/ethnic identity and self-esteem variable, the size of the effect was d = − 0.3775, p < .01, interpreted as falling between a small and medium (moderate) effect.

Hypothesis 2. Such an effect of transracial/transethnic adoption on racial and ethnic identity and self-esteem combined will be in the negative direction; i.e., indicators of racial or ethnic identity and self-esteem will be lower in transracially/transethnically adopted children compared to same-race/same ethnic group adoptees.

As noted above, the effect, on the composite dependent variable, was in the negative direction so that the alternative hypothesis was supported as stated.

A circumstance having relevance to these results should be mentioned. This had to do with the way racial identity was defined in interpreting responses on the Twenty Statements Test in one of the included studies (McRoy & Zurcher, 1983). A decision was made, in the present review, to interpret respondents' reference to race, on this measure, as indicative of a negative effect of transracial adoption. This was based on McRoy and Zurcher's conclusion that transracially-adopted children are more conscious of their racial group and adoptive status "since their physical dissimilarity to their family and peers is a constant reminder" (1983, p. 128). They are believed to be more likely to use racial self-descriptors than same-race adopted children because of this. However, a number of considerations may go into the use and analysis of race as a self-descriptor. These will be discussed later. In the meantime, it should be noted that, as an alternative, when a positive sign was assigned to the effect size of this same study, effect sizes decreased ($d = -0.2055$, $p < .001$, $d = -0.3500$, $p < .001$, and $d = -0.2831$, $p < .001$) for the composite of the twenty-nine dependent measure effect sizes, for the sixteen dependent measure effect sizes for racial/ethnic identity alone, and for the composite study level effect size for the combined racial/ethnic identity and self-esteem variable respectively, but remained statistically significant and in the negative direction.

Hypothesis 3. The above outcomes will be maintained when racial/ethnic identity and self-esteem are analyzed separately.

This hypothesis was supported in the case of racial/ethnic identity but not in the case of self-esteem. When the size of the effect of transracial/transethnic adoption was analyzed separately, the effect size on racial/ethnic identity increased, still in the negative direction ($d = -0.5220$, $p < .001$). However, size of the effect on self-esteem was minimal, in the positive direction, and not statistically significant ($d = 0.0845$, $p = .6676$).

Hypothesis 4. Racial/ethnic identity and self-esteem will decrease with increasing age in transracially/transethnically-adopted children.

Because of the small number of studies measuring effect on self-esteem, the effect of age was analyzed only for its effect on racial/ethnic identity.

A regression analysis was not performed so that it was not possible to analyze the linear effect of age on racial/ethnic identity or on self-esteem in transracially/transethnically adopted children. When a categorical model was calculated with *age* as a study quality, the model fit the effect size correctly. The test was found to be significant [$Q(B) = 10.70$, $p < .01$], indicating that the means of the four age groups differed significantly and that age potentially moderated the findings regarding the effect of transracial/transethnic adoption on racial identity. Effect size for each age group was in the negative direction, with the strongest effect being in the late adolescence category. What is suggested here is that age can be expected to influence the effect of transracial/transethnic adoption; that is, that racial/ethnic identity may decrease as transracial/transethnic adoptees become older. Future studies should control for these phenomena.

Homogeneity Level (Q)

As was mentioned earlier, meta-analytic reviews are interested not only in the size and direction of the effect of the independent variable(s) but additionally in whether homogeneity existed between studies. Accordingly, Halvorsen writes: " . . . the homogeneity test tests the null hypothesis that the between-studies variance is no greater than would be expected due to sampling error alone" (1994, p. 432). In the case that statistically-significant differences exist, heterogeneity is said to exist among the studies for the qualities on which there is a statistically-significant effect size. In this review, heterogeneity was found. (See Table 3 for a description of overall homogeneity level.)

The statistically significant test for homogeneity, or the confirmation of heterogeneity among the studies which were included, is typically addressed in one, or both of two ways: analysis of study qualities around which heterogeneity existed, referred to as potential moderators, and analysis of outliers. *Outlier* in this instance refers to the case that would result in the largest reduction to the Q (homogeneity) statistic if it were removed from the analysis. The results of each will be discussed.

Potential Moderators

Each study quality which was coded originally was tested for a significant Q, meaning that heterogeneity existed in the meta-analysis with regard to that study quality. Study qualities with a significant Q level are considered potential moderators. In this review, potential moderators were age; publication source [Q(B) 8.36, $p < .05$]; year of publication [Q(B) 15.01, $p < .05$]; geographical recruitment area [Q(B) 8.36, $p < .05$]; and size of sample [Q(B) 4.79, $p < .05$].

For *publication source,* effect sizes were in the negative direction for studies published in journals and in books, with the largest effect being associated with studies published in journals. (The Andujo [1988] measures were included here and since these had the largest effect sizes throughout the review, and were considered an outlier, the size of their effect here is not unexpected.)

In the case of *year of publication,* four out of five categories had effect sizes in the negative direction. The strongest effect size was for 1985 and contained the study by Black (1985). It is difficult to interpret this finding especially since the four phases of the longitudinal study had to be combined into one study, representing one publication year (when there were actually four), so that dependence associated with this phenomenon is great. What should be considered, of course, is the influence of historical era on the experience of transracial/transethnic adoptees.

Where *geographical recruitment area* was concerned, the strongest effect sizes, also in the negative direction, were associated with the studies conducted in the west and midwest, suggesting that reduced racial and ethnic identity associated with transracial or transethnic adoption may be greater in these regions and should be considered in future studies.

Finally, effect sizes for both *sample size* categories (that is, 0-50 and 51 and over) were in the negative direction, with the strongest effect associated with studies containing sample sizes of 51 or more. This finding may be related to increased power that is associated with larger sample sizes. What is suggested is that the effect of transracial/transethnic adoption may be demonstrated with larger sample sizes so that attempts at insuring adequate samples should be made. See Cohen, 1988 for methods of calculating power associated with effect size, d.

Outliers

The criterion which was used for identifying outliers was identification of the case that would result in the largest reduction to the Q-statistic if it were removed. In this review, the outlier identified by the DSTAT program was the effect size associated with the Andujo (1988) study.

This was especially interesting since the sample sizes, comparison groups, ages of subjects, statistics, and measures are almost identical to the McRoy and Zurcher (1983) study. However, the size of the effect is much greater ($d = -1.3358$, $p < .001$ for study-level effect). The difference in ethnic or racial identity here between transethnically-adopted Mexican-American adolescents and same-ethnic group adoptees is a distinct and consistent one. Why the magnitude of the effect would be so much greater in this instance, compared to the African-American sample, is an area for future study. The element of biracial heritage may come into play here. None of the transethnic adoptees in the Andujo study were ethnically-mixed, whereas seventy-three percent of the transracial adoptees in the McRoy and Zurcher study were of mixed racial heritage. This may have meant that the Mexican-American adoptees in Caucasian families may have been more aware of their ethnic difference from the adoptive family (because of the physical and perhaps language dissimilarity) and, therefore more inclined to describe themselves by color and ethnicity. Hence, a stronger effect of transethnic adoption.

In addition to the above results, an overall effect size, calculated for the individual effect sizes for the sixteen racial/ethnic identity dependent measures in studies, was $d = -0.4402$. (See Table 4 for a stem and leaf plot of the individual effect sizes for these dependent measures of racial/ethnic identity.)

As was mentioned earlier, in order to maximize independence of effect sizes, overall study level effect size was calculated using the four phases of the longitudinal study as a single study. When the four phases were treated as a four separate studies, the effect size of transracial/transethnic adoption decreased slightly, both for the combined racial/ethnic identity/self-esteem

TABLE 4. Stem and Leaf Plot of Effect Sizes of Dependent Measures of Transracial/Transethnic Adoption on Racial/Ethnic Identity

```
+ .9 |
+ .8 |
+ .7 |
+ .6 | 8
+ .5 |
+ .4 | 1
+ .3 |
+ .2 | 6
+ .1 |
+ .0 | 2  3  6
- .0 |
- .1 |
- .2 | 0
- .3 | 4  7
- .4 |
- .5 |
- .6 | 3  6
- .7 |
- .8 |
- .9 |
-1.0 |
-1.1 | 5  6
-1.2 | 0  4
-1.3 |
-1.4 |
-1.5 |
-1.6 | 5
```

variable (d = -0.3122) and for racial identity separately (d = -0.3912). However, both remained statistically significant and in the negative direction.

DISCUSSION

Overall results indicate that future studies, similar in substance and methodology to those included in this review, can be expected to show a moderate effect, in the negative direction, of transracial/transethnic adoption on racial and ethnic identity. Age, historical context in which the study is conducted, the geographical region of the study, the size of the sample, and the level of racial/ethnic integration of the adoptees' lifestyle should be considered carefully in such studies. Controlling these variables is recommended.

The failure of this synthesis to obtain a statistically significant effect of transracial/transethnic adoption on self-esteem prevents generalization to other studies on this construct. Since the effect size, when self-esteem and racial/ethnic identity were disaggregated, was based on a synthesis which included only the dependent measures from two studies, it is difficult to interpret the results. However, the positive direction of the results, in the context of a substantial effect, in the negative direction, on racial/ethnic identity, raises questions regarding the relationship between racial or ethnic identity and self-esteem, under what conditions the two occur, and the age considerations which are endemic. Also raised are broader questions. For instance, the effect of transracial/transethnic adoption on racial/ethnic identity has tended to be studied within the context of concerns regarding self-esteem, based on theoretical propositions regarding the relationship between the two. However, issues raised by the National Association of Black Social Workers also included such factors as preparation for "survival in a racist society" and "the healthy development of oneself as a black person" (NABSW, 1972; cited in McRoy, 1989, p. 150). The outcome of this synthesis suggests that additional variables such as these may be important and should be incorporated in future research.

The heterogeneity across studies, which was noted in this review, may be related to variation among the measures which were used or even to the variation with which results were interpreted using the same measure. For example, in the use of the Twenty Statements Test by studies included in this review, there was variation in the interpretation of use of racial self-descriptors (McRoy and Zurcher, 1983), use of color as a self-descriptor (Andujo, 1988), and use of ethnic self-descriptor (Andujo, 1988). It would be interesting to determine under what condition each is perceived as an indicator of racial or ethnic identity and how results differ. It may be that the difference between racial identity and ethnic identity emerges in this variation and is an important area for further study.

Another area of interest is the part played by biracial identity in the experience of the transracial/transethnic adoptee. All of the transethnic adoptees in the Andujo study were Mexican American whereas 22 or 73% of the transracial adoptees in the McRoy and Zurcher study were described by the authors as racially-mixed. The question is whether biracial status had an effect on the outcomes noted. Unfortunately, information was not given, in most of the studies in this review, regarding the proportion of biracial adoptees among those transracially/transethnically adopted. However, this will be an important area for future study.

A final consideration is the influence of racial and /or ethnic environment outside of that of the immediate family. It has been suggested (McRoy, Zurcher, Lauderdale, & Anderson, 1984) that effect of transracial adoption may be mediated by the transracially-adoptive parents intentionally exposing their adoptees to situations in which they can develop greater racial/ethnic identity (for example, living in well-integrated neighborhoods, attending well-integrated schools, participating as a family in activities and organizations which involve large numbers of persons who are of the same racial or ethnic group as the transracially- or transethnically-adopted child). It was not possible to assess this as a possible moderator in the present review. This was because in all of the studies for which such data were given, transracially-adoptive families lived in predominantly white neighborhoods. However, in the third phase (1988) of the Shireman and Johnson longitudinal study, the effect size for thirteen-year-olds attending well-integrated junior high schools was in the positive direction on both measures. This suggests that, even while residing in predominantly white environments, regular participation in a school situation where members of their race were in a majority may have resulted in a heightening of racial identity in transracially-adopted African-American young adolescents.

Implications for Future Research and Intervention

Eagly and Wood (1994) discuss the benefit of the meta-analytic review for planning future research. They raise the importance of achieving a goal of certainty, or sureness, in conclusions which can be drawn from meta-analytic outcomes. The identification of moderators as influencing variables and mediators as causative mechanisms is useful in directing future research.

The present review raises several such directions. First, comparative studies of review phenomena, i.e., racial or ethnic identity and self-esteem, among different age groups, will be useful in further understanding the contribution of age. Regression analyses will be especially beneficial.

Second, an important direction will be an assessment of the association between racial/ethnic identity and self-esteem, including conditions under which both occur and considerations of age.

Third, the issues raised in the criticism of transracial adoption by the National Association of Black Social Workers should be revisited, with a goal of identifying the total effect of racial/ethnic identity failures. As noted above, these include identification of those qualities which are necessary for surviving in a society in which racism exists, and delineation of the components of a healthy sense of self as a black person.

Fourth, from a theoretical standpoint, it will be important to seek a commonly-accepted definition of racial identity and to distinguish between racial and ethnic identity, if necessary. Measures should then be evaluated for their construct validity, that is, for the extent to which different measures are assessing the same racial or ethnic identity construct.

Fifth, the influence of biracial heritage of transracial adoptees is a necessary consideration. How does biracial heritage affect the experience of transracial/transethnic adoption in the areas noted (i.e., racial/ethnic identity and self-esteem) and what influence does this experience have on the developmental tasks confronting transracial and transethnic adoptees who are of biracial heritage?

Sixth, the relationship between external environment and racial or ethnic identity should be studied carefully. Purposive samples may be sought of transracial adoptees who are living and/or regularly and actively participating in environments where members of their race are in a majority. The racial or ethnic identity of these adoptees might then be compared to that of transracial adoptees who are living and participating in predominantly Caucasian or Anglo environments.

Seventh, although source of recruitment was not a moderator in the results of this review, participants in transracial/transethnic adoption studies have tended to be volunteers, raising the possibility of a self-selection element in study outcomes. Creative methods of randomly selecting a sample should be considered. Of related importance is evaluating whether the families who are contacted and do not respond represent a subsample of interest.

Eighth, there is now a population of adults who were transracially- or transethnically-adopted. They represent an untapped source of data, especially with the use of qualitative methods, also an untapped source of information in this area, and should be strongly considered for study.

Ninth, theoretical consideration should be given to how the other potential moderators (in addition to age) which were identified in this review (publication source, year of publication, geographical recruitment region, and size of study sample) might influence the magnitude of the effect of review phenomena.

Tenth, future studies should, where possible, consistently incorporate additional variables which may be potential moderators. These may include the influence of being adopted, the age of adoptee at placement, the presence of same-race adoptive or biological siblings in the adoptive family, adoptive family functioning, and socioeconomic status.

Finally, the issues of the development of racial and ethnic identity and of the maintenance of a healthy self-concept as a member of an ethnic minority group are important in their entirety. They constitute an important area of inquiry, both within and beyond the transracial/transethnic adoption experience.

In summary, the controversy surrounding transracial/transethnic adoption remains centered on what is in the best interest of the children involved. The results of this review seem to indicate that the question of the best interests of children of ethnic minority groups is a broad one with many remaining research directions. It is a topic which is worthy of continued, careful study.

REFERENCES

References marked with an asterisk indicate studies included in the meta-analysis.

Aboud, F. E. (1987). The development of ethnic self-identification and attitudes. In J. S. Phinney & M. J. Rotheram (Eds.), *Children's ethnic socialization: Pluralism and development* (pp. 32-55), Newbury Park, CA: Sage Publications.

Adoption Assistance and Child Welfare Act of 1980, Pub. L. No. 96-272, δ 473, 94 Stat. 500 (1981).

Allen, W. E. (1976). The formation of racial identity in Black children adopted by white parents. *Dissertation Abstracts International.*

*Andujo, E. (1988). Ethnic identity of transethnically-adopted Hispanic adolescents. *Social Work, 33,* 531-535.

*Baker, M. E. (1992). *Psychological adjustment of adopted minority children.* Unpublished master's thesis, University of North Carolina at Chapel Hill.

Bayerl, J. A. (1977). *Transracial adoptions: White parents who adopted white children and white parents who adopted black children.* Unpublished doctoral dissertation, University of Michigan.

Berk, L. E. (1991). *Child Development* (Second edition). Boston: Allyn and Bacon.

*Black, S. E. C. (1985). *The perception of racial identity in transracial and inracial adoptees.* Unpublished master's thesis, University of Houston.

Bowles, D. (1993). Bi-racial identity: Children born to African-American and White couples. *Clinical Social Work, 21,* 417-428.

Brown, W. T. (1974). Racial devaluation among transracially adopted children. *Dissertation Abstracts International.*

Children's Defense Fund (1995). *The State of America's Children Yearbook: 1995.* Washington, DC: Author.

Clark, K. B. and Clark, M. P. (1958). Racial identification and preference in Negro children. In E. E. Maccoby, T. M. Newcomb, and E. Hartley (Eds.), *Readings in Social Psychology.* New York: Holt, Rinehart, and Winston, Inc.

DeBerry, K. M. (1991). *Modeling ecological competence in African American transracial adoptees.* Unpublished doctoral dissertation, University of Virginia.

Eagly, A. H. & Wood, W. (1994). Using research syntheses to plan future research. In H. Cooper & L. V. Hedges (Eds.), *The Handbook of Research Synthesis* (pp. 485-502). New York: Russell Sage Foundation.

Falk, L. L. (1970). A comparative study of transracial and inracial adoptions. *Child Welfare, 49,* 82-88.

Feigelman, W. & Silverman, A. (1983). *Chosen children: New patterns of adoptive relationships.* New York: Praeger Publishers.

Fitts, W. H. (1965). *Tennessee self concept scale manual.* Nashville, TN: Counselor Recordings and Tests.

Freivalds, S. A. (1994, November). *Transracial and inter-national adoption: The current state of research, practice and policy.* Paper presented at the Annual Conference of the National Council on Family Relations, Minneapolis, MN.

Grow, L. J. & Shapiro, D. (1974). *Black children-White parents: A study of transracial adoption.* New York: Child Welfare League of America, Inc.

Hall, J. A., Rosenthal, R., Tickle-Degnen, L., & Mosteller, F. (1994). Hypotheses and problems in research synthesis. In H. Cooper & L.V. Hedges (Eds). *The handbook of research synthesis* (pp. 17-28). New York: Russell Sage Foundation.

Halvorsen, K. T. (1994). The reporting format. In H. Cooper & L.V. Hedges (Eds.) *The handbook of research synthesis* (pp. 425-438). New York: Russell Sage Foundation.

Harris, A. & Wyrsch, B. (1974). *Adoptive situation of white families who have adopted black children: A descriptive study of transracial adoption in the St. Louis Metropolitan area.* Unpublished Masters Thesis, University of Missouri School of Social Work, St. Louis.

Hill, R. B. (1977). *Informal adoption among black families.* Washington, DC: National Urban League Research Department.

Johnson, B. T. (1989). *DSTAT: Software for the meta-analytic review of research literatures.* Hillsdale, NJ: Erlbaum.

Indian Child Welfare Act of 1978, δ 1214 (1980).

Indiana Department of Public Welfare (1991, Revised 1992). *Indiana Family and Children's Services Manual: Adoption (Appendix VVV and WWW).*

Karger, H. & Stoesz, D. (1990). *American social welfare policy.* New York: Longman.

Krebbs, N. E. (1972). *A comparison of characteristics of women who adopted a black child and women who stated an unwillingness to adopt a black child.* Unpublished doctoral dissertation, University of Oregon, Corvalis.

Kuhn, M. & McPartland, T. S. (1954). An empirical investigation of self attitudes. *American Sociological Review, 54*, 58-76.

Light, R. J., Singer, J. D., & Willett, J. B. (1994). The visual presentation and interpretation of meta-analyses. In H. Cooper & L. V. Hedges (Eds.), *The handbook of research synthesis* (pp. 439-454). New York: Russell Sage Foundation.

Lopez, E. (1970). *Anxiety, acculturation and the urban Chicano.* Berkeley: California Books.

McRoy, R. G. (1989). An organizational dilemma: The case of transracial adoptions. *The Journal of Applied Behavioral Science, 25,* 145-160.

McRoy, R. G. (1994). Attachment and racial identity issues: Implications for child placement decision making. *Journal of Multicultural Social Work, 3,* 59-74.

McRoy, R. G. (1994, November). *Transracial and international adoption: The Current State of Research, Practice and Policy.* Paper presented at the Annual Conference of the National Council on Family Relations, Minneapolis, MN.

*McRoy, R. G. & Zurcher, L. A. (1983). *Transracial and inracial adoptees: The adolescent years.* Springfield, IL: Charles C. Thomas.

McRoy, R. G., Zurcher, L. A., Lauderdale, M. L., & Anderson, R. E. (1984). The identity of transracial adoptees. *Social Casework, 65,* 34-39.

Multiethnic Placement Act of 1994, δ1224 (1995).

Priddy, D. & Kirgan, D. (1970). *Characteristics of white couples who adopted black-white children in the San Francisco bay area: A study of 24 couples.* Unpublished Master's thesis, University of California, Berkeley.

Ramsey, P. G. (1987). Young children's thinking about ethnic differences. In J. S. Phinney & M.J. Rotheram (Eds.), *Children's ethnic socialization: Pluralism and development,* Newbury Park, CA: Sage Publications.

Roosa, M. W. & Beals, J. (1990). Measurement issues in family assessment: The case of the family environment scale. *Family Process, 29,* 191-198.

Rotheram, M. J. & Phinney, J. S. (1987). Introduction: Definitions and perspectives in the study of children's ethnic socialization. In J. S. Phinney & M. J. Rotheram (Eds.), *Children's ethnic socialization: Pluralism and development.* Newbury Park, CA: Sage Publications.

Scarr, S. & Weinberg, R. (1976). IQ test performance of black children adopted by white families. *American Psychologist, 31,* 726-739.

St. Denis, G. C. (1969). Interracial adoption in Minnesota: Self-concept and child-rearing attitudes of Caucasian parents who have adopted Negro children. *Dissertation Abstracts International.*

*Shireman, J. F. & Johnson, P. R. (1975). *Adoption: Three alternatives* (Phase I). Chicago, IL: Chicago Child Care Society.

*Shireman, J. F. & Johnson, P. R. (1980). *Adoption: Three alternatives* (Phase II). Chicago, IL: Chicago Child Care Society.

*Shireman, J. F. & Johnson, P. R. (1986). A longitudinal study of black adoptions: Single parent, transracial, and traditional. (Phase III). *Social Work, 31,* 172-177.

*Shireman, J. F. (1988). *Family life project: A longitudinal adoption study (Growing up adopted: An examination of major issues. (Phase IV).* Chicago, IL: Chicago Child Care Society.

Simon, R. J. & Alstein, H. (1977). *Transracial adoption.* New York: John Wiley Sons.

Simon, R. J. & Alstein, H. (1981). *Transracial adoption: A follow-up.* Lexington, MA: Lexington Books.

Simon, R. J. & Alstein, H. (1987). *Transracial adoptees and their families: A study of identity and commitment.* New York: Praeger Publishers.

Simon, R. J. & Alstein, H. (1992). *Adoption, race and identity: From infancy through adolescence.* New York: Praeger Publishers.

Simon, R. J., Alstein, H., Melli, M. S. (1994). *The case for transracial adoption.* Washington, DC: The American University Press.

Spencer, M. (1985). Cultural cognition and social cognition as identity correlates of black children's personal-social development. In M. B. Spencer, G. K. Brookins, & W. R. Allen (Eds.) *Beginnings: The social and affective development of black children* (pp. 215-230). Hillsdale, NJ: Lawrence Erlbaum Associates.

Spitzer, S., Couch, C., and Stratton, J. (1966). *The assessment of the self.* Iowa City, IA: Sernoll, Inc.

*Vroegh, K. S. (1992, April). *Transracial adoption: How it is 17 years later.* (Phase V). Paper presented at the Annual Meeting of the American Psychological Association, San Francisco.

Wares, D. M., Wedel, K. R., Rosenthal, J. A., & Dobrec, A. (1994). Indian child welfare: A multicultural challenge. *Journal of Multicultural Social Work, 3,* 1-15.

Weinberg, R. A., Scarr, S., Waldman, I. D. (1992). The Minnesota transracial adoption study: A follow-up of IQ test performance at adolescence. *Intelligence, 16,* 117-135.

Williams, J. E. (1971). *Preschool Racial Attitudes Measure II (PRAM II): General information and Manual of Directions.* Winston-Salem, NC: Wake Forest University Press.

Williams, J. and Morland, K. (1976). *Race, Color, and the Young Child.* Chapel Hill: University of North Carolina Press.

*Womack, W. M. & Fulton, W. (1981). Transracial adoption and the black preschool child. *Journal of the American Academy of Child Psychiatry, 20,* 712-724.

Zastrow, C. H. (1977). *Outcome of black children-white parents transracial adoptions.* San Francisco: R & E Research Associates.

Formal Adoption
of the Developmentally Vulnerable
African-American Child:
Ten-Year Outcomes

Janet L. Hoopes
Leslie B. Alexander
Paula Silver
Gail Ober
Nancy Kirby

SUMMARY. This research presents an in-depth study of ten-year adoption outcomes for 24 developmentally vulnerable African-American infants and toddlers and their parents. Overall the families reported feeling well bonded and satisfied with their children's progress, their family life, and the adoption experience. For the most part, the chil-

Janet L. Hoopes is Professor Emerita, Department of Psychology, Bryn Mawr College. Leslie B. Alexander is Professor, Graduate School of Social Work and Social Research, Bryn Mawr College. Paula Silver is Assistant Professor at the Center for Social Work Education, Widener University, Chester, PA. Gail Ober is Executive Director, The Children's Aid Society of Pennsylvania, Philadelphia, PA. Nancy Kirby is Assistant Dean at the Graduate School of Social Work and Social Research, Bryn Mawr College.

This study was funded by The Children's Aid Society of Pennsylvania, Philadelphia.

An earlier version of this paper was presented at the Annual Program Meeting of the American Orthopsychiatric Association in May of 1995 in Chicago, Illinois. Drawing on this same data base, additional papers are in preparation.

[Haworth co-indexing entry note]: "Formal Adoption of the Developmentally Vulnerable African-American Child: Ten-Year Outcomes." Hoopes, Janet L. et al. Co-published simultaneously in *Marriage & Family Review* (The Haworth Press, Inc.) Vol. 25, No. 3/4, 1997, pp. 131-144; and: *Families and Adoption* (ed: Harriet E. Gross and Marvin B. Sussman) The Haworth Press, Inc., 1997, pp. 131-144. Single or multiple copies of this article are available for a fee from The Haworth Document Delivery Service [1-800-342-9678, 9:00 a.m. - 5:00 p.m. (EST). E-mail address: getinfo@haworth.com].

dren were also doing reasonably well and had quite positive self esteem. This was despite the fact that some children had learning disabilities, some of the early adolescent males displayed oppositional social behavior, and some parents reported apparent contradictory perceptions of family cohesion and coping. *[Article copies available for a fee from The Haworth Document Delivery Service: 1-800-342-9678. E-mail address: getinfo@haworth.com]*

While permanency planning for all children remains the predominant goal of child welfare services, there is compelling evidence that this goal is not being met, especially for African-American children (Barth & Berry, 1994; Pecora, Fraser, Nelson, McCroskey, & Meezan, 1995). This goal has been particularly elusive around formal adoption by two-parent, African-American families. There is an implicit assumption that informal adoption is both more prevalent and highly valued than formal adoption among African-Americans. Although Williams (1991) and Billingsley (1992) challenge this thesis, pointing out the long and highly valued tradition of formal adoption by African-Americans, there is almost no readily available clinical or research literature to support this claim (see Gurak, Smith, & Goldson, 1982, for an exception).

Similarly, while there have been recent efforts to examine outcomes for "special needs adoptions"–those where children are adopted when they are older (> 4) and where there may often be severe developmental and physical handicaps (Rosenthal & Groze, 1990), there has been little systematic investigation of adoption outcomes for the developmentally vulnerable infant experiencing a range of less dramatic, but still serious risk factors. These include prenatal or perinatal complications, a history of heritable disorders, early neglect or abuse, and multiple disruptions of maternal bonding. This is in spite of research on resiliency in children which demonstrates that some who experience a range of early trauma manage to survive reasonably intact (Luthar & Zigler, 1991). A variety of protective factors fostering resiliency has been identified (Anthony & Cohler, 1987; Garmezy, 1993; and Brooks, 1994), with a warm, accepting family consistently among these.

The research study described here is an exploratory investigation of outcomes related to family and child functioning and satisfaction for a small cohort of African-American families with developmentally vulnerable infants and toddlers. These children were adopted between 1975-79 by two-parent African-American families, and followed up in 1989. The majority of these children were placed for adoption between one and two years of age, with a range from one month to 5 1/2 years.

METHODS

Participants: A one-group, posttest only design was used. Participants were drawn from closed adoption files from the years 1975-79, in two urban, private non-profit agencies in a large metropolitan area. Adoptees in their later teenage years were excluded to minimize the impact on study findings of normal stresses of later adolescence, resulting in a sample of 24 adoptees, most of whom were between the ages of 10 and 13 at follow-up ten years later.

Within these age parameters, each adoptee was selected on the basis of a history of at least one early medical, social or physical risk factor which research and practice suggest may result in subsequent developmental and/or adjustment problems. From this pool of eligible families, 23 African-American families agreed to be interviewed.

Procedures: After informed consent was obtained, semistructured interviews were conducted with parents in their homes, lasting from 1-1/2 to 3 hours, including completion of standardized instruments. Twenty-three mothers and 13 fathers were interviewed. All interviews were tape-recorded and were conducted by two African-American interviewers, both experienced clinical social workers.

At the close of the parent interviews, permission was obtained to interview their adopted child in his/her home on a separate occasion, using audiotapes and the same interviewers who had interviewed their parents. Twenty-four children were studied (one family had 2 adopted children); 22 were interviewed. Seventeen were male and 7 were female. Most adoptees were between 10 and 13 years of age, although there were 5 males who were 14 or 15.

Measures: Based on the work of McRoy, Grotevant, and Zurcher (1988), Masten and Garmezy (1978), and Hoopes (1967), which has identified background, prenatal and perinatal difficulties, and neglect and abuse, as early risk factors, a twenty-four item index was developed to rate each child's developmental vulnerability prior to adoptive placement (see Table 1). Data about risk factors were drawn from closed case records. Two raters, using a random sample of 10 of these cases, agreed on the coding of risk factors 90% of the time. Each item in the index was scored dichotomously, the sum of which was used as a risk factor score. The possible range of scores was 1 through 24, with higher scores representing more risk factors. For this sample scores ranged from a low of 1 to a high of 17, with a mean of 8.5 and a standard deviation of 5. There were no significant differences by gender.

Risk factors were not weighted, as no single risk factor was expected to effect long range outcome disproportionately. Nor did we examine the

TABLE 1. Risk Factors

Birth Mother

    Age: < 18 or > 40

    History of health problems

    History of psychiatric illness

    History of Psychiatric Hospitalization

    Health problems during pregnancy

    Substance Abuse

    Prenatal care: None or 3rd trimester only

Infant

    Birth weight: < 2510 grams

    Delivery complications

    Prenatal Medical Problems

     Apgar-7 or <;

     Fetal Distress;

     Fetal alcohol syndrome;

     Fetal drug syndrome;

     Respiratory difficulties;

     Sepsis;

     Failure to thrive;

     Neurological problems;

    Evidence of abuse or neglect

    Evidence of abandonment

    Age at First Placement in foster care: 1 year or >

    Number of pre-adoption placements: 2 or >

    Age at adoption placement: 1 year or >

    Health problems at time of adoption placement

    Developmental Problems at time of adoption placement

singular effect of each risk factor on outcome since the literature is clear that "a cumulative risk model of development posits that adverse developmental outcomes can better be predicted by combinations of risk factors than by a single one" (Liaw & Brooks-Gunn, 1994, 361). Follow-up studies of at-risk infants have shown that higher cumulative risk factors lead to a greater number of behavior and learning problems, particularly in later childhood and adolescence (Zelkowitz Papageorgious, Zelazo, & Weiss, 1995; Liaw & Brooks-Gunn, 1994; Adams, Hillman, & Gaydos, 1994; Levy-Schiff et al., 1994; Sameroff, Seifer, Baldwin, A., & Baldwin, C., 1993; Coon, Carey, Corley, & Fulker, 1992; Brodzinsky & Steiger, 1991; McRoy et al., 1988; Richards, Ford, & Kitchen, 1987; Caputo, Goldstein, & Taub, 1981; Masten & Garmezy, 1978; Sameroff & Chandler, 1978; and Hoopes, 1967).

A major question of this study was the extent to which this risk sum score in early life predicted child functioning and self-esteem in later childhood and early adolescence. Child functioning was measured by *The Revised Child Behavior Checklist CBCL-R* (Achenbach & Edelbrook, 1983), which was completed by the parents and yielded a measure of social competence, the presence of behavior problems, and internalizing/ externalizing behavior. Self-esteem was assessed by the *Coopersmith Self-Esteem Inventory* (CSI, Coopersmith, 1987). In addition to these standardized measures, parental satisfaction with the child's health status, school performance, and overall adjustment was assessed from the interview material, using single item likert scales.

Of equal importance to this study was the question of family characteristics which may have acted as protective factors in fostering resiliency, leading to positive developmental outcomes for these children. Also explored was the degree of satisfaction with the adoption experience for these African-American families.

To assess family characteristics, several standardized measures were completed by the parents and, together with interview material, addressed the following questions:

(1) How well bonded were the families? Family theory suggests that the level of bonding perceived by family members serves as an indicator of a family unit's functioning (Olson, McCubbin, & Associates, 1983). *The FACES III Cohesion scale* (Olson et al., 1985) measured this dimension.

(2) How adaptable were the families in handling family roles and rules? Family adaptability has to do with the extent to which the family system is flexible and able to change. *FACES III Adaptability Scale* (Olson et al., 1985) assessed this dimension.

(3) What were the family problem-solving styles? What were the effective problem-solving and behavioral strategies utilized by families in difficult or problematic situations? The *F-COPES* (Olson et al., 1985) assessed this dimension.

(4) How satisfied were the parents with the adoptive experience? This was assessed on a 4-point likert scale from the interview data.

It is important to note that while some data collected in the parent interviews required retrospective recall, all of the measures reported on in this paper except for the risk sum index asked for parental assessment in the present – that is, at the time of their interview. As indicated previously, the risk sum index reflected risks prior to adoption placement.

RESULTS

How were these developmentally vulnerable children faring at follow-up? Parents reported generally high levels of satisfaction with their children's health status and with their overall adjustment. They were more concerned about their children's school adjustment. Almost one-half reported being either "not at all satisfied" or "a little satisfied" with their child's school performance. These concerns were undoubtedly related to the number of learning problems reported by the school to the parents and to the children's special class placements (8 of 24). While parents of non-developmentally vulnerable children without learning disabilities might have similar concerns, one would not expect such a preponderance of dissatisfaction. Further, learning problems are frequently reported in samples of adopted children, particularly when perinatal difficulties are known to have occurred (Brodzinsky and Steiger, 1991).

Regarding CBCL findings, norms for this checklist are presented in age $\times$ gender groupings for nonclinical and clinical samples. A T score of 50 is considered the nonclinical norm. Ratings higher than 50 for problem behaviors, internalizing and externalizing are indicative of greater problem behavior. Ratings lower than 50 for social competence indicate less social competence.

Only mothers' ratings are presented since so few fathers completed this rating scale. Mothers' reports indicated that they viewed both their younger (< 11) and older daughters (12-15) as socially competent (T = 51.5 and 50.0 respectively). Likewise they viewed their younger sons (< 11) as socially competent (T = 53.5). However, mothers perceived their older sons (12-15) as less socially competent and more similar to children referred for clinical services. Their T score of 36.5 is more than one SD below the norm score of 50.9.

Mothers' ratings on number of problem behavior symptoms, and on internalizing and externalizing behavior were at the norm for both younger daughters and sons (T = 57.0 and 50.8, respectively). Likewise ratings for internalizing (T = 50.5 and T = 49.0) and externalizing (T = 49.5 and T = 49.8) were within the norms for these younger children.

Ratings on older daughters (T = 60.4) were one SD above the norm of 50.6, indicating a trend toward more problem behaviors. Internalizing (T = 51.8) and externalizing (T = 55.6) scores did not differ from nonclinical norms. In the case of older sons, ratings for both behavior symptoms (T = 64.8) and externalizing (T = 62.5) were greater than one SD above nonclinical norms; internalizing scores (T = 60.7) were equal to one SD above the norm. This group of older boys received higher ratings for aggressive, antisocial and poorly controlled behavior, as well as more fearful, withdrawn and overcontrolled behavior.

Did the risk sum index predict these behavior ratings? None of the correlations between the risk sum and CBCL scores were significant but all were in the expected direction. Those children who had a higher risk sum score, i.e suffered more prenatal and perinatal problems, or more abuse and neglect, tended to be the children who were currently viewed by their mothers as less socially competent (e.g., having few close friends, involved in fewer sports and hobbies, r = − .47). These children also manifested a higher total number of behavior problems (e.g., sleep disturbances, stealing, disobedience, fearfulness, and restlessness (r = .34), and also scored higher on Achenbach's externalizing (r = .21) and internalizing (r = .40) dimensions.

Self-esteem scores for both boys and girls were almost identical to the normative group's Total Self-Esteem Score (Coopersmith, 1987). Thus despite behavior problems reported by some mothers, all children indicated normal levels of self-esteem. These results conform to literature on self-esteem with African-American youth (Cross, 1985; Porter & Washington, 1979). However, those children with higher risk sum scores manifested lower self-esteem.

Since the older boys presented more problems than the other children, we examined other specific data for these early adolescents. The mean risk sum for these 11 boys was somewhat lower than the mean of the larger group (6.7 vs. 8.5), but not significantly so, indicating that they were at no greater risk than the total sample.

However, one postnatal risk factor which research has shown to predict greater adjustment difficulties for adopted children is age at adoption placement (see Brodzinsky, 1993). Thus we did examine this single risk factor in the history of these 11 boys. They were, in fact, older at adoption placement compared to the total sample. Only 1 boy was placed at less than 1 year; 4 were placed between 1 and 2 years of age, and 6 were placed after 2 years, with ages ranging from 2 years, 4 months, up to 5 years, 9 months.

In the interview parents reported that psychological problems were diagnosed early in 7 of the 11 boys; learning problems were also reported in 7 of the 11 boys. Seven were in special class placements. This pattern for greater psychological difficulties for boys this age is consistent with other findings: "Boys adopted or nonadopted tend to be more vulnerable than girls to a number of psychological problems, especially disruptive disorders and academic problems" (Brodzinsky, 1993, 157). Yet race does not appear to be connected to such reported behavior problems. Rosenthal and Groze (1992) found no significant differences by race for reported behavior problems among special needs adoptees. Thus our findings support previously reported patterns.

Turning to family characteristics, at follow-up most families were intact. Marriages had remained stable, with only one separation and three divorces. The majority of mothers and fathers were working outside of the home, with modest median family incomes in the $25,000 to $35,000 range. Most of these families had no biological children; at the time of the original home study none had more than one adopted child. At follow-up, 10 families had more than one adopted child; few had foster children at either assessment point.

The results of FACES III indicated that both mothers and fathers scored at the norm for feelings of cohesion and bondedness. Comparing our data with Olson's family types, mothers conformed to Olson's norms: 15 (of 23) mothers reported feelings of either connectedness or comfortable separateness. Equal numbers of mothers scored in the extreme quadrants of disengagement or enmeshment (4 each). Fathers presented a somewhat different pattern (n's for fathers were quite small). Although the number reporting feelings of connectedness (4 of 13) was within the normative range, fewer reported comfortable separateness (2), and more (5) felt disengaged. Overall, however, the data support a perception of good bonding.

What were the patterns of adaptability in handling family roles and rules? Olson's (1985) norming sample was almost entirely white and middle class. Thus it is interesting to find that the African-American families in this study conformed to these norms. Overall scores for adaptability were at the norm indicating a capacity on the part of the parents for coping flexibly with rules and family roles. Within this overall presentation of adaptability, how did the patterns compare with Olson's norms? "Flexible" and "structured" are the predominant adaptive styles in Olson's schema. Seven mothers did report a structured style, but a larger number (11) reported a more extreme chaotic style, rather than the normative flexible style. Fathers, while conforming to the norm for structure (4 of 13), reported a more rigid extreme (4) rather than flexible (2) or chaotic (3) styles.

Olson has indicated that while it is important to examine the adaptability and cohesion patterns reported above, the critical factor in assessing both cohesion and adaptability may be how satisfied the families are with the styles they have developed within their family system. He also proposed that while different ethnic and cultural groups might show extreme styles, these families might still function well as long as family members were satisfied with their pattern of adaptability and cohesion. Accordingly, he devised the Family Satisfaction Scale. Using this scale, mothers, fathers and children in this study all reported high satisfaction with their family's degree of bonding and adaptability.

The problem-solving strategies employed by the parents in this study, as assessed by the F-COPES, covered the range of Olson's categories: acquiring social support, reframing, seeking spiritual support, mobilizing the family, and passive appraisal. Scores for both mothers and fathers in all categories were at the 50th percentile or higher (50 is the norm). Mothers reported utilizing social support (57), reframing (53) and seeking spiritual support (49). The more predominant strategies for mothers were mobilizing the family—such as seeking information and advice from the family doctor (74) and passive appraisal—if we wait long enough the problem will go away (85). Fathers showed similar strategies for social support (59), seeking spiritual support (58), and mobilizing the family (64). They were more likely than mothers to use reframing—e.g., facing the problems "head-on" and trying to get a solution right away (66) and passive appraisal (93).

Did the family characteristics for the group of 11 boys differ from those of the total sample? Cohesion and adaptability scores for these families were essentially the same as for the total sample. Mothers of the 11 older boys tended to utilize "mobilizing the family" strategies more (81) than the total sample and passive appraisal less (74), indicating more active strategies in coping with family problems.

In summary, all families expressed feelings of connectedness, were adaptable in dealing with family roles and rules, and used a variety of problem-solving strategies. Furthermore, the adoption experience had been highly satisfying for them. When questioned in the interview, the replies were extremely positive for both fathers and mothers. Fathers were "extremely satisfied" (82%) or "very satisfied" (18%). Mothers reported somewhat lower, but still basically high levels of satisfaction: "extremely satisfied" (77%) and "very satisfied" (23%). None of the parents indicated "little" or "no" satisfaction with the adoption experience.

DISCUSSION

In addition to the small N, there were several other limitations in this study which may have confounded our conclusions and limit its generalizability. First, there were no comparison groups of African-American biological children, or African-American adopted children without early risk factors. Additionally, we were not able to investigate the role that gender played in early adolescence for these children since there were only 2 girls in our sample in the 12-15 age range. We also were not able to validate the learning difficulties reported by parents with data such as teachers' ratings. Murray and Fairchild (1989), commenting on underachievement in African-American children, discussed the need for greater sensitivity to cultural differences and expectations which result in systemic inequalities in educational programs for African-American students, particularly in urban settings where most of the children in this study lived. Consistent with this appraisal is our finding that parents expressed frustration in obtaining help in educational planning for their children, a frustration common among many families in this country. We cannot rule out stressors in the school environment, such as perceptual biases on the part of teachers, which might have contributed to the reported learning problems of the study children.

Despite these limitations we found that the families in this study, largely intact at follow-up, with modest family incomes, demonstrated family cohesion and adaptability, indicating a connectedness, bonding and flexibility which provide the setting necessary for well functioning families with at-risk children. Mothers felt connected, yet comfortably separated, versus more extreme patterns of disengagement or enmeshment.

The fact that fathers appeared more disengaged perhaps reflected the fact that many fathers in these modest income homes were working long hours and often two jobs. Mirande (1991) in discussing ethnicity and fatherhood found that contrary to the traditional view of African-American fathers as absent or insignificant, most African-American fathers play an integral role in the family. But it also may be as Rosenthal and Groze (1992) suggested, that fathers looked for and experienced greater closeness with those outside of the nuclear family, which could account for our finding of paternal disengagement.

The families revealed distinct patterns in handling family roles and rules. Mothers showed a preference for both a structured style (the normative pattern) or a more chaotic style. Rosenthal and Groze (1992) reported similar results. These authors suggested that often with special needs children, a loose, somewhat chaotic style was more adaptive. Fathers, while also reporting a structured style, tended to favor a more rigid style.

Mirande (1991) discussed a similar phenomenon with other studies of African-American fathers who presented an authoritative parental pattern. The handling of roles, relationships and rules may need at times a loosely structured style, and at others, a more rigid style to be successful with the high-risk child where such flexibility becomes advantageous.

Parents reported a range of behavioral strategies for coping with problems and difficulties arising within the family. These families were able to take an active "mobilizing the family" or "tackling the problem directly" approach to problem solving, both of which may be needed in dealing with the day-to-day problems of the at-risk child. Parents of the older boys reported using these active strategies. In contrast, it was apparent that both mothers and fathers could also afford a more "laid back" approach to problems, and thus were more tolerant of difficulties, feeling sure that they would go away if they waited long enough, and thus were able to cope with a broader range of problems which these children presented.

The children in this study experienced a range of serious risk factors during infancy, though not at the level of severity of many "special needs" adoptees today (Rosenthal & Groze, 1990; Lightburn & Pine, 1992; Marx, 1990; Deiner, Wilson, & Unger, 1988; McKenzie, 1993; and Barth, 1994). The literature on resiliency indicates that such at-risk children can develop within normative levels when growing up in accepting families, with flexible, adaptive parenting styles and who manifest warmth, caring and optimism about their child's development (Garmezy, 1993). Mostly positive outcomes were reported for these children; the majority were attending regular school classes; girls and younger boys exhibited satisfactory social and behavioral adjustments; and all reported normal levels of self-esteem.

The older boys did present more difficult problem behaviors and were seen as less socially competent. While their total risk sum scores were not different from that of the larger group, these boys had been placed for adoption at an older age. Breaking early attachments and forming new ones at ages beyond two years can pose later difficulties. This kind of disruption may have meant a more difficult adjustment in their adoptive home and thus could have contributed to their learning problems and behavior difficulties. But also the literature has shown that boys generally and especially adopted boys, are at greater risk for disruptive behavior and learning problems (Brodzinsky, 1993; and Rosenthal & Groze 1990).

In summary, adoption was a satisfying experience for these African-American families, even with the problem behaviors manifested by the young adolescent males. As have other researchers (McKenzie, 1993; Rosenthal & Groze, 1992; Marx, 1990; and Deiner et al., 1988), we conclude that early risk factors may be overcome by positive family characteristics, such as those reported by these African-American families. The majority of children in this study had good long-term outcomes. For these African-American children who might otherwise have remained in foster care, the opportunity to grow up in a permanent family was indeed a positive outcome and an important finding at a time when there is much media coverage about failed adoptions and unhappy adoptive families.

REFERENCES

Achenbach, T. M., & Edelbrook, C. (1983). *Manual for the child behavior checklist and revised child behavior profile.* Burlington, VT: University of Vermont.

Adams, C. D., Hillman, N., & Gaydos, G. R. (1994). Behavioral difficulties in toddlers: Impact of sociocultural and biological risk factors. *Journal of Clinical Child Psychology 23,* 373-381.

Anthony, E. J., & Cohler, B. (Eds.). (1987). *The invulnerable child.* New York: The Guilford Press.

Barth, R. (1994). Adoption of drug exposed infants. In R. Barth, J. D. Berrick, & N. Gilbert (Eds.), *Child welfare research, review* (Vol.I) (pp. 273-294). NY: Columbia University Press.

Barth, R., & Berry, M. (1994). Implications of research on the welfare of children under permanency planning. In R. Barth, J. D. Berrick, & N. Gilbert (Eds.), *Child welfare research review* (Vol. I) (pp. 322-376). NY: Columbia University Press.

Billingsley, A. (1992). *Climbing Jacob's ladder: The enduring legacy of African-American families.* New York, NY: Touchstone Books.

Brodzinsky, D. M. (1993). Long-term outcomes in adoption. *The Future of Children, 3,* 153-167.

Brodzinsky, D. M., & Steiger, C. (1991). Prevalence of adoptees among special education populations. *Journal of Learning Disabilities, 34,* 484-489.

Brooks, R. B. (1994). Children at risk: Fostering resilience and hope. *American Journal of Orthopsychiatry, 64,* 545-553.

Caputo, D. V., Goldstein, K. M., & Taub, H. B. (1981). Neonatal compromise and later psychological development: A 10 year longitudinal study. In S. L. Friedman & M. Sigman (Eds.), *The psychological development of low birth weight infants* (pp. 353-385). Norwood, NJ: Ablex.

Coon, H., Carey, G., Corley, R., & Fulker, D. W. (1992). Identifying children in the Colorado Adoption Project at risk for conduct disorder. *Journal of the American Academy of Child and Adolescent Psychiatry, 31,* 503-511.

Coopersmith, S. (1987). *Self-esteem inventories.* Palo Alto, CA: Consulting Psychologists Press, Inc.

Cross, W. E. (1985). Black identity: Rediscovering the distinction between personal identity and reference group orientation. In M. B. Spencer, G. K. Brookins, & W. R. Allen (Eds.), *Beginnings: The social and affective development of black children* (pp. 151-174). Hillsdale, NJ: Lawrence Erlbaum Associates.

Deiner, P. L., Wilson, N. J., & Unger, D. G. (1988). Motivation and characteristics of families who adopt children with special needs: An empirical study. *Children and Youth Services Review, 8,* 15-29.

Garmezy, N. (1993). Children in poverty: Resilience despite risk. *Psychiatry, 56,* 127-134.

Groze, V., & Rosenthal, J. A. (1991). A structural analysis of families adopting special-needs children. *Families in Society: The Journal of Contemporary Human Services, 72,* 469-481.

Gurak, D. T., Smith, D. A., & Goldson, M. F. (1982). *The minority foster child: A comparative study of Hispanic, Black and White Children.* Monograph No. 9. Bronx, NY: Hispanic Research Center, Fordham University.

Hoopes, J. L. (1967). *An infant rating scale: Its validation and usefulness.* New York, NY: Child Welfare League of America.

Levy-Schiff, R., Einat, G., Har-Even, D., Mogilner, M., Mogilner, S., Lerman, M., & Krikler, R. (1994). Emotional and behavioral adjustment in children born prematurely. *Journal of Clinical Child Psychiatry, 23,* 323-333.

Liaw, F., & Brooks-Gunn, J. (1994). Cumulative familial risks and low-birth-weight children's cognitive and behavioral development. *Journal of Clinical Child Psychology, 23,* 360-372.

Lightburn, A., & Pine, B. (1992, May). *Adoption of children with disabilities and chronic illness: Implications for policy and practice.* American Orthopsychiatry Association, Poster Session.

Luthar, S. S., & Zigler, E. (1991). Vulnerability and competence: A review of research on resilience in children. *American Journal of Orthopsychiatry, 61,* 6-22.

Marx, J. (1990). Better me than somebody else: Families reflect on their adoption of children with developmental disabilities. *Journal of Children in Contemporary Society, 2*(3-4), 141-174.

Masten, A., & Garmezy, N. (1978). Risk, vulnerability and protective factors in developmental psychology. In J. Anthony & B. Cohler (Eds.), *The invulnerable child.* New York: The Guilford Press.

McKenzie, J. (1993). Adoption of children with special needs. *Future of Children, 3*(1), 62-66.

McRoy, R. H., Grotevant, H. D., & Zurcher, L., Jr. (1988). *Emotional disturbance in adopted adolescents: Origins and development.* New York: Praeger.

Mirande, A. (1991). Ethnicity and fatherhood. In F. W. Bozett & S. M. H. Hanson (Eds.), *Fatherhood and families in cultural context* (pp. 53-82). NY: Springer Publishing Co.

Murray, C. B., & Fairchild, H. H. (1989). Models of black adolescent under-achievement. In R. L. Jones (Ed.), *Black adolescents* (pp. 229-245). Berkeley, CA: Cobb & Henry Publishers.

Olson, D., McCubbin, H. I., & Associates (1983). *Families: What makes them work.* Beverly Hills, CA: Sage Publications.

Olson, D., McCubbin, H. I., Barnes, H., Larsen, A., Muxen, M., & Wilson, M.

Family inventories (Rev. ed.). (1985). Family Social Science, St. Paul, MN: University of Minnesota.

Pecora, P. J., Fraser, M. W., Nelson, K. E., McCroskey, J., & Meezan, W. (1995). *Evaluating family-based services.* NY: Aldine De Gruyter.

Porter, J., & Washington, R. (1979). Black identity and self-esteem: A review of studies of black self concept, 1965-1978. *Annual Review of Sociology, 5,* 53-74.

Richards, A., Ford, G., & Kitchen, W. H. (1987). Extremely low-birthweight infants: Neurological, psychological growth and health status beyond five years of age. *Medical Journal of Australia, 147,* 476-481.

Rosenthal, J. A., & Groze, V. (1990). Special needs adoption: A study of intact families. *Social Service Review, 64,* 475-505.

Rosenthal, J. A., & Groze, V. (1992). *Special needs adoption.* New York: Praeger.

Rosenthal, J. A., Groze, V., & Curiel, H. (1990). Race, class, and special needs adoption. *Social Work, 35,* 532-539.

Sameroff, A., & Chandler, M. (1978). Reproductive risk and the continuum of caretaking casualty. In J. Anthony & B. Cohler (Eds.), *The invulnerable child.* New York: The Guilford Press.

Sameroff, A. J., Seifer, R., Baldwin, A., & Baldwin, C. (1993). Stability of intelligence from preschool to adolescence: The influence of social and family risk factors. *Child Development, 64,* 80-97.

Werner, E. E., & Smith, R. S. (1992). *Overcoming the odds: High-risk children from birth to adulthood.* Ithaca, NY: Cornell University Press.

Williams, C. C. (1991). Expanding the options in the quest for permanence. In J. E. Everett, S. S. Chipungu, & B. R. Leashore (Eds.), *Child welfare: An africentric perspective* (pp. 266-289). New Brunswick, NJ: Rutgers University Press.

Zelkowitz, P., Papageorgious, A., Zelazo, P. R., & Weiss, M. J. S. (1995). Behavioral adjustment in very low and normal birth weight children. *Journal of Clinical Child Psychology, 24,* 21-30.

Key Issues in Adoption Legislation:
A Call for Research

Kerry J. Daly
Michael P. Sobol

SUMMARY. This paper examines the underlying assumptions associated with two key areas of adoption legislation where there is variation across jurisdictions and calls for change. These legislative issues are consent and openness. In each area, there is very little social research which might otherwise offer insight into how to best formulate legislation in a way that would serve the needs of various members of the adoption experience. The primary goal of this paper is to consider key legal issues associated with consent and openness and make recommendations for how research might provide important information that could serve as guides for a legislative re-evaluation of these areas. *[Article copies available for a fee from The Haworth Document Delivery Service: 1-800-342-9678. E-mail address: getinfo@haworth. com]*

Any analysis of adoption legislation in North America is likely to face three challenges. First, there is the difficulty in studying the diversity in the adoption laws which fall under state or provincial jurisdiction. There

---

Kerry J. Daly is Associate Professor in the Department of Family Studies, and Michael P. Sobol is Professor in the Department of Psychology, both at the University of Guelph, Ontario, Canada. They have a combined experience of 25 years doing adoption research. They are the authors of *Adoption in Canada* (1993) and have published articles on adoption in the *Journal of Marriage and the Family, Family Relations* and *Journal of Social Issues*.

[Haworth co-indexing entry note]: "Key Issues in Adoption Legislation: A Call for Research." Daly, Kerry J., and Michael P. Sobol. Co-published simultaneously in *Marriage & Family Review* (The Haworth Press, Inc.) Vol. 25, No. 3/4, 1997, pp. 145-157; and: *Families and Adoption* (ed: Harriet E. Gross and Marvin B. Sussman) The Haworth Press, Inc., 1997, pp. 145-157. Single or multiple copies of this article are available for a fee from The Haworth Document Delivery Service [1-800-342-9678, 9:00 a.m.-5:00 p.m. (EST). E-mail address: getinfo@haworth.com].

145

are 62 different sets of adoption laws in North America. Second, one must contend with the underlying assumptions that have given shape to such a wide range of statutes. At one level, this diversity is fully expected. Every government is a product of its unique environment: its social structure, economic experience, cultural history, geography, and accumulated wisdom. These factors enter into any discussion of these issues. A third and final challenge is that adoption law is undergoing radical transformations because of significant changes in the number and kinds of placements (Bachrach, Adams, Sambrano, & London, 1990; Flango & Flango, 1993; Sobol & Daly, 1994) and the values and beliefs held by the various members of the adoption experience. Specifically, there are fewer healthy infants being brought forward for adoption, growing numbers of international adoptions and a move toward greater openness in the adoption experience. While community attitudes play an important role in shaping legislation, quite often there is no accompanying empirical evidence that can provide guidelines to the legislative process. As Hemphill, McDaniel and Kirk (1981, p. 510) have noted, while "social trends are impinging on legal adoption dynamics" one can "cite very little substantive research" in the formation of adoption law. While this assertion was made some time ago, there is a resounding similarity for legislating adoption today.

The purpose of this analysis is to examine the underlying assumptions associated with two key areas of adoption legislation. These legislative issues are consent and openness. Following the analysis of the assumptions associated with consent and openness, recommendations will be offered for how research might guide a legislative re-evaluation of these areas.

CONSENT

The issue of consent is the legal pivot in adoption law. When a law alters the history and dynamics of a blood relationship, there must be safeguards against misunderstanding or abuse. Massachusetts was one of the first North American jurisdictions to have an adoption statute (MacDonald, 1984). Implemented in 1851, all that was necessary to obtain an adoption was the acceptance by a court of a petition from the adoptive parents and a letter of consent from the birth parents. If the court was satisfied that the adopting parents were fit to raise and educate the child, the petition was accepted. By the late 1800s, the provinces of Nova Scotia (1896) and New Brunswick (1873) had mirrored this legislation.

Historically, there has been an increasing respect for a child's right to self-determination. In the U.S. for example, "Uniform State Laws" were adopted in many jurisdictions and these shifted the emphasis from seeing children as "property" to people with rights (Schwartz, 1983). There was also a corresponding recognition that a child's right to choose and to consent would have to be supported in order for this right to be exercised. At the other end of this spectrum is consideration, by a court, of the child's "best interests." This is the ultimate prerogative of the courts in both Canada and the U.S. Under the *parens patriae* authority, the state acts on behalf of children who are either too young or disabled to decide themselves, even with supports.

The requirement that children consent to decisions affecting their life is what the law refers to as a necessary but not a sufficient condition. Because of the ever-looming presence of the best interests principle, the child's consent or refusal is seldom solely determinative of the outcome. However, legislation and judges are increasingly eliciting the views of children and giving serious weight to them. As the children's ages increase, their consent becomes ever more determinative. The law implicitly recognizes the necessity of voluntary consent by birth parents. In order to prevent ill-advised or hasty consent, a variety of safeguards are typically provided.

Six such statutory provisions have been identified (Katarynych, 1991): a time period following a child's birth during which the parent is not permitted to sign a consent; a period immediately following the signing of the consent, within which birth parents can change their minds; a requirement that counselling around decision making be offered to birth parents by authorized professionals; a requirement that the consent be witnessed by an authorized representative of the state; a provision of special protection for a parent; e.g., in Ontario, the requirement that the Official Guardian be satisfied that the consent reflects the true and informed wishes of any parent less than 18 years of age; and, a requirement that the judge, before whom the adoption application is presented, be satisfied that every person who has given consent understands the nature and effect of an adoption order. These safeguards are designed mainly for the protection of adoptees and birth parents.

Post-Birth Waiting Period

There are two "cooling off" periods recognized by provincial and state laws—the period just after birth, and the period following consent, when that consent may be withdrawn. For post-birth consent, the law in some jurisdictions recognizes that a certain period is necessary when no consent is to be permitted because of the emotional volatility in the period immediately following recent childbirth. There is, however, tremendous variation in the length of time that is allocated for this cooling off period. In Canada, this time frame ranges from none at all in two provinces and one of the territories (i.e., Alberta, Quebec and the Yukon) to 14 days in Prince Edward Island and 15 days in Nova Scotia. In the United States, while 3-5 days appears to be the norm, here again, there is tremendous variation (National Committee for Adoption, 1989). In many states, consent may be given immediately (e.g., Alabama, Alaska, Florida, Georgia, Idaho, Kansas, Maine, Michigan, Minnesota, Montana, New York, North Carolina, Oklahoma, Oregon, South Carolina, Tennessee, Texas and Utah, Vermont, Wisconsin and Wyoming). Similar to Canada, there are other states that have a 15 day cooling off period (Maryland and Rhode Island).

What criteria determine the waiting time period in each case? What are the implications for the birth mother of a lengthy wait period as contrasted with none at all? There is no research on this issue. There are many stories about the consequences of consent hastily given; that is, birth mothers attempt to revoke consent. There has been little attention to the empirical determination of the relationship between time and the resolution of the crisis of adoption placement. Research which closely analyzes the phenomenological experience that birth mothers have immediately following the birth has the potential to provide insight into the optimum waiting period. Specifically, this could involve a detailed narrative analysis of birth mothers' stories. Hearing their stories over time has the advantage of providing insight into the changing meanings and dynamics of their consent decisions. For example, what are birth mothers' perceptions of consent change before, during and after the placement experience? Qualitative work that is done in collaboration with hospital and social work staff could map and identify critical events, stages and emotional states associated with the provision of consent.

Post-Consent Withdrawal Period

An examination of laws in the area of the post-consent waiting period reveals disparity in how states and provinces treat consent withdrawal. Four different categories are evident: withdrawal within a specified time period immediately following the giving of consent; withdrawal up to but not after placement of the child; withdrawal at anytime prior to the signing of the final adoption order; and legislative silence on the issue.

There is a range across the United States with respect to the post-consent withdrawal period. At one extreme, the adoption consent is irrevocable in at least 13 states. In four states, there is legislative silence on the issue.[1] The most common time frame, adopted by about one third of the states, is 10 to 30 days. At the other extreme, either birth parent can withdraw from the consent decree up to 90 days in Maryland. In Rhode Island the birthparents can petition the court to revoke consent within 12 months of termination of birth parent rights.

Within Canada, there is a similar diversity with respect to these laws. In five of the provinces, consent can be withdrawn within the 10-30 day time frame (Yukon, Ontario, Alberta, Quebec, Newfoundland). In four provinces (New Brunswick, Nova Scotia, British Columbia and Saskatchewan) withdrawal is permitted, provided there has been no placement. In Manitoba, Prince Edward Island and the Northwest Territories, there is no legislation with respect to withdrawal of consent.

Withdrawal of consent is most contentious in jurisdictions where the law is silent or ambiguous because it is more likely to result in an adversarial contest for custody of the child. Even in these jurisdictions, withdrawal of consents is usually not granted unless there is evidence that the consent was given under duress or it can be demonstrated that it is ultimately not in the best interests of the child.

Schwartz (1983) has pointed out that contested adoption cases often involve contradictory psychological testimony, statutory limitations and judicial actions that are in conflict with child development research. As a result, decisions are made that are not always in the child's best interests. Furthermore, although adoption law is based on the best interests principle, it is "vague, indeterminate, and speculative . . . [and it] obfuscates numerous competing and often contradictory interests" (Schwartz, 1991, p. 171). This is a precarious situation for all parties to the adoption. When cases are contested, the child's best interests are likely to be compromised in some fashion, regardless of who "wins," by virtue of the traumatic upheaval associated with the court process.

It is difficult to demonstrate that the needs and interests of children vary fundamentally from one jurisdiction to the next. It is not clear how providing for late withdrawal of consent is in the best interests of a child's need for stability and permanency. It is difficult to imagine how the absence of relevant legislation in Manitoba, Rhode Island's removal of the child from adoptive parents within a one year period or Florida's lack of a time limitation up to placement could be based on evidence of unique and indigenous psyches of children from each locale. The interests of children, birth parents and adoptive parents could be dealt with more uniformly. The optimal time for the revocation of consent can be found by data found in court records, agency experience and "expert" wisdom. While there may be a tendency to regard the jurisdictional tradition as the right way, the needs and interests of all parties in the adoption would be better served by an objective evaluation of these standards.

There is also a need to examine the legislative underpinnings concerning the extent to which consent is informed. Informed consent, as a legal term, is rooted in medical practice and has been used to describe the obligations of a physician to explain procedures, discuss risks, benefits and discomforts, disclose alternatives and answer any questions so that a patient has the ability to make an informed choice (Castel, 1978). However, informed consent is applicable to any situation if three conditions are met: a service or benefit is provided; a person is disempowered in some way; and, the service provider is correspondingly empowered to undertake an intrusive act. In the case of adoption, the alleged benefit to birth parents is relief of the burden of child rearing. The adoption facilitators perceive themselves as providing a variety of professional services which support the alleged benefit to all parties. The parents' consent must be informed because they are about to release their fundamental right to have the state preserve and protect their biological offspring. This right enters domestic law through article 23 of the *International Covenant on Civil and Political Liberties,* which states that "the family is the natural and fundamental group unit of society and is entitled to protection by society and the State." To relinquish a fundamental right such as preservation of one's family requires that disclosure be complete and comprehensible. Jurisprudence recognizes this well in the field of medicine but not equally well in the adoption process. Considering the importance of informed consent in adoption, the way most state and provincial laws deal with the ingredients of informed consent supports this conclusion.

There is tremendous variation in the requirements for informed consent. While many jurisdictions provide no guidelines at all, others give very explicit and detailed accounts of what is necessary for consent. The Ontario legislation states that parents may not give consent until they have been advised of the right to withdraw consent, have been informed when the adoption order is to be made, have obtained non-identifying information and have been informed of the possibility of participating in the adoption register. The parent must also be given the opportunity to seek counselling and independent legal advice with respect to the consent. Where the parent is a minor, the Official Guardian of the province must be satisfied that the consent is fully informed and that it reflects the true wishes of the birth parents. When consent comes from a child in Ontario (over the age of seven) there is a mandatory requirement that it not be given in the absence of an opportunity to obtain independent legal advice and counselling. In Alberta, the Director of Adoption Services or a designate must witness the consent and be satisfied that the consenter has the capacity to understand and appreciate the nature and consequences of the consent and that this consent represents the true and informed wishes of the person signing it. Further, the Director must inform the signer of the possibility to withdraw consent, disclose all information required by the statute, and notify the person of the right to be given notice of the adoption order. Alberta's legislation is detailed and specific. It includes terms such as "capacity," "understand," "appreciate," "nature" and "consequences," each of which has been judicially scrutinized. For example, the term "understand" is defined as cognitive and the term "appreciate" is defined to include an emotional component and an analysis of knowledge or experience component.

If, as stated earlier, consent is the legal pivotal point of adoption, it must be clarified and explained more closely according to its basic elements. There are two areas of research that would assist in the development of legal guidelines for the provision of informed consent. First, there is a need to examine the implications of child development for the provision of consent in adoption cases. There is a tendency in law to treat birth mothers as lacking developmental differentiation. Yet, birth mothers who are asked to provide consent span the full range of reproductive years. Surely the criteria for informed consent need to be attentive to these developmental changes. Research that identifies the cognitive, emotional and social needs of birth mothers at various stages of development can act as a basis for guidelines that are more sensitive to the diversity of birth mother experience when giving consent. This is especially important for younger birth mothers who may not fully appreciate what they are being asked to consent to and who are unable, either by age or mental development, to understand the process. Second, while the rights of the biological father have traditionally been overlooked in adoption practice, this situation has now changed so that in many jurisdictions, there is an insistence on their informed consent as well (Schwartz, 1986). There is, however, very little research which can serve as a basis for understanding the birth father experience. Studies are needed to examine the full range of experiences that birth fathers have in the pregnancy decision: what are their perceptions of control and entitlement? What unique challenges do they have in the adoption experience? What are their developmental changes? An analysis of current experiences could serve to identify essential components to direct the provision of informed consent for birth mothers and fathers of all ages.

OPENNESS

Inasmuch as openness is currently one of the most important changes in adoption practice, it is an imprecise construct. Several distinctions are warranted at the outset. First, as discussed by others in this volume, there is a wide spectrum of openness practices. These can range from giving birth parents detailed, but non-identifying information to help them in the selection of adoptive parents to the full disclosure of identifying information that can be used as a basis for setting up meetings with the adoptive parents before and after placement. A second distinction concerns the timing of openness strategies. One strategy which is increasing in current adoption practice is to arrange the adoption placement with an openness agreement between biological and adoptive parents that allows for meetings, the regular exchange of information or some kind of negotiated contact. From a different perspective, openness is a strategy for those who have entered into a closed or "sealed" adoption in the past but who, in light of the move towards openness in current practice, wish to access their own sealed records. The first strategy may avoid subsequent misunderstandings about the parties' degree of access to each other because they have come to a negotiated agreement about what level of openness is desired. However, the second strategy is typically more contentious because it gives rise to a clash between agreements that were made in different historical contexts.

While both of these strategies indicate greater philosophical acceptance of openness in practice, they contrast sharply with the legislative tradition of secrecy which still informs much of professional adoption workers' practice and its legislative framing. For example, adoption legislation continues to be shaped by the principle of "relinquishment" which is rooted in an ethos of shame and secrecy. Although secrecy was noticeably absent from early adoption legislation (MacDonald, 1984), Garber (1985) has noted that pregnant girls placed their babies for adoption in order to avoid the shame of "illegitimacy," while childless couples were eager to adopt in order to avoid the shame of their "incompleteness." Only by carrying out the adoption ritual in complete secrecy with the pretence by all parties that the adoptive parents could rightfully claim the child as their own, was the shame successfully avoided. Kirk (1964), in his landmark work *Shared Fate,* referred to this as "the equivalence doctrine" where adoptive families worked at the pretence of being a family "as if" the child were born to them. This pretence was firmly established in adoption laws in most jurisdictions by the 1930s (Cook, 1992). These laws included measures such as the amendment of birth certificates to give adoptees the surname of the adopting parents. In law, the equivalence doctrine continues to be upheld, for as Cook (1992) has suggested, "contemporary adoption statutes continue to emphasize confidentiality . . . and require complete cessation of the rights, responsibilities and privileges of natural family members after adoption" (p. 491).

As this would suggest, it appears that the principles of legislation have fallen out of step with the movement in practice towards more openness. There are at least three major forces that created this gap between practice and legislation. *One force* has to do with the kinds of adoptions that are being facilitated: with the decline in infant adoptions and the rise in older, special needs and international adoptions, the difference of adoption is more public from the start and the pretence too difficult to establish or maintain (Sobol & Daly, 1994). *The second force* for the increase in the amount of openness can be attributed to birth mothers who desire more control over the management of the placement and who no longer accept "relinquishment" as a psychological reality (Sobol & Daly, 1992). *The third force* is that the professional community, as a whole, has gradually embraced the philosophy of "acknowledgement of difference" (Kirk, 1964) and, as a result, has gradually increased the degree of openness that they use in the facilitation of adoptions. In our own research on 347 public and private service providers in Canada, all types of service providers rated open adoptions as at least "moderately successful" (Daly & Sobol, 1993).

Many questions remain, however, about the legislative implications of these more open adoption practices. Who decides on the level of openness? How do we manage the changing nature of needs in the adoption relationship? What is the role of the adoption practitioner in the life long experience of an adoption relationship? To answer these questions, there is a need for research that recognizes openness not as an event but as an ongoing *process*. It is an ongoing set of rights and attitudes that are subject to changing needs and unanticipated turns. Impassioned intentions at the time of placement can develop into a very different set of behaviours after the child has settled into the adoptive family home. Longitudinal research (see for example Gross in this volume) that traces some of the developmental changes associated with openness arrangements is desperately needed.

Research suggests that openness is viewed positively by birth parents and adoptive parents (Berry, 1991; McRoy, Grotevant & White, 1988; Winkler & van Keppel, 1984). However, there is little evidence to provide insight into the adopted child's experience of openness. Triseliotis (1991) does find that adoptees in open arrangements are able to distinguish among different kinds of parental relationships and still maintain loyalty to adoptive parents. However, the sample is small and limited in its generalizability. Given the centrality of the "best interests of the child" in adoption legislation, there is an urgency to have detailed studies of the effects of openness arrangements for the adopted child. One reason for the paucity of this research is that openness practices are a relatively recent phenomenon. We are now at a stage where a generation of children has been raised with openness agreements. Important research on openness is currently under way (Grotevant, McRoy, Elde, Fravel, 1994). However, given the revolutionary nature of the changes associated with increasing openness, there needs to be a much wider effort to look at all of its ramifications. Of particular importance is the need to examine how adopted children have responded to the openness arrangements. Do adoptees think openness serves in their best interests?

Questions about a legislative approach to openness need to be attentive to the emphasis placed by service providers on the voluntary and negotiated nature of openness agreements. The appropriate level of openness in any situation is going to be determined by a variety of factors not able to be incorporated into legislation. For example, the degree of openness will vary by the amount of pre-placement counselling about openness available to both birth and adoptive families, the age of the child, and the motives for the adoption of all parties involved. Monolithic standards which seek to govern how these complex adoptive relationships are established and managed will probably not work. What may be important is an option in the law for a skilled mediator to negotiate openness agreements that are responsive to the changing needs of the birth parents and the adoptive family. For example, in our own research we found that verbal agreements were more successful because they seemed to be more flexible and responsive to the emerging developmental needs of all parties to the adoption (Daly & Sobol, 1993). Currently, written agreements have no standing in law in either Canada or the U.S. (see Cook, 1992, p. 488-89 for case law examples).

In spite of the move towards openness in practice, the legacy of relinquishment or the complete breaking of ties remains a central tenet of the laws governing adoption in North America. Consequently, many agencies continue to operate within legal constraints that are not supportive of openness. As we have argued here, research which explores the implications of openness for all members of the adoption experience should direct these overdue legislative changes.

A discussion of implementing openness in current placements carries with it the thornier problem of what to do with adoptions from the past that were entered under very different conditions and beliefs. In these cases, the ideology and practices of the past come into direct conflict with current beliefs and service directions. Many institutional custodians of adoption continue to cite statutes, some more than half a century old, as a basis upon which to deny any family information to adoptees or birth parents who are searching for their biological kin. Among those affected is a large group of people who entered into adoption contracts with the belief and legislative reassurances that adoptions based on the principle of confidentiality are the best way to have a successful adoption. There are also those who champion the benefits of open adoption—both in practice and research. Caught between those who oppose opening previously closed adoptions and those who argue for greater openness in today's adoptions are adult adopted persons and birthparents who are often frustrated in their attempt to get answers about themselves and their biological roots.

As the Adoption Rights Movement has gained momentum in recent years, there has been a drive to make access to information easier in many jurisdictions. However, in most states and provinces, access to identifying information continues to be severely restricted. While active registries have been developed to assist in the search for biological families, these are often bogged down in bureaucratic overload because of the effort required on the part of staff to locate the non-registered party. While some states have adopted measures to make access to information easier (Harrington, 1986), typically this is information that is non-identifying or of a medical nature. Access to identifying information is usually only available upon reaching the age of majority, and then, only with the mutual consent of the adoptee and the birth parent.

Research can help determine the impact of opening the records. While the protection of rights from agreements in the past plays a key role in maintaining the status quo, there needs to be a close examination of the experiences of adoption parties involved in such contacts (successful and not). For example, if adoptees were given the legal right to have access to identifying information when they reach the age of majority, how does this affect the experience of reunion? What is the impact on birth parents and their own established families of having to surrender their promised secrecy? To what extent do searching adoptees successfully achieve their goals when approaching a reticent birth parent? While there is tremendous pressure to open access to these records, we know little about the social psychological impact or dynamics that might be expected in such situations (but see Fraser 1997 and Modell 1997 in this volume).

CONCLUSION

Consent and openness have been cornerstone focal points in existing adoption legislation. However, there is tremendous diversity with respect to how these are legislated across North America and there are dramatic changes in practice that reflect new and diverse ways of thinking about these issues. While changes in practice do affect changes in the law (and the reverse), there are many unanswered questions which only research can address to guide legal reconsiderations.

There are wide discrepancies in the state and provincial laws pertaining to consent. Several key areas of research would be particularly useful for determining whether greater uniformity in consent laws is warranted. First, there needs to be a closer examination of key events and stages in the post-birth experience of birth mothers in order to identify the optimum cooling off period. Second, legislation concerning revocation of consent would benefit from a critical analysis of case files that demonstrate the implications of revoking consent at various points in time. Third, developmentally sensitive research about "informed" consent might help to move this legislation from its current static grounding.

Several forces have moved the practice of openness in adoption beyond its legislative underpinnings. As jurisdictions examine their legislation to be consistent with cultural changes and current adoption practice, important research questions need to be addressed. First, the experience of openness as an unfolding process needs examination. Specifically, how do needs, interests and perceptions of entitlements change over time from the original negotiated agreement? Are there protective safeguards that are effective in successful openness arrangements? Are there limits to openness that should be legally enforced? Second, what are the most effective tools for managing even legally buttressed openness agreements? If not legally protected, should openness arrangements be written or verbal? All such research should also take into account the effects of various openness strategies on the adopted child. Finally, with respect to the opening of sealed records, what are the social psychological impacts on all participants in the adoption?

While research cannot provide all answers needed to revise adoption legislation, it can provide useful guidelines to better reflect the different circumstances of current practice in the field.

REFERENCES

Bachrach, C.A., Adams, P., Sambrano, S., & London, K.A. (1990). *Adoption in the 1980's: Advance data from vital and health statistics (No. 181)*. Hyattsville, MD: National Center for Health Statistics, Public Health Service.

Berry, M. (1991). The practice of open adoption: Findings from a study of 1396 adoptive families. *Children and Youth Services Review, 13*, 379-395.

Castel, J.G. (1978). Nature and effects of consent with respect to life and the right to physical and mental integrity in the medical field: Criminal and private law aspects. *Alberta Law Review, 293*.

Cook, L.W. (1992). Open adoption: Can visitation with natural family members be in the child's best interest? *Journal of Family Law, 30*, 471-492.

Daly, K. & Sobol, M. (1993). *Adoption in Canada: Final Report*. Ottawa: National Welfare Grants, Health and Welfare Canada.

Flango, V.E., & Flango, C.R. (1993). Adoption statistics by state. *Child Welfare, 72,* 311-319.

Garber, R. (1985). *Disclosure of adoption information*. Report of the Special Commissioner, Ministry of Community and Social Services, Government of Ontario.

Grotevant, H., McRoy, R.G., Elde, C., & Fravel, D.L. (1994). Adoptive family system dynamics: Variations by level of openness in the adoption. *Family Process, 33,* 125-146.

Harrington, J.D. (1986). Adoption and the state legislatures, 1984-1985. *Public Welfare, 44,* 18-25.

Hemphill, S., McDaniel, S., & Kirk, H.D. (1981). Adoption in Canada: A neglected area of data collection for research. *Journal of Comparative Family Studies, 12,* 509-515. 19

Katarynych, H.L. (1991). Adoption. In N. Bala, J.P. Hornick, & R. Vogl (Eds.), *Canadian Child Welfare law: Children. Families and the State.* Toronto: Thompson Educational Publishing Inc.

Kirk, H.D. (1964). *Shared Fate.* New York: The Free Press.

MacDonald, John A. (1984). Canadian adoption legislation: An overview. In P. Sachdev (Ed.), *Adoption: Current issues and trends.* Pp. 43-62. Toronto: Butterworths.

McRoy, R. Grotevant, H. & White, K. (1988). *Openness in Adoption: New practices. New Issues.* New York: Praeger.

National Committee for Adoption (1989). *Adoption Factbook: United States Data, Issues, Regulations and Resources.* Washington, DC: National Committee for Adoption.

Schwartz, L.L. (1983). Contested adoption cases: Grounds for conflict between psychology and the law. *Professional psychology: Research and practice. 14,* 444-456.

Schwartz, L.L. (1986). Unwed fathers and adoption custody disputes. *The American Journal of Family Therapy, 14,* 347-354.

Schwartz, L.L. (1991). Religious matching for adoption: Unravelling the interests behind the "Best Interests" standard. *Family law quarterly, 25,* 171-192.

Sobol, M. & Daly, K. (1992). The adoption alternative for pregnant adolescents: Decision making, consequences and policy implications. *Journal of Social Issues, 48,* 143-161.

Sobol, M.P., & Daly, K.J. (1994). Canadian adoption statistics, 1981-1990. *Journal of Marriage and the Family, 56,* 493-499.

Triseliotis, John. (1991). Maintaining the links in adoption. *British Journal of Social Work, 21,* 401-414.

Winkler, R., & van Keppel, M. (1984). Relinquishing mothers in adoption: Their long term adjustment. *Institute of Family Studies Monograph, 3.* Melbourne: Inst. of Family St.

Bonding and Attachment in Adoption: Towards Better Understanding and Useful Definitions

Kenneth W. Watson

SUMMARY. The meaning of the words "bonding" and "attachment" as terms related to human connections are examined from an historical perspective and as important tools in the field of adoption. For over three decades there has been confusion between the two words and about the processes which they represented. Because adoption, by definition, changes the usual patterns of family connections, it is especially important that there be common agreement about terminology. Clinical observations have led to the discrete definitions proposed here. The words are defined, for utilitarian purposes, in a way that underscores the qualitative differences. The result is a tool that can improve placement decisions, help resolve controversial custody cases, reduce tensions among the families to which an adopted child has connections, and provide concrete assistance to children in their efforts to learn how to make significant attachments. *[Article copies available for a fee from The Haworth Document Delivery Service: 1-800-342-9678. E-mail address: getinfo@haworth.com]*

Over the past forty years few issues in infant and child development have generated as much public interest and professional disagreement as

Kenneth W. Watson was formerly Assistant Director of Chicago Child Care Society. Now retired, he has written and published extensively over a 30-year period.

[Haworth co-indexing entry note]: "Bonding and Attachment in Adoption: Towards Better Understanding and Useful Definitions." Watson, Kenneth W. Co-published simultaneously in *Marriage & Family Review* (The Haworth Press, Inc.) Vol. 25, No. 3/4, 1997, pp. 159-173; and: *Families and Adoption* (ed: Harriet E. Gross and Marvin B. Sussman) The Haworth Press, Inc., 1997, pp. 159-173. Single or multiple copies of this article are available for a fee from The Haworth Document Delivery Service [1-800-342-9678, 9:00 a.m. - 5:00 p.m. (EST). E-mail address: getinfo@haworth.com].

159

bonding and attachment. John Bowlby, the person most clearly identified with the subject of attachment, wrote in the "Epilogue" of his monumental three volume work:

> Intimate attachments to other human beings are the hub around which a person's life revolves, not only when he is an infant or a toddler or a schoolchild but throughout his adolescence and in his years of maturity as well, and on into old age. From these intimate attachments a person draws his strength and enjoyment of life and, through what he contributes, he gives strength and enjoyment to others. These are matters about which current science and traditional wisdom are one. (Bowlby, 1980, p. 441)

Disagreement with Bowlby's claim about the centrality of attachment throughout life has been voiced from many quarters. The British psychiatrist Anthony Storr (1988) has rebutted Bowlby's basic philosophical premise. He claims that society's pre-occupation with interpersonal relationships has interfered with the privacy and isolation that are important to the human creative process. Others, like Rutter (1972) and Eyer (1992) have questioned the empirical evidence upon which attachment theory is based.

In spite of such critics, both the significance of intimate interpersonal relationships and the importance of early caretaking in learning how to make such attachments have become canons of the child welfare and mental health professions. The capacity to form attachments has become a criterion of healthy maturity, and "Reactive Attachment Disorder" appears in the American Psychiatric Association's *Diagnostic and Statistical Manual of Mental Disorders, Fourth Edition* (1994).

In adoption there can be little question that how children are connected to other people and the significance and meaning of those connections are critical components of theory, practice, and policy. By definition, adopted children have connections to two different families, one by genes, ancestry, and birth, and the other by law and ongoing parental nurturing. A persistent problem, however, is that the words *bonding* and *attachment* have become a part of professional jargon and the popular lexicon without definition or common agreement about their meanings. Both words have been used indiscriminately to describe a child's connections to either family. In reporting controversial adoption cases such as "Baby Jessica" and "Baby Richard" the media discuss whether or not a child has bonded to a family or is capable of forming attachments. Child welfare agencies and the courts weigh the same issues in making placement decisions. Birth and adoptive parents compete over the relative strength of the bond or the attachment that a child has to them. Increasingly social workers, parents, and therapists worry about children's attachment disorders.

The premise of this paper is that the confusion between these two terms and the lack of a clear definition of either has interfered with effective adoption services. In the absence of empirical evidence, it seems useful to examine current theory and to establish some *utilitarian* definitions that will distinguish between bonding and attachment in ways that will better meet children's needs. If adoption workers, adoptive, foster, and birth families, and mental health practitioners can agree to the suggested definitions, better placement decisions will be made on behalf of children in care, controversial custody cases can be resolved more easily, the connections of adopted children to both of their families will be accommodated better, adoption searches will be facilitated, and children with attachment disorders can be treated more effectively.

ATTACHMENT THEORY AND THE CONFUSION OF TERMS

Because infants cannot directly share with us how they experience human connections or learn to make them, theories about this process have been based on three other sources of information: (1) ethology, or the observations of animals and their evolution in their environments (e.g., Lorenz, 1935, and Harlow, 1963); (2) psychoanalytic reconstructions based upon interpretations of material from adult patients (e.g., Winnicott, 1964, and Klein, 1952); and (3) research based on direct observations of developing infants (e.g., Kagan, 1984, and Stern, 1985).

The boundaries among these three approaches are blurred. Part of Bowlby's genius was his ability to weave psychoanalytic concepts into an ethological framework. One legacy of this interweaving, however, has been a lack of clarity about what the terms bonding and attachment mean and a history of the careless use of both words. Few authors define the terms, most use the words interchangeably, and some run the words together using *bonding-and-attachment* as a single word.

As a young psychiatrist, Bowlby became interested in human attachment because of his concern about children raised in institutions. He noted that some of them seemed unable to make intimate and lasting relationships. He was aware of the observations of imprinting among young birds that led Lorenz (1935) to believe that not only was there an inborn instinct for the young to form attachments, but there was also a critical period of time when such attachments could be formed. Lorenz had noted that if a young bird was exposed to the object of attachment before or after that particular period, no attachment would be formed. Bowlby speculated that the inability of children to make attachments might be because they also had missed opportunities to form solid attachments to nurturing figures at a critical period in their early lives.

In his essay, "The Origins of Attachment Theory," Bowlby (1988) traces the influences that led to his position, among which were the writings on infant attachment of psychoanalysts D. W. Winnicott (1964) and Melanie Klein (1952). Bowlby incorporated their insights into an ethological perspective, concluding that in humans, as in other animals, attachment behaviors evolved from an instinctual survival mechanism designed to keep caretakers close by. He proposed that humans were born with the instinctual drive for attachment just as they were born with the drive for feeding and sex.

Bowlby related the instinctual base of an infant's earliest connections to bonding in animals, yet he never clearly distinguished such a connection from learned attachment behaviors. As late as 1980, when the differences between bonding and attachment were being noted by others (e.g., Rutter, 1981), Bowlby wrote, "During the course of healthy development attachment behaviour leads to the development of affectional bonds or attachments, initially between child and parent and later between adult and adult" (Bowlby, 1980, p. 39).

Several years earlier Rutter (1972) offered a thoughtful review and appraisal not only of Bowlby's work but of attachment literature up to that time. He concluded that there was a body of research that supported the importance of three elements if infants were to learn how to make attachments: (1) prompt and consistent response to the infant's needs, (2) a limited number of caretakers, and (3) mutual interaction between a caretaker and the child, with the caretaker both initiating patterns of interaction, and being alert and sensitive to the infant's signals.

It was in 1972 that Klaus and his associates (Klaus, Jerald, Kreger, McAlpine, Steffa, & Kennell, 1972) reported what has been perhaps the most controversial contribution to the research in the area of bonding and attachment. They identified the period immediately after a child's birth as a critical time in the bonding process and stressed the importance of mothers having contact at that time with their infants. The study generated extensive media attention and professional response. It lent support to changes in some maternity hospitals that had traditionally separated a mother from her child right after birth to allow time for each to recuperate. It upset parents who were denied early intimate contact with their children because of the child's low birth weight or medical complications.

This research also had implications for adoptive parents and for adoption agencies. Since adoptive parents, by definition, enter their adopted children's lives as primary caretakers at some point after the children's birth, the research suggested that they were not going to be able to form as secure bonds with their children as were birth parents who had experienced immediate contact with their children right after birth. This contradicted both the experience of adoption agencies who had been successfully placing special needs children, many of whom had been denied early contact with their birth parents and consistent caretaking during infancy, and earlier research by Kadushin (1970). While he did not specifically address the importance of immediate contact between new born infants and their birth mothers, Kadushin had laid the groundwork for the placement of children with special needs by documenting that adoption could reverse earlier childhood trauma.

Even 20 years later the study by Klaus and his associates (Klaus, Jerald, Kreger, Steffa, & Kennell, 1972) was controversial. Eyer (1992) not only raised serious questions about the validity of the study, but argued that the widespread acceptance of its conclusions not only reflected and served the political agenda of medical professionals eager to maintain close supervision of obstetric practice, but also sustained gender-incriminating views of maternal deprivation. Eyers's analysis is interesting for its historical context and the political import of conceptual issues. This concept, however, still informs much recent research (e.g., Byng-Hall, 1995), so the history of its refinement and its continued clarification, which is the concern of this paper, remains warranted.

As early as 1981 Rutter, after a careful review of the literature on early maternal-infant care, suggested that attachment was, perhaps, not a unitary concept. He wrote that

> there is a difference between attachment behaviour and persisting bonds. Infants show a general tendency to seek attachments to other people (Robertson and Robertson, 1971). However the contact of bonding implies selective attachment (Cohen, 1974) which persists over time even during a period of no contact with the person with whom bonds exist. (Rutter, 1981, pp. 142-143)

The following year Klaus and Kennell (1982) acknowledged that in their earlier writings they had contributed to the confusion between the two terms. The importance of differentiating between bonding and attachment was coming into focus.

By that time the direction of research on attachment had shifted. The focus on ethology and psychoanalytic reconstructions was being replaced by an emphasis on observed infant development. Not only was the instinctual basis for attachment being questioned, but Freud's (1938) view that there were separate, sequential, discrete phases each of which a child must master to progress steadily through childhood, and Mahler's (1975) idea that early child development was a gradual process of separation and individuation were being challenged.

Stern (1985) proposed that an infant's first order of business was to create a sense of a core self and core others. His research indicated that infants functioned independently from birth and suggested that major developmental changes were the result of the infant's gaining new senses of self which Stern labeled the emergent self, the core self, the subjective self, and the verbal self. Stern saw these not as successive phases that replaced one another. Rather he postulated that once formed each sense of self continued to function, to grow, and to coexist with the others through-out life. With the infant very much at the center of his thinking, Stern wrote,

> At various levels, attachment is a set of infant behaviors, a motiva-tional system, a relationship between mother and infant, a theoretical construct, and a subjective experience for the infant in the form of "working models" (of the caretaker in the infant's mind). (Stern, 1985, p. 25)

Nothing in Stern's theories, however, contradicted Rutter's (1972) ear-lier conclusions that if infants were to learn how to make attachments their needs had to be met quickly and consistently in mutually interactive rela-tionships with a limited number of caretakers.

DEFINITIONS OF BONDING AND ATTACHMENT

If we follow Carroll's pronouncement, "When I use a word . . . it means just what I choose it to mean . . . " (Carroll, 1865, stanza 61), we are free to define bonding and attachment as we wish. Because of existing confusion Bourguignon and Watson (1987) suggested defining the terms in a way that would distinguish them by identifying the unique characteristics of each. Reitz and Watson (1992) pointed out that if the words were defined as *qualitatively different* and therefore not *quantitatively comparable,* birth parents and adoptive parents would struggle less about whose connection to the child was stronger and adopted children would be less conflicted about having a meaningful allegiance to both families.

We can easily make such a clear distinction by logically extending Bowlby's ethological theoretical formulation. We can define bonding, then, not strictly as a function of genetic coding, but as a significant relationship between people that happens without the knowledge or conscious effort of those involved and not as the result of a learned skill. If we build on the child development literature, we can define attachment as the learned ability to make psychologically rooted ties between people that gives them significant meaning to each other. According to these definitions, bonding and attachment are not interchangeable terms and the qualitative difference means that their emotional intensity cannot be compared.

Bonding, then, just happens. Children are bonded to other people without choice and such bonds continue without ongoing involvement or effort on the part of the participants. Attachments do not just happen. Children must learn the skill of making attachments during the first years of their life and do so as a result of mutual interaction with a limited number of primary caretakers. Once learned, the skill of making attachments is transferable, but since an attachment is made by choice and conscious effort, it can be ended by choice or by atrophy.

This theory suggests children must learn how to disengage from attachments just as they had to learn how to make them. Disengagement skills involve learning to cope with loss and are acquired once a child has established the capacity to make attachments—usually sometime during the third year of life. Without acquiring the skill to disengage, children would soon be encumbered with accumulated attachments that were no longer developmentally appropriate. They would not then have the emotional energy to develop and maintain new connections.

Kinds of Bonding

If bonding is a sense of being connected to someone without conscious effort, intent, or awareness of how it happened, the number of different kinds of human bonds is limited. Perhaps no more than four different kinds are possible: genetic bonding, birth bonding, traumatic bonding, and transference bonding.

Genetic bonding. Genetic bonding occurs because those who share common genes share a built-in sense of connection through their common ancestry and certain inherited common characteristics. The greater the number of common genes shared, the greater the connection. Such a connection is clear to identical twins, and to a lesser extent is recognized by fraternal twins, by siblings who have common parentage, and by children and their birth parents.

Birth bonding. Birth bonding involves not only common genes but also a shared experience during pregnancy and birth which is unique to that mother and that infant. There is perhaps no more vital and intense connection than that of an embryo in the womb who is physiologically dependent upon the expectant mother for space, blood, oxygen, and food. The womb is also the embryo's total psychological environment, and there is increasing evidence that events there may have influence beyond the uterus. DeCasper (cited in Donovan and McIntyre, 1990, p. 5) established that newborns do remember something about their earlier environment. Verny and Kelly (1981) write, "We know now that the unborn child is an aware, re-acting human being who from the sixth month on (and perhaps even earlier) leads an active emotional life" (p. 12).

While it can be documented that pre-natal activities on the part of the expectant mother can dramatically affect the physiology of the developing embryo, it is less easy to assess the extent to which parental attitudes and expectations may influence the kind of relationship that will exist between mother and child following birth. Klaus and Kennell (1976) suggest that there are pre-natal adaptive tasks that enhance the in uterus bonding process. While a mother's anticipation and perceptions of her expected baby may affect the way in which she begins the attachment process, if we accept the earlier conceptualization of bonding, they can have no effect on the bonding process. By definition, bonding cannot be influenced by conscious input.

Traumatic bonding. Traumatic bonding happens when strangers unexpectedly experience a common trauma which connects them to each other. One thinks of those who end up as hostages or surviving together in a lifeboat after a ship wreck. With no conscious effort, and perhaps against their wishes, the intensity of the traumatic experience generates a bond. Recent literature has suggested the traumatic bond as one of the factors that may keep a young victim from disclosing sexual abuse or from testifying against an adult perpetrator (deYoung and Lowery, 1992).

Transference bonding. Transference bonding takes its name from the psychoanalytic concept of transference. It refers to the kind of immediate connection that strangers may develop based on their unconscious responses to each other. These responses, which stem from the past relationships that each has had with other significant people, draw two strangers together for reasons that neither can explain. While not everyone has experienced such a bond, those who have are apt to say that they feel they have known all of their lives someone whom they have just met, or that they immediately feel related to a stranger as if to a long-lost brother or sister.

IMPLICATIONS FOR ADOPTION

The value of these definitions lies in their pragmatic use. If we accept the suggested definitions and the distinction between bonding and attachment and the importance of the first three years of life in learning how to make attachments, the adoption related issues identified at the beginning of this paper become easier to resolve.

Assessment of Attachment Capacity

The assessment of the capacity of children to make connections is unrelated to whom they happen to be bonded. It becomes instead the assessment of the acquired skill of forming attachments. Assessing this capacity is based on three things: (1) the history of the child's caretaking experiences during the first three years; (2) the child's developmental level, with particular attention to the capacity for interpersonal engagement, the level of trust, and regressive behavior which suggest earlier unmet needs; and (3) direct observation, both of the nature and the appropriateness of the child's response to offers by the observer to engage in a relationship and of the child's relationship with a significant current caretaker and any reaction to separation from this caretaker.

Likewise, the assessment of parents as potential caretakers for children with attachment difficulties should focus on the first three years of the prospective parents' developmental histories and their pattern of relationships throughout their lives—things such as the relationships with family members; exploration of their significant friendships, both current and long term; the degree of intimacy in their present marital relationship, or, if single, the degree to which intimate relations are important and how the need for such intimacy is being met; and their tolerance for people who do not like to get too close.

Adoption Custody Cases

Custody issues involving adopted children need to be resolved as quickly as possible. The guiding principle must be the recognition that such matters are adult issues that should be settled promptly by the adults involved. Any pain the adults do not absorb will be passed along to the children. That means that the adults involved should opt for mediation, not litigation; for accommodation rather than polarization. It means they must accept that adoption never eliminates a child's earlier family connections or replaces them with a brand new family. Adopted children who are at the center of custody disputes have legitimate connections to both sets of parents. We know from clinical experience in custody matters related to divorce and remarriage that when children have more than two parents, their best interests are served when those adults are able to cooperate with each other.

The law, reflecting a prevailing society value, is that children have the right to grow up with their birth parents unless those parents have opted out or been deemed unfit. In adoption custody disputes, it is common for the caretaking parents (usually parents hoping to adopt) and their attorneys to claim that the children involved have now bonded to those parents and would suffer irreparable damage were that bond to be broken. While such children may have strong and viable attachments to those caretaking families, with the distinction suggested here, their genetic and birth bonds are to their birth parents.

Since there is no way to compare the relative strengths of these two kinds of connections, the clinical issue becomes one of assessing attachment. The pain of the child's move is related to his or her loss of the caretaking parents. The appropriate questions relate to attachment concerns such as the age of the child, where in the process of attachment the child is at the time of the move, how to help the child with regression in that process that might be caused by the move, and how to help the child cope with the impact of the loss of those he or she has come to love.

Searching

Searching in adoption is increasingly being recognized as a natural part of the adoption process. As Brodzinsky, Schechter, and Henig (1992) write,

> We are often asked, "What percentage of adoptees search for their birth parents?" And our answer surprises most people: "One hundred percent." In our experience, all adoptees engage in a search process. It may not be a literal search, but it is a meaningful search nonetheless. It begins when the child first asks, "Why did it happen?" "Who are they?" "Where are they now?" (p. 79)

The reasons for the search are many, but in part the search is driven by the birth bond—the sense of a meaningful connection that adopted persons and their birth parents feel for each other. Adoptive parents are sometimes threatened by their adopted off-springs' wish to search; and many adopted adults are reluctant to undertake a search, or do so clandestinely, out of a concern that searching implies a sense of disloyalty to their adoptive parents. Birth parents, too, are sometimes reluctant, and say that their reluctance is based on a wish not to interfere with the relationship between the adoptive parents and the adopted person. These concerns reflect not only thoughtfulness but the threat that the child's dual family membership presents and the sense of underlying competition that the two sets of parents may feel toward each other.

An awareness that a bond exists between adopted persons and their birth families, especially their birth mothers, and the acceptance that such a bond is different from the attachment that exists between adopted persons and their adoptive families, reduces tension. Adoptive parents, however much they are attached to their adopted children, can never go back and give birth to them. Birth parents, no matter how strong the bond they feel to children to whom they gave birth but lost to adoption, can never go back and rear those children who have been reared already. Neither set of parents can undo the child's connection to the other parents—nor need this concern them. That there are two kinds of significant connections involved which cannot be in competition is reassuring, and ought to be part of the preparation for adoption for everybody.

Treatment of Attachment Disorders

If infants get consistently good care from a limited number of caretakers in the context of mutually interactive relationships, by the time they are three years old they have learned both how to become attached and how to manage separation from those to whom they have become attached. The capacity to make attachments once learned is never lost. Children who have not had this kind of care during these three years, and this is true of most children who come into foster care or adoption beyond that age, usually have attachment disorders.

According to Watson (1994) there are three categories of attachment disorders. Children whose early attachment processes have been interrupted, unhealthy, or sporadic are *inadequately attached children*; those whose caretaking was at a subsistence level, lacking consistency and affectional interaction with caretakers are *non-attached children*; and those whose early caretaking had been going well for their first 12 to 24 months until the process was interrupted by the sudden, inexplicable loss of the caretaking parent (perhaps by death, a sudden move, or by sexual abuse by the trusted adult) are *traumatized children*.

Theory about how attachments are formed provides the structure for the treatment of attachment disorders. To learn to attach, children need security, stability, good nurture, and respect for their evolving selves. Lacking those ingredients, they will suffer a developmental delay in the attachment process. Although the developmentally favorable time for children to learn attachment is between the ages of birth and three, if attachment is not learned then, it can be learned later. As with some other skills, like language acquisition, children will not learn it as easily or as well as if they had learned it earlier. The further chronologically removed a child is from the developmentally right time, the more difficult becomes the task. The most useful component for the successful treatment of children with attachment disorders, however, remains a safe, stable environment with consistent, effective nurturing. A well-functioning family with adults who make attachments easily can usually help children with attachment disorders make up many of the earlier deficits, even those children whose problems may require additional therapeutic input.

Adoptive parents, beyond meeting the ongoing nurturing and developmental needs of their adopted child, can also provide a belated opportunity for the children to learn how to make attachments. Since the treatment goal is focused on meeting the earlier unmet needs, such caretakers must be able not only to accept, but to welcome, regressive behavior in the child in order to make affectual contact. This means that the families must have a high level of tolerance for immature behavior—which frequently means disturbing symptoms. Recognizing the symptom as the child's coded message for an earlier unmet need provides the caretakers with opportunities to meet those needs.

Providing new experiences, either to correct those that occurred or to fill in developmental gaps that were missed, is more difficult with older children. Their ability to express earlier infantile needs and allow parents the opportunity for a remedial response often runs contrary to the current development issues with which they are coping. The good news, however, is that the remedial efforts of the caretaking adults have symbolic significance once the child has psychologically accomplished the capacity to think in more symbolic ways, generally around the age of five. That means that a little time spent lovingly rubbing sun screen lotion on the back of a nine-year-old can help make up for a whole lot of missed oiling as an infant.

Sometimes older children and those who have suffered a severe attachment trauma may need supplementary treatment outside the family. This out-patient treatment may be cognitively oriented, behaviorally adaptive, or emotionally intrusive, and the parents should always be involved. The treatment of attachment difficulties is directed toward (1) helping a child understand what has happened earlier and giving that experience new meaning; (2) consciously teaching a child ways to act that will encourage others to seek attachments; (3) helping a child learn to live more comfortably with attachment limitations; or (4) providing planned intensive interpersonal treatment experiences that are designed to break into a person's defenses of control or manipulation and access the rage which blocks close attachments (the holding or rage reduction techniques).

This last approach is becoming more popular, particularly in treating adolescents. Keck and Kupecky (1995), in discussing the treatment of children with severe attachment disorders, write,

> Holding is a process that often reactivates delayed development. It is a vehicle that allows an intensive interpersonal relationship to develop, and consequently promotes, nurtures, and supports growth. Holding therapy does not result in a "quick fix" but rather a "'jump start." The child and therapist can access feelings that would not be available through talk therapy alone. (p. 157)

For some children the nature or degree of their symptoms, dual diagnostic considerations, their age, or the lack of a suitable family resource may mean that some sort of group or institutional care is indicated. With respect to the attachment disorder, the base of treatment remains the same: provide a stable nurturing, interactive environment; view symptoms as communications about developmental gaps; offer opportunities for symbolic reparenting; and utilize other appropriate therapeutic approaches. Whenever possible, the family in which such a child most recently lived or, if return to that family is not indicated, the family to which it is hoped the child will be moving, should be active participants in the treatment.

There is an additional technique which may allow some young adults who have had lifetime attachment difficulties to learn how to attach. Some young adults with attachment disorders who have become parents may learn how to attach by teaching their children how to make attachments. This can be effective if the parents can be taught about the importance of attachments and also have a hands-on opportunity to learn techniques in parenting classes. In learning how to effectively interact with their babies as they hold, feed, bathe, oil, powder, diaper, or play with them, the parents can symbolically have some of their own attachment deficits filled.

CONCLUSION

Human connections through bonding and attachment are different. Clarifying the difference for those who are part of an adoption triad or who are professionals reduces tension and frees energy and time to bring about more effective services for children.

A child's first bond is to his or her birth mother. Children also have genetic bonds to their fathers, their siblings, and others with whom they share a gene pool. They may also develop bonds through a shared traumatic experience or through a transference process. Whatever the source of the bonding, nothing can ever dissolve the bonds. Unlike this automatic bonding process, children have to learn how to make attachments. Once they have developed this capacity they are free to choose the people with whom they wish to make significant attachments in order to add meaning and pleasure to their lives. In adoption, birth parents, adoptive parents, and professionals need to respect the bonds that children have and help them with the development of critical attachment skills.

REFERENCES

American Psychiatric Association. (1994). *Diagnostic and statistical manual of mental disorders* (4th ed.). Washington, DC: Author.

Bourguignon, J. P. & Watson, K. W. (1987). *After adoption: a manual for professionals working with adoptive families*. Chicago: Illinois Department of Children and Family Services.

Bowlby, J. (1980). *Loss*. New York: Basic Books.

Bowlby, J. (1988). The origins of attachment theory. *A secure base: parent-child attachment and healthy human development* (pp. 20-38). New York: Basic Books.

Brodzinsky, David., Schechter, Marshall, & Henig, Robin (1992). *Being adopted: the lifelong search for self.* New York: Doubleday.

Byng-Hall, John (1995). Creating a secure family base: some implications of attachment theory for family therapy. *Family Process 34*: 45-58.

Carroll, Lewis (1885). *Alice's adventures in wonderland.*

Cohen, L. J. (1974). The operational definition of human attachment, *Psychological Bulletin 81,* 107-217.

DeCasper, A. J., cited in Donovan, D. & McIntyre, D. (1980). *Healing the hurt child.* New York: W. W. Norton & Company.

deYoung, M. & Lowery, J. (1992). Traumatic bonding: clinical implications in incest. *Child Welfare, 71,* (2) 165-175.

Eyer, D. (1992). *Mother-Infant bonding: a scientific fiction.* New Haven, CT: Yale University Press.

Freud, Sigmund (1938). *The basic writings of Sigmund Freud.* New York: The Modern Library.

Harlow, H. (1963). The maternal affection system, *Determinants of infant behavior,* Vol. II. London: Menthuen.

Kadushin, A. (1970). *Adopting older children.* New York: Columbia University Press.

Kagan, J. (1984). *The nature of the child.* New York: Basic Books.

Keck, Gregory C., & Kupecky, Regina M. (1995). *Adopting the hurt child: hope for families with special needs kids.* Colorado Springs, CO: Piñon Press.

Klaus, M., Jerauld, P., Kreger, N., McAlpine, W., Steffa, M., & Kennell, J. (1972). Maternal attachment: the importance of the first postpartum days. *New England Journal of Medicine, 286* (9), 460-463.

Klaus, M. H. & Kennell, J. H. (1976). *Maternal-Infant bonding.* St. Louis, MO: The C. V. Mosby Company.

Klaus, M. H. & Kennell, J. H. (1982). *Maternal-Infant bonding* (2nd ed.). St. Louis, MO: The C. V. Mosby Company.

Klein, M. (1952). *Developments in psychoanalysis.* London, Hogarth Press.

Lorenz, K. (1935). Der Kumpan in der Umvelt des vogles, *Journal of Ornithology,* Berlin, 83. English translation, Companions as factors in a bird's environment, in C. H. Shiller (Ed.) (1957), *Instinctive behavior.* New York, International University Press.

Mahler, Margaret, Pine, F., & Furer, F. (1975). *The psychological birth of the human infant.* New York: Basic Books.

Reitz, Miriam, & Watson, Kenneth (1992). *Adoption and the family system: strategies for treatment.* New York: Guilford Press.

Robertson, J. & Robertson, J. (1971). Young children in brief separation: a fresh look. *Psychoanalytic study of the child, Vol. 26,* 164-31.

Rutter, Michael (1972). *Maternal deprivation reassessed.* New York: Penguin.

Rutter, Michael (1981). *Maternal deprivation reassessed* (2nd ed.). New York: Penguin.

Stern, Daniel (1985). *The interpersonal world of the infant.* New York: Basic Books.

Storr, Anthony (1988). *Solitude: a return to the self.* New York: The Free Press.

Verny, Thomas, & Kelly, John (1981). *The secret life of the unborn child.* New York: Dell.

Watson, Kenneth (1994). *Substitute care providers: helping abused and neglected children.* Washington, DC: U.S. Department of Health and Human Services, Administration for Children and Families, National Center on Child Abuse and Neglect.

Winnicott, D. W. (1964). *The child, the family, and the outside world.* London: Penguin.

The Consequences
of Placing versus Parenting
Among Young Unmarried Women

Pearila Brickner Namerow
Debra Kalmuss
Linda F. Cushman

SUMMARY. This paper compares the consequences of placing versus parenting for young women who experienced a non-marital teenage pregnancy. We examined whether placers were faring better, worse or no differently from parenters four years after giving birth. The findings clearly indicate that relative to parenting, resolving a teenage pregnancy by relinquishing one's infant for adoption is a positive choice resulting in more favorable outcomes on a broad variety of sociodemographic and social psychological outcomes. At the bivariate level, on virtually every outcome except feelings about the pregnancy resolution decision, placers fared significantly better than parenters. When control was introduced for sociodemographic background factors and several post-birth mediators, the differences in

Pearila Brickner Namerow is Associate Professor of Public Health, Debra Kalmuss is Associate Professor of Public Health, and Linda F. Cushman is Assistant Professor of Public Health in the Center for Population and Family Health at the Columbia University School of Public Health. Their research interests include the causes and consequences of adolescent childbearing, and factors related to women's contraceptive and reproductive decisions.

This research was supported by Grants APR-000942 and APR-000960 from the Office of Population Affairs, U.S. Department of Health and Human Services.

[Haworth co-indexing entry note]: "The Consequences of Placing versus Parenting Among Young Unmarried Women." Namerow, Pearila Brickner, Debra Kalmuss, and Linda F. Cushman. Co-published simultaneously in *Marriage & Family Review* (The Haworth Press, Inc.) Vol. 25, No. 3/4, 1997, pp. 175-197; and: *Families and Adoption* (ed: Harriet E. Gross and Marvin B. Sussman) The Haworth Press, Inc., 1997, pp. 175-197. Single or multiple copies of this article are available for a fee from The Haworth Document Delivery Service [1-800-342-9678, 9:00 a.m. - 5:00 p.m. (EST). E-mail address: getinfo@haworth.com].

sociodemographic outcomes and feelings about the pregnancy resolution decision remained unchanged. However, the differences between
placers and parenters on virtually all of the remaining social psychological outcomes, were explained by their varying marital, fertility
and welfare experiences since the birth of the index child. *[Article
copies available for a fee from The Haworth Document Delivery Service:
1-800-342-9678. E-mail address: getinfo@haworth.com]*

Adoption is a process whose primary function depends upon one's
position in the adoption triad. For adoptive parents and adopted children,
its aim is family formation, whereas for birth mothers it is pregnancy
resolution. Research about adoption has focused more on its family formation than on its pregnancy resolution function. We have learned much
about how adoptive children and parents fare, but, as discussed below, we
know comparatively little about the consequences of adoption for birth
mothers. In this paper, the focus is on the social psychological and life
outcomes associated with choosing adoption as a means of resolving a
teenage pregnancy. Specifically, we compare and contrast the life situations of two groups of young women who had a non-marital teenage birth
four years previously; one group who placed their infants for adoption and
another who parented their babies.

Adoption as a pregnancy resolution alternative has been cast in two
different lights. From one perspective it is viewed as a positive alternative
for women that allows those who have mistimed or unwanted pregnancies
to delay parenting until they are ready for and desirous of this role (Bachrach et al., 1992; Donnelly & Voydanoff, 1991; Herr, 1989; Klerman,
1983; McLaughlin, Manninen, & Winges, 1988; McLaughlin, Pearce,
Manninen, & Winges, 1988; National Committee on Adoption, 1989;
Resnick, 1984). Such a delay provides the opportunity for cognitive and
emotional growth and development, relationship building, and activities
that will enhance women's socioeconomic status, including additional
schooling, paid employment, and marriage. Each of these outcomes
associated with delayed parenting are beneficial for the mother as well as
for the child.

A second perspective portrays relinquishing one's infant for adoption
as a traumatic experience that may have short- as well as long-term negative consequences for birth mothers. The focus here is on the feelings of
loss, grief and regret associated with relinquishment that may negatively
affect a birth mother's emotional and psychological well-being, her subsequent marital and fertility-related life outcomes, and ultimately her level
of socioeconomic attainment (Deykin et al., 1984; Pannor et al., 1978;
Rynearson, 1982; Sobol & Daly, 1992; Watson, 1986).

Research on the consequences of relinquishment for birth mothers has been limited. Studies have utilized several different sources of data: clinical data, convenience samples, large-scale survey data sets, and agency data. The first two sets of studies are based on small, non-representative samples of relinquishers with no comparison group of parenters (Burnell & Norfleet, 1979; Deykin et al., 1984; Millen & Roll, 1985; Pannor et al., 1978; Rynearson, 1992). Moreover, a subset of these studies is based on women who are likely to have had a difficult adjustment to placing their child; those in psychotherapy as well as those who have joined birth mother support groups (Deykin et al., 1984; Millen & Roll, 1985; Rynearson, 1992). It is not surprising that these studies report long-lasting negative psychological outcomes of relinquishment. In addition, because they are retrospective in design, it is unclear whether the poor psychological functioning of the birth mothers was a consequence of their relinquishment decision, or whether it was due to other causes that preceded this decision.

Another approach to exploring the consequences of adoption for birth mothers has utilized nationally representative survey data to compare the characteristics of women who relinquished versus those who kept and reared their babies. Based on data from the National Survey of Family Growth, it was concluded that relinquishers were less likely to live in poverty and to receive public assistance and were more likely to complete high school than were women who had a premarital birth and parented their babies (Bachrach, 1986). While this study utilized a nationally representative fertility data set and contained a comparison group of parenters, its analyses are limited by the small number of relinquishers (60) in the sample.

Another set of studies has employed data from agencies serving pregnant women: prenatal clinics, adoption agencies and maternity residences (Kalmuss et al., 1992; McLaughlin, Manninen, & Winges, 1988; McLaughlin, Pearce, Manninen, & Winges, 1988). Consistent with Bachrach's work, these studies found that young women who relinquished their children fared more positively than those who parented on a wide variety of sociodemographic outcomes such as school enrollment, employment status, income, public assistance, and rapid subsequent pregnancies. However, they were indistinguishable from parenters on social psychological outcomes such as self-esteem, personal efficacy, satisfaction with life, emotional support, and level of optimism regarding life at age 30. The only outcome measure where relinquishers fared less well was satisfaction with their pregnancy resolution decisions. While both parenters and placers in each of these studies reported high levels of satisfaction with their decisions, relinquishers were significantly less satisfied than parenters.

In this paper, we extend our previous work on the consequences of resolving a teenage pregnancy by relinquishing one's infant for adoption. Our earlier research examined the short-term consequences of parenting versus placing at six months post-birth. In this analysis, we will compare the life situations and experiences at four years post-birth of women who placed versus those who parented their babies. The longer post-birth interval allows time for placers and parenters to have made changes in their lives regarding: educational and employment status, income and receipt of public assistance, marital and partner status and subsequent fertility. Their perceptions and feelings about their lives may have changed over the years as well. These changes may have increased, decreased or had no effect upon the previously observed differences in short-term life outcomes of placers and parenters. The goal of this paper is to assess how parenters and placers differ in their sociodemographic and social psychological life outcomes four years after having a non-marital teenage birth.

METHODOLOGY

Study Design and Sample

This analysis is based on data from a longitudinal study of the determinants and consequences of pregnancy resolution decision making among teenagers. The study focused on two pregnancy resolution alternatives; parenting or placing one's infant for adoption. The design of the study involved interviews: during the last trimester of pregnancy, and then again at six months and four years post-birth. To be eligible for the study, women had to be aged 21 or younger, unmarried, not of Hispanic origin, and in their last trimester of pregnancy.

A total of 592 pregnant teenagers were recruited into the study, 54% of whom were parenters and 46% of whom were placers. Of these women, 527 (89%) were re-interviewed at the first follow-up, and 406 (76%) at the four year follow-up. Fifty-seven percent of the women interviewed at the four year follow-up had parented their infants and 43% had placed them for adoption.

Studying adoption among young pregnant women brings several methodological challenges. The most critical is to generate a sufficiently large sample of young women choosing adoption. Using data from the National Survey of Family Growth, Bachrach et al. (1992) estimate that between 1982 and 1988, two percent of the babies born to never married women were relinquished for adoption. Moreover, there is no national adoption data collection system from which it might be possible to draw a random sample of young women who have relinquished their babies. Therefore, when planning the sample the need to identify a sizeable number of young women who intended to place their infants was prioritized.

Women were recruited from three types of programs for pregnant teenagers. The majority of respondents (75%) came from maternity residences, followed by prenatal clinics (17%) and adoption agencies (8%). The source of recruitment differed for placers and parents. Virtually all placers (92%) were recruited from residences, while parenters were recruited from both residences (61%) and prenatal clinics (39%). The fact that such a large proportion of the sample was recruited from maternity residences limits the generalizability of our findings. Moreover, we are unable to estimate the extent of this problem because there are no baseline statistics on the proportion of pregnant teenagers overall, let alone placers and parenters specifically, who live in maternity residences. Thus, to be conservative, generalizability of these findings should be limited to relinquishers who reside in maternity residences during their pregnancy and to parenters from residences and maternity clinics.

In Table 1, we present a profile of the pre-birth characteristics of the 406 women included in the final sample, as well as a comparison of those who chose to relinquish versus to parent their babies. The mean age at

TABLE 1. Percentage Distribution of the Sample by Selected Pre-Birth Characteristics, According to Pregnancy Resolution Decision

	Total Sample (N = 406)	Placers (N = 231)	Parenters (N = 175)
Mean age at index pregnancy**	17.06	17.42	16.79
Race**			
African-American	27.8	6.9	43.7
White	72.2	93.1	56.3
Family received public assistance while R was growing up**	22.6	5.8	35.6
Lived with both biological parents at age 14**	48.2	56.8	41.8
Graduated from high school at Round 1**	40.9	58.9	27.3

**p < .01

their index teenage pregnancy was 17.06 for the entire sample. Seventy-two percent of the sample was white, 28% were African-American, nearly one-quarter had grown up in a family that received public assistance (22.6%), almost half had lived with both biological parents at age 14 (48.2%), and 41% had graduated high school prior to the index teenage birth.

The results in Table 1 indicate that the pre-birth characteristics of placers were significantly different from those of parenters. Placers were slightly older at the index pregnancy, and were overwhelmingly more likely to be white than African-American. Ninety-three percent of the placers were white as compared to 56% of the parenters. In addition, placers were more likely to have lived with both of their biological parents while growing up, and were more than twice as likely to have completed high school by that pregnancy. Finally, parenters were more than six times as likely to have lived in a family that received public assistance while they grew up. In short, young women who resolved the index teenage pregnancy by parenting came from more disadvantaged backgrounds than did those who placed their babies for adoption.

MEASURES

Dependent Variables. This study examined two primary domains of dependent variables: sociodemographic and social psychological outcomes. The former include: educational attainment, a trichotomous measure of highest degree obtained that distinguishes respondents with less than a high school degree, a terminal high school degree, and a post-secondary degree, and a continuous measure of years of school completed; school enrollment, whether respondents are currently enrolled in school, and whether they have been enrolled since the birth of the index child; educational aspirations, the highest year of school that respondents plan to complete; employment status, whether respondents are currently employed; relationship status, whether respondents are married, cohabiting and whether they are separated or divorced; and fertility status, whether respondents had been pregnant since the index birth, whether they have had an abortion since that birth, and the number of live births they have had since then.

The social psychological outcomes focus on feelings about the pregnancy resolution decision, psychological well-being, life satisfaction and future outlook. We use two indicators of comfort with the decision to parent or place. The first measures level of regret about the decision using a 4-point scale ranging from no regret at all (1) to a lot of regret (4). The second measures whether respondents reported that they would definitely choose the same pregnancy resolution option again.

The measures of psychological well-being are based on two sub-scales of Ware's 18-item Mental Health Inventory (Veit & Ware, 1983; Ware et al., 1984). We selected the depression and general positive affect subscales as most directly related to the types of psychological consequences of adoption that have been described in the literature. The items in each subscale are based on feelings during the past month, and response categories range from none of the time (1) to all of the time (5). The three items in the depression subscale assess the extent to which in the past month respondents have felt: low or very low in spirits, downhearted and blue, and have been moody or brooded about things. The five items in the general positive affect scale assess the extent to which respondents have been: a happy person, cheerful and lighthearted, able to relax without difficulty, calm and peaceful, and the extent to which their daily lives have been full of things that were interesting to them.

The life satisfaction items were measured with a 4-point scale ranging from very dissatisfied (1) to very satisfied (4). We included measures of overall life satisfaction, satisfaction with one's job, and satisfaction with one's financial situation. In addition, we included a scale assessing the quality of a woman's relationship with her current partner. This scale was composed of four items assessing the frequency with which respondents: confide in their partner, quarrel with their partner, have regrets that they are married to/in a relationship with their partner, think that things with their partner are going really well. The response categories for these items were: never, rarely, sometimes, and often. The items were summed so that a high score on the scale reflected positive relationship quality.

To assess women's perceptions about their future lives, we asked them to think about the likelihood that they would achieve the following outcomes by age 30; complete the amount of schooling that they desire, have enough money to live comfortably, have the kind of job they want, and be happily married. Responses to each question were coded on a 4-point scale ranging from very unlikely (1) to very likely (4). Responses to these items were summed to form a scale assessing the extent to which respondents hold a positive future outlook.

Independent Variables. The key independent variable in this analysis is whether respondents had placed their infant for adoption or parented their infant four years previously. In addition, in the multivariate models, we control for the following background factors that differentiated placers and parenters: race, age of respondents at Round 1 (i.e., during the index pregnancy), whether they had completed high school at Round 1, whether respondents were living with both of their parents at age 14, and whether they received public assistance while growing up.

BIVARIATE ANALYSIS

Our preliminary descriptive analyses will use data from six months and four years after respondents experienced a non-marital teenage birth. This information will be used to compare and contrast the life situations of those who parented versus those who placed their infants for adoption. While our primary focus is on differences between the two groups at the four year follow-up, the earlier data will enable us to assess change over time both within and between groups.

Sociodemographic Outcomes. To establish the context of these women's lives at four years post-birth, we begin with an examination of their experiences and current status in four key sociodemographic spheres: education, work, marriage and fertility. The results in Table 2 indicate that placers have completed more schooling than parenters at both follow-up points. For example, at six months post-birth, two-thirds of the placers as compared to less than half (43%) of the parenters had completed high school. At four years post-birth, both groups had increased their educational attainment, with over two-thirds of the parenters and more than nine-tenths of the placers (71% and 91% respectively) having completed high school. Despite these gains, the differences remained substantial, with more than three times as many parenters (29%) as placers (9%) having completed less than high school by four years after their non-marital teenage birth.

The pattern of differential educational attainment is similar for post-secondary schooling as well. While few women in either group continued on for a post-secondary degree, placers were more than four times as likely to have completed a two year college degree as parenters (12.5% versus 3%). No parenters and only seven placers had completed a bachelors college degree by four years post-birth.

The results in Table 2 indicate that the association between pregnancy resolution decision and the second educational outcome, school enrollment status changed over time. Placers were significantly more likely to have attended school within the first six months of birth than were parenters. At four years post-birth, this difference was no longer significant; parenters were as likely to have returned to school as were placers. Moreover, rates of current school enrollment declined over time for both groups of young women, from 43% to 33% for parenters and from 59% to 36% for placers (results not shown). The decline was steeper for placers

TABLE 2. The Bivariate Relationships Between Pregnancy Resolution Choice and Sociodemographic Outcomes at Six Months and Four Years Post-Birth

	6 MONTHS		4 YEARS	
	PARENT	PLACE	PARENT	PLACE
SOCIODEMOGRAPHIC OUTCOMES				
Educational attainment**,**				
Less than high school	56.7	32.4	28.6	9.1
High school	42.9	66.5	68.4	78.3
Associates/Bachelors Degree	.4	1.2	3.0	12.5
Attended school in interval since reference date*,NS	51.9	63.0	81.8	86.2
Educational aspirations**,**	14.1	15.5	15.5	16.2
Currently employed**,**	29.2	69.4	46.7	69.9
Ever received welfare since reference date---,**	—	—	75.6	16.1
Currently receiving welfare**,**	62.0	4.0	47.2	6.9
Currently married**,*	11.2	1.7	21.8	31.0
Currently cohabiting**,**	12.9	4.0	19.7	9.8
Currently separated/divorced/widowedNS,NS	0.0	1.2	13.9	9.2
Ever pregnant since reference dateNS,**	2.1	1.2	67.4	41.6
Abortion since reference date---,**	—	—	16.5	5.7
Number of live births since reference date---,**				
0	—	—	50.6	67.8
1	—	—	38.1	26.4
2	—	—	11.3	5.7

*p < .05
**p < .01
NS Non-significant
--- These variables were not included in the six month post-birth interview.

because they were substantially more likely to be enrolled within six months of birth than were parenters.

Finally, the pattern of association between pregnancy resolution decision and the final outcome in this domain, educational aspirations, remained the same over the two time periods. At both follow-ups, placers held significantly higher educational aspirations than did parenters. Educational aspirations increased over time for both groups, but particularly so for parenters.

Regarding employment status, the results in Table 2 indicate that at both time periods young women who placed their infants for adoption were significantly more likely than those who parented to be currently employed for pay. While the differences in the work status of parenters and placers were significant at both follow-ups, they were most dramatic in the period immediately following the birth, when far more placers (69%) than parenters (29%) were employed outside the home. This difference narrowed to almost half of the parenters (47%) and 70% of the placers at four years post-birth. The narrowing of this difference may in part be due to varying levels of available support from kinship networks within the two groups. Although the need for child care clearly makes obtaining employment more difficult for parenters, this barrier may be partially offset by greater availability of kin and family support among this group.

Pregnancy resolution decision is related to the receipt of public assistance in a constant fashion across the two time periods. At both time periods, parenters were substantially more likely than placers to be receiving public assistance. However, the data in Table 2 also indicate that the trends in public assistance status over time vary by pregnancy resolution group. Specifically, the percent of women currently receiving public assistance increased slightly for placers, from 4% to 7%, between six months and four years post-birth, whereas it decreased for parenters (from 62% to 47%) during the same time period. It is likely that some parenters, particularly those who have had no additional children, were able to move off public assistance during the interval. Some placers, on the other hand, may have had a non-marital birth during the interval, and thus have experienced a transition onto welfare.

The pattern of association between pregnancy resolution decision and relationship status also changed over time. At six months post-birth, although the majority of both groups had not yet married, parenters were significantly more likely to be married, or cohabiting than were placers. At this time there was no difference between the groups in the percent who were separated or divorced. By four years post-birth, while a much larger percentage of both groups were married, placers were more likely than parenters to be legally married, while parenters were more likely to be cohabiting, separated or divorced.

Finally, there is a strong association between prior pregnancy resolution decisions and subsequent fertility over time. At six months post-birth, there were no fertility differences between the two groups. This is not surprising given the brief interval for pregnancies to occur. By four years post-birth, however, there were several significant differences in fertility outcomes. Parenters were more likely to have been pregnant, to have had an abortion and to have had at least one live birth than were placers. Finally, among those women who had a subsequent birth, placers were more likely to have had a marital and parenters a non-marital birth (results not shown).

Social Psychological Outcomes. The next issue that we will examine is how placers and parenters perceive their lives at four years post-birth. A logical starting point is to examine their feelings about their pregnancy resolution decision. The results in Table 3 indicate that while the overall level of satisfaction among both groups was quite high, at both time periods, parenters were significantly more satisfied with their pregnancy resolution decision than were placers. At six months post-birth, 88% of the parenters versus 70% of the placers said that they were very certain that they would make the same decision again. The results are very similar at four years post-birth, with 91% of the parenters versus 78% of the placers offering that response.

Focusing on regret regarding their pregnancy resolution decision, at six months post-birth, 85% of the parenters reported no regret and only 1% reported a lot of regret as contrasted to 37% of the placers indicating no regret and 17% indicating a lot of regret. By four years post-birth, more than 90% of the parenters versus two-thirds of the placers reported no regret and 3% of the parenters versus 10% of the placers reported a lot of regret. One of the striking findings regarding regret is the sharp decrease over time among placers, with the proportion reporting no regret increasing from one-third to two-thirds between the two time periods.

Comparisons of the psychological well-being of placers and parenters on measures of depression and general positive affect are limited to data collected four years after birth. At that time placers scored significantly lower on the depression scale than did parenters, and higher on the scale assessing general positive affect. That is, placers reported feeling moody, downhearted, and in low spirits less often than did parenters. Conversely, they more often reported perceiving themselves to be: a happy person, cheerful and light-hearted, calm and peaceful, able to relax without difficulty, as well as perceiving that their life was full of things that were interesting to them.

In terms of life satisfaction, placers were significantly more satisfied with all but one domain of their lives at both time periods. They reported greater levels of overall life satisfaction as well as satisfaction with their work, and their financial situation. The results also indicated that at four years post-birth, the quality of placers' relationships with their partners was significantly higher than that of parenters.

TABLE 3. The Bivariate Relationships Between Pregnancy Resolution Choice and Social Psychological Outcomes at Six Months and Four Years Post-Birth

	6 MONTHS		4 YEARS	
	PARENT	PLACE	PARENT	PLACE
FEELINGS ABOUT PREGNANCY RESOLUTION DECISION				
Amount of regret about pregnancy resolution decision**,**				
None	85.0	37.0	92.2	65.5
A little	7.7	23.1	3.5	13.2
Some	6.0	22.5	1.7	10.9
A lot	1.3	17.3	2.6	10.3
Would definitely make the same decision again**,**	88.3	69.9	90.9	78.1
OTHER SOCIAL PSYCHOLOGICAL OUTCOMES				
Mean on depression scale---,*	—	—	2.0	1.8
Mean on general positive affect scale---,**	—	—	3.4	3.7
Mean life satisfaction*,**	3.3	3.5	3.3	3.6
Mean financial satisfaction**,**	2.5	3.1	2.5	2.9
Mean work satisfaction**,**	3.1	3.4	3.3	3.6
Mean quality of relationship with partner---,**	—	—	3.3	3.6
Future outlook – life at 30**,**	14.3	15.2	13.7	14.6

*$p < .05$
**$p < .01$
--- These variables were not included in the six month post-birth interview.

Finally, we assessed the differences in respondents' future orientation, or their perceptions of the likelihood that they would achieve their goals in a variety of life domains (education, work, marriage, financial security) by age 30. At both time periods, placers were significantly more optimistic than were parenters. However, the level of optimism decreased over time for both groups as they moved closer to reaching 30 years of age.

In sum the bivariate differences observed at six months persist at four years post-birth. Placers fare as well or better than parenters on virtually all of the outcome measures. Placers' status and experiences in each of the sociodemographic domains, education, employment, marriage and fertility, put them on a trajectory toward higher ultimate socioeconomic attainment than do the experiences of parenters. Moreover, placers are more satisfied with their lives in general as well as with specific domains of their lives than are parenters. They are less likely to be depressed, and are more optimistic about their future life prospects as well. It is only in satisfaction with their pregnancy resolution decision that placers lag behind parenters. This suggests that by four years after a first non-marital teenage pregnancy, we do not see evidence of an equalization between the objective or the subjective life situations and future prospects of young women who placed versus those who parented their babies.

MULTIVARIATE ANALYSIS

The next step in this analysis is to assess whether the observed bivariate differences in the objective and subjective life outcomes of teenagers who place their infants for adoption versus those who rear their babies persist in a multivariate context. Prior research has established that pregnant teenagers who choose to place their infants differ from those who choose to parent on key background characteristics (Bachrach, 1986; Bachrach et al., 1990; Bachrach et al., 1992; Kalmuss et al., 1991; McLaughlin, Manninen & Winges, 1988; McLaughlin, Pearce, Manninen & Winges, 1988; Namerow et al., 1993; Resnick et al., 1990). It is therefore possible that the observed differences in the life outcomes of parenters and placers may be due to these pre-existing differences in background characteristics rather than to the effects of their pregnancy resolution decisions per se. To assess this possibility, we will estimate a set of multivariate models that include pregnancy resolution behavior, as well as controls for race, family structure while growing up, receipt of public assistance while growing up, age at index pregnancy, and educational level at index pregnancy, measured by whether respondents had completed high school.

Table 4 presents findings from these multivariate analyses for selected sociodemographic outcomes. Controlling for background differences between placers and parenters has only a minor impact on the effect of pregnancy resolution behavior. Specifically, while placers are no longer more likely than parenters to be married or working for pay, after controlling for background characteristics, they remain more likely to have higher educational attainment and aspirations, are less likely to have had a pregnancy or a live birth in the four years since the index birth, and are less likely to be currently receiving public assistance.

TABLE 4. Logistic and OLS Regression Models of Sociodemographic Outcomes at Four Years Post-Birth

	Educational Attainment	Educational Aspirations	Current Work	Current Marriage	Current Welfare	Subsequent Pregnancy	Subsequent Birth
Pregnancy resolution decision (parent/place)	.655**	.603*	.392	−.104	−1.718**	−.862**	−.861**
Race (African-American/White)	−.282	−.479	.607*	1.110**	−1.078**	−.074	.292
Age at Round 1	.046	−.066	.206*	.127	.036	.055	.101
Completed high school at Round 1	.947**	.616	.989**	.092	−.497	−.580	−.549
Lived with both parents at age 14	.194	.030	.125	−.556*	.223	−.354	−.386
Received public assistance while growing up	−.692**	−.682	−.805**	−.898*	1.266**	.010	−.443
Constant	11.206	16.902	2.915	−3.760	−.457	.112	−1.426
R²	.30	.05	——	——	——	——	——
F	26.115	3.241	——	——	——	——	——
−2* log likelihood	——	——	454.9	385.8	334.4	480.2	486.4

*p < .05
**p < .01

A similar pattern emerges when we examine the association between pregnancy resolution decision and the social psychological outcomes in a multivariate context. The results in Table 5 indicate that, by and large, placers continue to fare better than parenters. The only change from the bivariate context is that once controls are added for background characteristics, placers and parenters no longer differ on their scores on the depression subscale. However, placers continue to have higher scores on: the general positive affect subscale, overall satisfaction with life, satisfaction with their jobs and their financial situation, the quality of their relationships with their partners, and on the positive future outlook scale.

The one negative effect of relinquishing one's infant on social psychological outcomes persists within a multivariate context as well. Placers are less positive about their pregnancy resolution decision than are parenters. They report greater levels of regret about the decision and are less likely than parenters to indicate that they would definitely make the same pregnancy resolution decision again.

Although these multivariate findings clearly indicate that the four year post-birth differences in the life outcomes of placers and parenters are not primarily due to differences in their background characteristics, they do not offer insights into why their outcomes are so disparate. The final set of analyses is designed to address this question.

Our approach is to focus upon several post-birth variables that potentially mediate the relationship between young women's pregnancy resolution decision and their subsequent life outcomes. As mediators, these variables would not only differentially characterize the post-birth experiences of placers and parenters, but would also be associated with subsequent life outcomes for the two groups of young women. In this analysis, we will explore the role of three potential mediating variables: subsequent fertility, post-birth marital status and post-birth receipt of public assistance. As noted above, placers and parenters differed significantly on each of these outcomes at four years after birth. Placers were more likely to be married, and less likely to have had a subsequent live birth or to have received welfare. Given the important effects that marital, fertility and welfare status have on the nature and quality of women's lives, it is plausible that differences between placers and parenters in these areas partially account for the varying sociodemographic and social psychological outcomes reported above.

Thus, in our final models of the sociodemographic outcomes, in addition to controls for background factors that pre-dated the decision to parent or place, we also control for the potential mediating effects of both marital status and subsequent fertility. We do not control for receipt of

TABLE 5. Logistic and OLS Models of Social Psychological Outcomes at Four Years Post-Birth

	Regret	Same Decision	Depression	General Positive Affect	Life Satisfaction	Financial Satisfaction	Work Satisfaction	Quality of Life Relationship	Life Outlook
Pregnancy resolution decision (parent/place)	.468**	−1.12**	−.011	.215*	.267**	.263*	.218*	.203**	.715**
Race (African-American/White)	−.017	.478	−.208	.003	.242*	.160	.092	−.002	−.320
Age at Round 1	−.006	−.161	.043	−.011	.002	−.005	.017	−.007	−.104
Completed high school at Round 1	−.029	.826	−.286*	.257*	.066	.209	−.070	.137	.613
Lived with both parents at age 14	−.034	.046	−.124	.102	−.041	.065	−.038	.065	.316
Received public assistance while growing up	−.095	.322	.147	.038	.043	−.289*	−.259*	−.049	−.057
Constant	1.319	4.336	1.432	3.453	3.013	2.481	3.061	3.394	15.387
R2	.08	——	.05	.07	.08	.10	.06	.08	.06
F	5.328	——	3.121	4.705	5.142	6.66	3.328	3.899	3.391
−2* log likelihood	——	291.6	——	——	——	——	——	——	——

*p < .05
**p < .01

welfare in these models since its timing could not be precisely pinpointed relative to the sociodemographic outcomes under consideration.

Table 6 presents results from these re-estimated models for educational attainment, fertility status, and receipt of welfare, the outcomes on which parenters and placers differed when background factors were controlled. The results of these models are very consistent. With the exception of educational aspirations, the differences between placers and parenters on each outcome remain significant even after controlling for post-birth marital status, and fertility. Thus, the difference in educational attainment between parenters and placers cannot be explained by the fact that placers are less likely to have a subsequent birth and might thus be more able to continue their schooling. Similarly the fact that placers are less likely to receive public assistance is not entirely explained by the fact that they are more likely to be married and less likely to have a subsequent birth. Finally, the differences in subsequent fertility between placers and parenters is not due to the differential post-birth marital status of these two groups.

Table 7 presents results from the re-estimated models for the social psychological outcomes. These models contain controls for post-birth marital status, subsequent fertility, and receipt of welfare. Since all of the social psychological outcomes are measured at the four year follow-up,

TABLE 6. Logistic and OLS Regression Coefficients for the Effects of Pregnancy Resolution Behavior on Selected Outcomes Net of Selected Background and Post-Birth Variables[a]

Educational attainment	.525**
Educational aspirations	.445
Currently receiving welfare	−1.610**
Subsequent pregnancy[b]	−.903**
Subsequent live birth[b]	−.909**

[a]Race, age, Round 1 educational attainment, family structure, receipt of public assistance while growing up, post-birth marital status, and post-birth fertility status.

[b]Subsequent fertility is not included as a control variable in this model.

**p < .01

TABLE 7. Logistic and OLS Regression Coefficients for the Effects of Pregnancy Resolution Behavior on Selected Outcomes Net of Selected Background and Post-Birth Variables

	Sociodemographic Background, Marital Status, and Subsequent Fertility	Sociodemographic Background, Marital Status, Subsequent Fertility, and Receipt of Welfare
Feelings about the pregnancy resolution decision		
Amount of regret	.287**	.328**
Make same decision again	−1.100**	−1.3705**
General well-being	.126	--
Life satisfaction	.154**	.182
Financial satisfaction	.197	--
Work satisfaction	.186	--
Quality of relationship	.200**	.218**
Life outlook at age thirty	.153**	.387

**$p < .01$

establishing the timing of receipt of welfare relative to these outcomes is not problematic as it was above. Including the welfare variable, which indicates whether the respondent has received welfare within the past four years, serves as a reasonable indicator of post-birth poverty status. The findings indicate that the post-birth controls do not explain the relationship between pregnancy resolution decision and comfort with that decision. Even with controls for young women's post-birth marital, fertility and welfare status, placers remain less comfortable with their pregnancy resolution decision than do parenters.

The outcome domains in which the post-birth variables do have mediating effects are psychological well-being, life satisfaction, and future outlook. With the exception of quality of relationship with partner, the differences between placers and parenters are no longer significant on these outcomes when we control for the mediating factors. Specifically, when post-birth marital and fertility status are controlled, placers and parenters no longer differ on: measures of general positive affect, or satisfaction with their financial situation and their jobs. Thus, the differences between parenters and placers in these domains four years after birth appear to be due to their different marital and fertility experiences after the index pregnancy. Finally, the differences in overall life satisfaction and in positive outlook regarding their lives at age thirty do not retain significance once welfare status is in the model. This suggests that placers are more likely to be satisfied with their lives overall and more optimistic about what their lives will be like when they reach thirty, in part, because they are less likely to be living in poverty.

CONCLUSIONS

The purpose of this paper was to gain a better understanding of the consequences for birth mothers of relinquishing an infant for adoption. We approached this issue by comparing two groups of women who had experienced a non-marital teenage pregnancy; one group who relinquished their infants for adoption and another who parented their babies. We examined whether placers were faring better, worse or no differently from parenters four years after giving birth, on a variety of sociodemographic and social psychological outcomes. We then explored whether the observed differences were due to the realities of placing versus parenting per se, or whether they were due to differences in the background characteristics of these two groups of young women which pre-dated their pregnancy resolution decisions.

The bivariate and multivariate results indicate that young women who place their infants for adoption generally fare as well or better than those who parent their babies. The bivariate differences between the two groups are straightforward. On virtually every outcome measure except feelings about the pregnancy resolution decision, placers fared significantly better than parenters. In the sociodemographic domains, placers have higher levels of educational attainment and aspirations, are more likely to be currently employed, are more likely to be married and less likely to be cohabiting, are less likely to have received welfare since the index birth or to currently be receiving welfare, and finally are less likely to have had a subsequent pregnancy, abortion or birth.

The differentials in social psychological outcomes are equally striking at the bivariate level. With the exception of feelings about the pregnancy resolution decision, placers fare significantly better on all outcomes. These include: depression, positive affect, overall life satisfaction, satisfaction with work and finances, quality of relationship with partner, and optimism about one's future life prospects. It is only on feelings about one's pregnancy resolution decision that placers are less satisfied than parenters.

The overall nature of these results did not change substantially when we estimated multivariate models to assess the association between pregnancy resolution behavior and life outcomes, while controlling for differences in background characteristics. Placers continued to fare better on the majority of sociodemographic and social psychological outcomes. However, as in the bivariate findings, placers fared significantly worse than parenters on feelings regarding their pregnancy resolution decision.

Next considered are the roles of marital, fertility and welfare status following the pregnancy resolution decision as potentially important mediators of the subsequent life outcomes among these two groups of women. These mediators influence the sociodemographic outcomes, social psychological outcomes, and feelings about the pregnancy resolution decision in unique ways. The differences between placers and parenters on key sociodemographic outcomes persisted, with placers enjoying more favorable outcomes than parenters. Moreover, placers continued to fare significantly worse than parenters with respect to their feelings regarding their pregnancy resolution decision. However, with only one exception, all of the other differences between placers and parenters on social psychological outcomes were mediated by differences between the groups on post-birth marital, fertility and welfare experiences. Quality of respondent's relationships with their partners is the only remaining social psychological outcome that was not mediated by the post-birth experiences. That is, even after controlling for these mediating variables, placers continued to have significantly higher quality partner relationships than parenters. This may be due to the fact that while all of the parenters were raising a child, only one-third of the placers were doing so by the four year follow-up. There is a large body of research that has documented that marital quality is lower among couples with children than among those who are not raising children (Belsky, Lang & Rovine, 1985; Belsky, Spanier & Rovine, 1983; Cowan et al., 1985; Feldman & Nash, 1984; Goldberg, Michaels & Lamb, 1985; Waldron & Routh, 1981).

The findings from this study clearly indicate that relative to parenting, resolving a teenage pregnancy by relinquishing one's infant for adoption is a positive choice resulting in more favorable outcomes on a broad variety of sociodemographic and social psychological outcomes. This is consistent with the literature on the consequences of teenage childbearing, which has repeatedly found that women who delay childrearing have more favorable education, fertility and socioeconomic outcomes than do teenage mothers. From this perspective, the adoption option appears to be a reasonable choice for pregnant young women who wish to postpone parenting.

The only arena in which relinquishers fare worse than parenters is on comfort with their pregnancy resolution decision. Without trying to minimize this finding, it is important to consider that nearly two-thirds of the placers experienced no regret four years later, and that nearly four-fifths of them said that they would definitely make the same decision again. A balanced description of the feelings of placers would be that as a group they are quite positive about their pregnancy resolution decision, but not as positive as parenters. It should also be considered that the differences in feelings between the two groups may be partly reflective of social norms. It is certainly more socially acceptable for a young woman to report regret about relinquishing than about parenting. Thus, teenagers who chose to parent may have been less willing, and those who relinquished more willing, to admit their feelings of regret about their pregnancy resolution decision.

POLICY RECOMMENDATIONS

Several policy recommendations can be gleaned from these findings. First, young pregnant women who are considering adoption need thorough counseling regarding this decision. One goal of this counseling should be to identify women who may be at high risk of regret about their decision, since at four years post-birth, placers who reported regret scored higher on depression and lower on overall life satisfaction than those reporting no regret. The counseling should explicitly address the possibility that a woman may experience regret about her decision to relinquish, and that the likelihood of this occurring is greater for young women who choose adoption than for those who choose childrearing. Finally, these findings indicate that in order to minimize the amount of regret and dissatisfaction that these women experience, only young women who are very clear about their desire to place their child for adoption should be encouraged to carry through with their plan.

The implications of these findings extend beyond counseling programs for women who want to relinquish their infants. Currently, pregnant teenagers faced with unintended pregnancies do not traditionally receive complete pregnancy resolution counseling. In most instances, adoption is neither discussed nor considered (Mech, 1986). Similarly, adoption is not routinely included in many sex education and family life curricula. Although it is likely that far more teenage pregnancies will continue to be resolved through abortion than through adoption, there will always be substantial numbers of young women with unintended or mistimed pregnancies for whom abortion is either unavailable or unacceptable. Our results indicate that it would be in the best interests of these women for pregnancy resolution counselors to fully and fairly discuss the adoption option. Regardless of whether it prompts larger numbers of women to choose adoption, over time it might increase the extent to which adoption is identified and considered as an acceptable option for and by pregnant teenagers. This, in turn, may ultimately lead to changes in attitudes and behaviors regarding this pregnancy resolution alternative.

REFERENCES

Bachrach, C.A. (1986). Adoption plans, adopted children, and adoptive mothers. *Journal of Marriage and the Family* 48:243-253 (May).

Bachrach, C.A., P.F. Adams, S. Sambrano, & K.A. London. (1990). Adoption in the 1980's. *Advance Data From Vital and Health Statistics of the National Center for Health Statistics* U.S. Dept. of Health and Human Services. 181.

Bachrach, C.A., K.S. Stolley, & K.A. London. (1992). Relinquishment of premarital births: Evidence from National Survey data. *Family Planning Perspectives* 24(1):27-48 (Jan/Feb).

Belsky, J., M.E. Lang, & M. Rovine. (1985). Stability and change in marriage across the transition to parenthood: A second study. *Journal of Marriage and the Family* 47:855-865.

Belsky, J., G. Spanier, & M. Rovine. (1983). Stability and change in marriage across the transition to parenthood. *Journal of Marriage and the Family* 45:567-577.

Burnell, G.M., & M.A. Norfleet. (1979). Women who place their infant up for adoption: A pilot study. *Patient Counselling and Health Education* 169-172 (Summer/Fall).

Cowan, C.P., P.A. Cowan, G. Heming, E. Garrett, W.S. Coyish, H. Curtis-Boles, & A.J. Boles, III. (1985). Transitions to parenthood: His, hers, and theirs. *Journal of Family Issues* 6:451-482.

Deykin, E.Y., L. Campbell, & P. Patti. (1984). The postadoption experience of surrendering parents. *American Journal of Orthopsychiatry* 54(2):271-280 (April).

Donnelly, B., & P. Voydanoff. (1991). Factors associated with releasing for adoption among adolescent mothers. *Family Relations* 40(4):404-410.

Feldman, S.S. & S.C. Nash. (1984). The transition from expectancy to parenthood: Impact of the firstborn child on men and women. *Sex Roles* 11:84-92.

Goldberg, W.A., G.Y. Michaels, & M.E. Lamb. (1985). Husbands' and wives' patterns of adjustment to pregnancy and first parenthood. *Journal of Family Issues* 6:483-504.

Herr, K. (1989). Adoption versus parenting decisions among pregnant adolescents. *Adolescence* 24:795-799 (Winter).

Kalmuss, D., P.B. Namerow, & U. Bauer. (1992). Short-term consequences of parenting versus adoption among young unmarried women. *Journal of Marriage and the Family* 54:80-90 (Feb).

Kalmuss, D., P.B. Namerow, & L. Cushman. (1991). Teenage pregnancy resolution: Adoption versus parenting. *Family Planning Perspectives* 23:17-23.

Klerman, L.V. (1983). Adoption: A public health perspective. *American Journal of Public Health* 73(10):1158-1160 (Oct).

McLaughlin, S.D., D.L. Manninen, & L.D. Winges. (1988). Do adolescents who relinquish their children fare better or worse than those who raise them? *Family Planning Perspectives* 20(1):25-32.

McLaughlin, S.D., S.E. Pearce, D.L. Manninen, & L.D. Winges. (1988). To parent or relinquish: Consequences for adolescent mothers. *Social Work* 33(4):320-324.

Mech, E.V. (1986). Pregnant adolescents: Communicating the Adoption Option. *Child Welfare League of America* 65(6):555-567 (Nov/Dec).

Millen, L., & S. Roll. (1985). Solomon's mothers: A special case of pathological bereavement. *American Journal of Orthopsychiatry* 55(3):411-418.

Namerow, P., D. Kalmuss, & L. Cushman. (1993). The determinants of young women's pregnancy-resolution choices. *Journal of Research on Adolescence* 3(2):193-215.

National Committee on Adoption. (1989). *1989 Adoption Factbook* Washington, DC: Author.

Pannor, R., A. Baran, & A.D. Sorosky. (1978). Birth parents who relinquished babies for adoption revisited. *Family Process* 17:329-337 (Sept).

Resnick, M.D. (1984). Studying adolescent mothers' decision making about adoption and parenting. *Social Work* 29:4-10.

Resnick, M.D., R.W. Blum, J. Bose, M. Smith, & R. Toogood. (1990). Characteristics of unmarried adolescent mothers: Determinants of child rearing versus adoption. *American Journal of Orthopsychiatry* 60(4):577-584 (Oct).

Rynearson, E. (1982). Relinquishment and its maternal complications: A preliminary study. *American Journal of Psychiatry* 139:338-340.

Sobol, M.P., & K.J. Daly. (1992). The adoption alternative for pregnant adolescents: Decision making, consequences, and policy implications. *Journal of Social Issues* 48(3):143-161.

Veit, C.T., & J.E. Ware. (1983). The structure of psychological distress and well-being in general populations. *Journal of Consulting and Clinical Psychology* 51(5):730-742.

Waldron, H., & D.K. Routh. (1981). The effect of the first child on the marital relationship. *Journal of Marriage and the Family* 43:785-788.

Ware Jr., J.E., W.G. Manning Jr., N. Duan, K.B. Wells, & J.P. Newhouse. (1984). Health status and the use of outpatient mental health services. *American Psychologist* 39:1090-1100.

Watson, K. (1986). Birth families: Living with the adoption decision. *Public Welfare* 5-10.

Adopted Adults:
Comparisons with Persons
Raised in Conventional Families

William Feigelman

SUMMARY. With archival data from the National Longitudinal Study of Youth, this study compares the adult behavior patterns of adoptees (N = 101) and children raised in all other types of attenuated nuclear families (N = 3,949) with those raised till age 18 by both biological parents (N = 6,258).

Both adoptees from intact two-parent families and those raised in all other types of disrupted nuclear families showed a higher incidence of problem behaviors during adolescence than children raised exclusively by both bio-parents. This was in terms of the following dimensions: delinquency, youth crime, and the use of alcohol and drugs. Later, during adulthood, the educational attainments, job statuses, and levels of marital stability of those growing up in all types of disrupted nuclear families lagged behind those raised by both birth parents. At the time when most respondents were entering their thirties, those growing up in attenuated nuclear families were also more likely to report symptoms of depression.

Adoptees, too, showed some, but much less clear evidence of long-term difficulties arising from their more turbulent adolescent

---

William Feigelman is Chair and Professor of Sociology, Nassau Community College, Garden City, NY 11530.

A preliminary version of this paper was presented at the Conference on Adoption Research held at Cornell University, Ithaca, New York, October 7-8, 1994. The author is grateful for the thoughtful comments of Richard Barth which were very valuable in making the present revision.

[Haworth co-indexing entry note]: "Adopted Adults: Comparisons with Persons Raised in Conventional Families." Feigelman, William. Co-published simultaneously in *Marriage & Family Review* (The Haworth Press, Inc.) Vol. 25, No. 3/4, 1997, pp. 199-223; and: *Families and Adoption* (ed: Harriet E. Gross and Marvin B. Sussman) The Haworth Press, Inc., 1997, pp. 199-223. Single or multiple copies of this article are available for a fee from The Haworth Document Delivery Service [1-800-342-9678, 9:00 a.m. - 5:00 p.m. (EST). E-mail address: getinfo@haworth.com].

experiences, compared to those growing up with both bio-parents. By their late twenties and early thirties adoptees reported more instances of cohabitation prior to marriage and more females seemed to report lower levels of marital happiness. Yet, in most all other aspects surveyed—such as the recent use of drugs, educational attainments, job holding, employment successes, asset accumulations, home ownership and marital stability, they appeared much like those raised in intact bio-parent families.

Like their counterparts from all types of disrupted nuclear families, adoptees showed a need for greater social services—especially during adolescence—to overcome psycho-social problems emerging at that time. In the absence of having such care, long-term dysfunctional consequences are more likely to occur, especially for those raised in all other types of attenuated nuclear families. *[Article copies available for a fee from The Haworth Document Delivery Service: 1-800-342-9678. E-mail address: getinfo@haworth.com]*

INTRODUCTION

The vast majority of the research on the adjustments of adopted persons has been based upon studies of children, especially upon infants and preteenagers. Adolescents have been exposed to a lesser degree of research scrutiny. Hardly any studies have assessed adoptive outcomes among American adults. Most of the limited literature on adopted adults has focused upon adult adoptees who have or have not searched for their biological parents. The search issue has dominated the very sparse literature on adopted adults.

The studies of adopted adolescents have generally concluded that adoptees are more problem-prone than their nonadopted counterparts reared in families with biological parents. In a literature review article of the long-term outcomes of adoption David Brodzinsky concludes,

> as a group they [adoptees] are more vulnerable to various emotional, behavioral and academic problems than their nonadopted peers living in intact homes with their biological parents. (p. 153, Brodzinsky, 1993)

Brodzinsky bases his conclusions on findings showing higher rates of substance abuse, eating disorders, learning disabilities, aggression, delinquency, academic and social deficiencies, among other problems, found in clinical and in nonclinical studies of adoptees. Brodzinsky acknowledges that most of this evidence comes from clinical studies, which may not be the fairest test of this hypothesis.

Among the various reasons why adoptive parents with problem children may be more prone to seek treatment and thus may be overrepresented among the ranks of clinical patients could be past parental connections with the adopting agency. Thus, epidemiological studies become a more effective test of assessing whether the adoptee is more problem-prone than non-adopted persons.

The proof of this association is less clear when viewing the available nonclinical data. Several studies cited by Brodzinsky find no evidence of increased psychological problems among adoptees (Mikawa and Boston, 1968; Norvell and Guy, 1977; Stein and Hoopes, 1985). And, another study done in Sweden, which may not be entirely comparable to U.S. conditions and laws, showed mixed evidence of adoptees' problem-proneness, depending upon the age of the adolescent (Bohman and Sigvardsson, 1990).

In contrast, several studies completed among younger adopted children (ages 6 through 12 year olds), undertaken in school settings, found more academic deficiencies, less socially acceptable behavior and more delinquency among adopted respondents than among the nonadopted ones (Brodzinsky et al., 1984; Brodzinsky et al., 1987). Another study found evidence from parental reports of lower academic accomplishment and higher numbers of behavior problems among adopted children than from the parents of the nonadopted (Zill, 1985).

Theoreticians of adoption have posited that adoptees suffer from a sense of "genealogical bewilderment" or a "confused sense of identity" and that this is a developmental issue most adopted persons must confront as they enter into adulthood (Lifton, 1994; Sorosky, Baran and Pannor, 1979). If such an issue is fundamental to growing up adopted, then such identity seeking and turmoil would be manifested in more dysfunctional conduct compared to the nonadoptee as the adoptee moves from childhood into adulthood.

These contradictory findings and theoretical predictions do not enable us to accept that adopted adolescents are more problem-prone. More supportive data will be needed to accept this conclusion. In this paper I raise and study questions about how the adult life course of adopted people may vary from others who were non-adopted.

This study adds evidence relevant to the issue of adoptee problem-proneness and to the theoretical conceptualization of adoptees' vulnerable self-identities.

METHOD

This study is based upon data from the National Longitudinal Study of Youth. NLSY is a longitudinal research project begun in 1979. The initial sample included 12,686 respondents who were then between the ages of 14 and 21. NLSY interviews respondents annually, as they move through the life cycle. They trace respondents' employment histories, family lives and child raising activities. NLSY has been administered by the National Opinion Research Center at the University of Chicago. There is a 90 percent rate of continuing participation. Consequently, these highly reliable data have been used by large numbers of social scientists.

Each original NLS sample was designed to represent the civilian noninstitutionalized population at the time of its initial survey. Each age-sex cohort studied was represented by a multistage probability sample drawn by the Bureau of the Census. This survey also oversampled African American and Hispanic respondents. For a fuller description of the NLS methods and sampling procedures readers are advised to see: *NLS User's Guide* (1994).

In 1988, for the first time, NLSY respondents were asked about their early childhood residence patterns: whether they had always lived till age 18 with both biological parents; this was true for 6,258 respondents, and whether they had ever lived four months or longer with adoptive parents; 195 respondents reported being adopted. The remaining 3,949 respondents grew up in a variety of attenuated nuclear families: lived with stepparents, in foster homes, with other family members, in institutional settings, independently, or in some combination of these alternative family living arrangements. With nonresponses and survey attrition over this nine year period, the original 12,686 was reduced to a total of 10,402 potentially useable cases.

From the original sample of 195 adopted respondents two important subgroups were excluded: (1) adoptees who were adopted by their stepparent(s); and (2) adoptees who did not live together with both parents consistently during their first seventeen years. Thirty-seven adoptees reported living with a step-parent during their childhood years. Since many of these cases were instances where a step-parent had adopted their partner's child, these special cases of adoption were omitted from the analysis. Fifty-seven additional respondents reported not living continuously with both parents during their first 17 years. These cases, also, were removed from the analysis, leaving 101 subjects.

The study plan called for matching adoptees as closely as possible with those raised by both bio-parents. Much as I was reluctant to diminish the already meager numbers of adoptees, I wanted to make a comparison among those growing up in intact bio-parent families, those who were adopted who were raised in intact two-parent adoptive families and those who grew up in all other types of family living arrangements. The proceeding analysis compares these three groups.

STATISTICAL PROCEDURES

In this analysis I used chi square significance tests to gauge the association between the primary independent variable–family type–and the various dependent variables of interest. Each of the dependent variables was run against the trichotomized independent variable of family type. Asterisks are used in the accompanying tables to show whether the association was significant at the .05 or .001 probability levels.

Like most significance test statistics chi square is greatly affected by sample size differences. Slight differences (of at least 5 percent or more) between large sample subgroups will ordinarily show statistically significant differences. In the case of differences between a smaller sized subgroup (of the adoptees) and one of the larger subgroups, substantial subcategory differences–of greater than 20 percent or more–will often be needed to achieve statistical significance.

The sample of adoptees was smaller than we might have desired. Yet, it is of analytical importance to know whether the differences between the adoptees and those raised by both bio-parents were greater than chance. Consequently, separate chi square significance tests were completed for each hypothesized relationship in a bivariate association contrasting adoptees with those raised by both bio-parents. These chi squares are reported with plus signs. One plus signifies the chi square probability approached, but failed to achieve the .05 level, with a probability level falling between .06 and .15. A double plus sign shows the conventional probability level, of less than .05.

RESULTS

Table 1 presents data on demographic characteristics of three groups of respondents. Those from attenuated nuclear families tend to be slightly younger than the other two groups of respondents. Slightly more females are noted among those raised in step- and other type families. More males are among adoptees raised in intact adoption families. Inasmuch as the gender differences between subgroups could prove to be a confounding factor in relation to such activities as criminal behavior, gender specific comparisons of the dependent variables are made.

Whites are over-represented among adoptees while African Americans

TABLE 1. Demographic Characteristics of Children Raised by Both Birth-Parents, Adoptees from Intact Two-Parent Families and Children Raised in Step- and Other Families

Percentage / N

	Both Birth Parents	Intact Adopted	Step- and Other Families	Base N
Age (in 1979) **				
14-16	33.5 / 2098	36.6 / 37	38.7 / 1529	3664
17-19	39.2 / 2453	33.3 / 34	38.1 / 1504	3991
20-22	27.3 / 1707	29.7 / 30	23.2 / 916	2653
Sex *				
Males	50.3 / 3146	57.4 / 58	47.7 / 1882	5086
Females	49.7 / 3112	42.6 / 43	52.3 / 2068	5222
Race ** ++				
White	74.0 / 4598	87.1 / 88	59.3 / 2330	7016
Black	20.8 / 1296	8.9 / 9	34.9 / 1372	2677
Other	5.2 / 323	4.0 / 4	5.8 / 227	554
Father's Education ** ++				
< HS	42.0 / 2433	34.8 / 31	46.3 / 1359	3823
HS	32.0 / 1855	25.8 / 23	36.7 / 1078	2956
SomeColl	9.8 / 571	11.2 / 10	7.7 / 226	807
Coll+	16.2 / 938	28.1 / 25	9.4 / 275	1238
Father's Occupation (in 1979) ** +				
Prof/Manager	27.0 / 1387	40.5 / 32	18.5 / 392	1811
Sales/Clerical	9.1 / 469	7.6 / 6	7.8 / 166	641
Skilled Manual	26.0 / 1335	24.1 / 19	27.6 / 586	1940
Less Skill Man	27.2 / 1395	20.3 / 16	34.6 / 733	2144
Unskill Manual	10.6 / 542	7.6 / 6	11.5 / 244	792

*   Chi square probability < .05
**   Chi square probability < .001
+   Bivariate Chi square probability > .06 and < .15
++ Bivariate Chi square probability < .05

Source: National Longitudinal Study of Youth, 1979-92

are over-represented in step- and other kinds of families. Fathers of adoptees are more likely to be well educated and in higher status occupations
than the other groups of children (Table 1). In contrast, children in step-
and other kinds of families were more likely to have fathers who held
lower status positions and were less well educated compared to the other
groups of youth respondents. Such differences reflect trends in adoption
practice which self-select more upper status persons to eventually become
adoptive parents. And these differences are also linked to the economic
conditions that bring more lower status and minority member families into
the ranks of dissolved households.

Among adoptees, step- and other type of family-raised children—compared
to those raised by both birth parents—there are higher rates of anti-social
behavior, drug and alcohol use and crime (Tables 2 and 3).

Table 3 did not show statistically significant differences in drinking to
intoxication among the three groups in the 1982 survey. But, by 1988,
drinking to intoxication was more pronounced among the step- and other
kind of families' children than among those raised by both birth parents.

Table 3 also shows that those raised in step- and other type families still
drank more heavily, consumed other drugs and had more problems
associated with their drug use (compared to bio-parent raised children)
even when respondents began to approach middle age. Yet, the evidence in
Table 3 is less clear about the persistence of higher drug and alcohol use
and its associated problems among the adoptees. The only places where
statistically significant differences emerged between the adoptees and
those raised in intact bio-parent families, was in relation to questions about
drug and alcohol use over the life course.

An important item which could confound any differences in antisocial
behavior linked to family structural differences, is gender differences in
the original samples. Readers will recall Table 1 showed adopted respondents more likely to be male than the other two subgroups. Table 4 controls for the gender difference specifying the differences separately for
male and female respondents. While it may not have been supported on
each and every comparison, it still showed a similar pattern of differences
when respondents were divided into their separate gender groups. Differences of growing up in diverging family structures still seemed linked in
the same way to higher crime participation and delinquency among separated male and female respondents. Of course, the rates of criminal participation were far lower for the women, compared to those for the men.

Tables 5 and 6 show differences in educational attainments by 1992,
current job holding, unemployment, job status, pay differentials between
our various groups of respondents: those raised by both birth parents,

TABLE 2. Delinquency and Crime During the Past Year Among Children Raised by Both Birth-Parents, in Intact Adoption Families and Children Raised in Step- and Other Families

Percentage / N

	Both Birth Parents	Intact Adopted	Step- and Other Families	Base N
Ran away from home (A) (Z) ** ++				
Yes	6.3 / 129	18.9 / 7	14.0 / 253	340
No	93.7 / 1928	81.1 / 30	86.0 / 204	3211
Skipped school days (A) (Z) **				
Yes	43.9 / 902	51.4 / 19	52.8 / 768	1689
No	56.1 / 1155	48.6 / 18	47.2 / 686	1859
Fought at school or work (B) **				
Yes	25.8 / 1540	30.6 / 30	32.2 / 1191	2761
No	74.2 / 4429	69.4 / 68	67.8 / 2509	7006
Shoplifted (B) ** ++				
Yes	24.8 / 1482	35.7 / 35	29.6 / 1095	2612
No	75.2 / 4484	64.3 / 63	70.4 / 2603	7150
Stolen property (> $50) (B) **				
Yes	4.3 / 256	7.1 / 7	7.1 / 264	527
No	95.7 / 5706	92.9 / 91	92.9 / 3429	9226
Ever charged with illegal act (B) ** ++				
Yes	7.6 / 460	13.0 / 13	14.4 / 549	1022
No	92.4 / 5628	87.0 / 87	85.6 / 3258	8973
Attacked someone with intent to injure or kill (B) **				
Yes	8.4 / 502	9.2 / 9	13.4 / 497	1008
No	91.6 / 5467	90.8 / 89	86.6 / 3199	8755

(A)   1979 Survey
(B)   1980 Survey   (Z)   Among under age 18 population

++   Bivariate Chi square probability < .05
**   Chi square probability < .001

Source: National Longitudinal Study of Youth, 1979-80

TABLE 3. Alcohol, Drug Use and Drug-Related Crime During Past Year Among Children Raised by Both Birth-Parents, in Intact Adoption Families and Children Raised in Step- and Other Families

Percentage / N

	Both Birth Parents	Intact Adopted	Step- and Other Families	Base N
Smoked marijuana / hashish (A) ** ++				
Never	56.5 / 3358	44.8 / 43	49.0 / 1795	5196
Once	8.1 / 479	7.3 / 7	10.0 / 368	854
Twice or more	35.4 / 2106	47.9 / 46	41.0 / 1500	3652
Sold hard drugs (A) **				
Yes	1.9 / 110	3.1 / 3	3.0 / 110	223
No	98.1 / 5828	96.9 / 94	97.0 / 3556	9478
During last 30 days, took 6 or more alcoholic drinks when drinking (B)				
Never	39.0 / 1572	35.1 / 26	40.7 / 973	2571
Once	16.7 / 673	10.8 / 8	15.7 / 376	1057
Twice or more	44.3 / 1782	54.1 / 40	43.6 / 1044	2866
Drinking ever interfere w/job (B) ** ++				
Yes	1.9 / 107	6.3 / 6	2.4 / 84	197
No	98.1 / 5493	93.8 / 90	97.6 / 3380	8963
Felt aggressive or cross while drinking (C) * +				
Yes	16.9 / 721	23.3 / 17	19.2 / 496	1234
No	83.1 / 3535	76.7 / 56	80.8 / 2094	5685
During last 30 days taking 6 or more alcoholic drinks when drinking (D) *				
Never	47.2 / 1997	37.0 / 27	45.5 / 1175	3199
Once	15.9 / 675	16.4 / 12	14.3 / 368	1055
Twice or more	36.9 / 1562	46.6 / 34	40.2 / 1037	2633
Felt aggressive or cross while drinking (D) ** +				
Yes	12.5 / 529	19.2 / 14	16.5 / 427	970
No	87.5 / 3705	80.8 / 59	83.5 / 2155	5919

TABLE 3 (continued)

	Both Birth Parents	Intact Adopted	Step- and Other Families	Base N
Afraid you might become				
an alcoholic (D) **				
Yes	6.0 / 255	8.2 / 6	9.1 / 236	497
No	94.0 / 3977	91.8 / 67	90.9 / 2345	6389
Occasions used cocaine (lifetime) (D) ** ++				
Never	75.1 / 4592	58.6 / 58	68.5 / 2657	7307
Once or twice	8.9 / 543	13.1 / 13	10.6 / 412	968
Three or more	16.0 / 980	28.3 / 28	20.9 / 812	1820
Have you found that you				
have to drink more to				
get the same effect (E) **				
Yes	13.5 / 531	18.8 / 12	15.3 / 355	898
No	86.5 / 3403	81.3 / 52	84.7 / 1968	5423
Have you ever lost ties				
with family or friends				
because of your drinking (E) ** ++				
Yes	3.0 / 119	10.9 / 7	5.5 / 127	253
No	97.0 / 3815	89.1 / 57	94.5 / 2197	6069
(among lifetime users)				
Use of marijuana/				
hashish, last year (F) **				
Yes	34.0 / 902	36.7 / 22	39.9 / 687	1611
No	66.0 / 1752	63.3 / 38	60.1 / 1036	2826
(among lifetime users)				
Use of cocaine,				
last year (F) **				
Yes	35.2 / 388	27.6 / 8	45.9 / 360	756
No	64.8 / 714	72.4 / 21	54.1 / 424	1159

(A)	1980 Survey	(C)	1984 Survey	(E)	1989 Survey
(B)	1982 Survey	(D)	1988 Survey	(F)	1992 Survey

*	Chi square probability < .05
**	Chi square probability < .001
+	Bivariate Chi square probability > .06 and < .15
++	Bivariate Chi square probability < .05

Source: National Longitudinal Study of Youth, 1979-92

TABLE 4. Crime During the Past Year Among Children Raised by Both Birth-parents, in Intact Adoption Families and Children Raised in Step and Other Families, Controlled by Sex

Percentage / N

Among Males Only

	Both Birth Parents	Intact Adopted	Step- and Other Families	Base N
Fought at school or work (B) **				
Yes	38.3 / 1140	42.1 / 24	44.2 / 774	1938
No	61.7 / 1834	57.9 / 33	55.8 / 978	2845
Shoplifted (B) ** +				
Yes	27.9 / 828	36.8 / 21	33.0 / 577	1426
No	72.1 / 2143	63.2 / 36	67.0 / 1171	3350
Stolen property (> $50) (B) ** +				
Yes	7.1 / 212	12.3 / 7	12.2 / 212	431
No	92.9 / 2754	87.7 / 50	87.8 / 1532	4336
Ever charged with illegal act (B) **				
Yes	12.1 / 370	15.5 / 9	23.5 / 425	804
No	87.9 / 2676	84.5 / 49	76.5 / 1383	4108
Attacked someone with intent to injure or kill (B) **				
Yes	12.3 / 365	12.3 / 7	18.4 / 321	693
No	87.7 / 2606	87.7 / 50	81.6 / 1426	4082

Among Females Only

	Both Birth Parents	Intact Adopted	Step- and Other Families	Base N
Fought at school or work (B) **				
Yes	13.4 / 400	14.6 / 6	21.4 / 417	823
No	86.6 / 2595	85.4 / 35	78.6 / 1531	4161
Shoplifted (B) * ++				
Yes	21.8 / 654	34.1 / 14	26.6 / 518	1186
No	78.2 / 2341	65.9 / 27	73.4 / 1432	3800

TABLE 4 (continued)

Among females only	Both Birth Parents	Intact Adopted	Step- and Other Families	Base N
Stolen property (> $50) (B) *				
Yes	1.5 / 44	0.0 /	2.7 / 52	96
No	98.5 / 2952	100.0 / 41	97.3 / 1897	4890
Ever charged with illegal act (B) ** ++				
Yes	3.0 / 90	9.5 / 4	6.2 / 124	218
No	97.0 / 2952	90.5 / 38	93.8 / 1875	4865
Attacked someone with intent to injure or kill (B) **				
Yes	4.6 / 137	4.9 / 2	9.0 / 176	315
No	95.4 / 2861	95.1 / 39	91.0 / 1773	4673

(B)	1980 Survey
*	Chi square probability < .05
**	Chi square probability < .001
+	Bivariate Chi square probability > .06 and < .15
++	Bivariate Chi square probability < .05

Source: National Longitudinal Study of Youth, 1979-80

those from intact adoption families and those raised in step- and other type families. Since gender is such an important correlate to job holding and job-related successes, we separated this analysis into two parts, one for men and one for women.

Again, the results showed much the same pattern for both sexes. Compared to their bio-parent and intact adoption raised child counterparts, step- and other type family-raised children showed lower educational attainments, more unemployment, lower earnings and lower status occupations. The only convergent point in this six dimension assessment was in the area of job satisfaction: similar levels of job satisfaction were reported by all subgroups.

When the intact adoption males are contrasted with those raised by both bio-parents, several differences can be noted: more adoptees report getting some college training, but not completing college; this was statistically significant with chi square in the separate comparison of adoptees and

TABLE 5. Educational Attainments, Job Status, Job Satisfaction and Pay Differentials in 1992 Between Children Raised by Both Birth-Parents, in Intact Adoption Families and Children Raised in Step- and Other Families

Percentage / N

For Males Only

	Both Birth Parents	Intact Adopted	Step- and Other Families	Base N
Education ** ++				
< HS	12.9 / 342	3.9 / 2	22.7 / 337	681
HS	45.3 / 1199	45.1 / 23	46.4 / 688	1910
SomeColl	20.1 / 531	33.3 / 17	19.4 / 287	835
Coll+	21.7 / 575	17.6 / 9	11.5 / 171	755
Occupation **				
Prof/Manager	28.6 / 705	29.5 / 13	22.4 / 285	1003
Sales/Clerical	12.6 / 311	18.2 / 8	11.0 / 140	459
Skilled Manual	20.3 / 502	27.3 / 12	20.3 / 259	773
Less skill Man	26.5 / 654	15.9 / 7	32.9 / 419	1080
Unskill Manual	12.0 / 295	9.1 / 4	13.5 / 172	471
Job Satisfaction				
Like very much	44.3 / 1113	41.3 / 19	42.8 / 566	1698
Like somewhat	47.6 / 1196	47.8 / 22	47.0 / 622	1840
Dislike somewhat	6.5 / 164	6.5 / 3	7.3 / 96	263
Dislike very much	1.7 / 42	4.3 / 2	2.9 / 39	83
Current Employment Status **+				
Employed	85.3 / 2260	74.5 / 38	76.4 / 1134	3432
Unemployed	6.6 / 175	13.7 / 7	7.6 / 113	295
Out of labor force	5.7 / 152	7.8 / 4	12.1 / 179	335
Military	2.3 / 62	3.9 / 2	4.0 / 59	123
Weeks unemployed last 12 mo. **				
None	80.3 / 2091	74.0 / 37	74.2 / 1075	3203
1-20	14.3 / 373	22.0 / 11	16.8 / 243	627
21-52	5.4 / 141	4.0 / 2	9.0 / 131	274
Hourly pay **				
< $5.00	9.0 / 210	11.9 / 5	13.9 / 169	384
Bet $5 & $10	37.9 / 886	33.3 / 14	46.1 / 559	1459
Over $10	53.1 / 1241	54.8 / 23	39.9 / 484	1748

    **   Chi square probability < .001
    +   Bivariate Chi square probability > .06 and < .15
    ++   Bivariate Chi square probability < .05

Source: National Longitudinal Study of Youth, 1992

TABLE 6. Educational Attainments, Job Status, Job Satisfaction and Pay Differentials in 1992 Between Children Raised by Both Birth-Parents, in Intact Adoption Families and Children Raised in Step- and Other Families

Percentage / N

For Females Only

	Both Birth Parents	Intact Adopted	Step- and Other Families	Base N
Education ***				
> HS	8.6 / 222	15.2 / 5	19.8 / 324	551
HS	42.6 / 1097	36.4 / 12	46.4 / 759	1868
SomeColl	25.7 / 663	30.3 / 10	23.0 / 376	1049
Coll+	23.1 / 596	18.2 /6	10.9 / 178	780
Occupation ***				
Prof/Manager	36.2 / 764	38.5 / 10	28.0 / 357	1131
Sales/Clerical	34.5 / 727	38.5 / 10	33.4 / 426	1163
Skilled Manual	2.0 / 42	0.0 /	2.4 / 30	72
Less skill Man	9.7 / 204	3.8 / 1	24.2 / 153	358
Unskill Manual	17.6 / 371	19.2 / 5	24.2 / 309	685
Job Satisfaction				
Like very much	48.3 / 1016	42.3 / 11	44.9 / 569	1596
Like somewhat	42.9 / 899	50.0 / 13	40.7 / 516	1428
Dislike somewhat	6.9 / 145	3.8 / 1	9.1 / 115	261
Dislike very much	2.1 / 45	3.8 /1	5.3 / 67	113
Current Employment Status ***				
Employed	71.8 / 1853	72.7 / 24	65.5 / 1075	2952
Unemployed	5.6 / 145	0.0 /	7.4 / 122	267
Out of labor force	22.2 / 573	27.3 /9	26.7 / 438	1020
Military	.4 / 11	0.0 /	.4 / 7	18
Weeks unemployed last 12 mo. ***				
None	84.1 / 2138	90.9 / 30	78.1 / 1260	3428
1-20	11.9 / 303	6.1 /2	16.4 / 265	570
21-52	4.0 / 102	3.0/1	5.5 / 88	191
Hourly pay ***				
< $5.00	16.6 / 334	16.7 / 4	23.3 / 284	622
Bet $5 & $10	44.1 / 890	41.7 / 10	48.8 / 595	1495
Over $10	39.3 / 792	41.7 / 10	28.0 / 341	1143

** Chi square probability < .001

Source: National Longitudinal Study of Youth, 1992

those raised by both bio-parents; higher levels of unemployment were also reported among the male adoptees; this approached significance in a similar two subcategory comparison.

The employment/education patterns for NLSY females were not entirely congruent to the male pattern of responses. Compared to their peers raised by both bio-parents, women who grew up in step- and other kinds of families were more likely to drop out of school, have lower occupational prestige statuses, gained less money and had more and longer periods of unemployment. Yet, adopted females showed similar education/ employment as those raised by both bio-parents. None of these six variable comparisons approached statistical significance with chi square in a separate contrast of adoptees and those raised by both bio-parents.

Table 7 shows the asset accumulations of all three groups of respondents. As expected, males and females raised in step- and other kinds of families showed the lowest levels of asset accumulations of all three subgroups. When adopted males were compared with those raised by both bio-parents, asset accumulations remained substantially alike. Comparing adopted females with those by both natural parents, again, showed a similar pattern of asset accumulations. None of the four variable comparisons of these groups of men and women showed any differences of any magnitude approaching statistical significance with chi square in separate contrasts of adoptees and those raised by both bio-parents.

Table 8 shows clear divergences in fertility and child bearing among the three subgroups of NLSY females. Greater percentages of both birth-parent raised females and adoptees had never been pregnant compared to the women raised in step- and other family living arrangements. The most fertile subgroup of all were step- and other family raised children. By 1992–now between the ages 27 and 34–71 percent of step- and other family raised children had two or more pregnancies, compared to only about 55 percent among female adoptees and 57 percent of birth-parent-raised children.

Delaying pregnancy was most common among the both birth-parent raised females and the adoptees; over 30 percent of both groups had their first pregnancy after age 22. For women growing up in step- and other type families, having one's first child before age 18 was most common. In all the aspects surveyed here, the fertility patterns of females adoptees were much like those raised by both birth parents.

Owing partly to their earlier timing of fertility, more children of step- and other type families had greater numbers of abortions, stillbirths and miscarriages compared to the other two groups of women. Initially, those from intact adoption homes seemed to be more likely to have abortions

TABLE 7. Asset Accumulations Among NLSY Respondents (For Self and Spouse) by 1992 Between Those Raised by Both Birth-Parents, in Intact Adoption Families and Children Raised in Step- and Other Families

Percentage / N

For Males Only

	Both Birth Parents	Intact Adopted	Step- and Other Families	Base N
Estimated market value of owned residential property **				
< $50,000	28.1 / 310	16.7 / 4	37.8 / 154	468
$51 to $100K	40.2 / 443	54.2 / 13	35.9 / 146	602
Over $100K	31.7 / 350	29.2 / 7	26.3 / 107	464
Total amount of money assets **				
< $5000	59.2 / 1053	58.3 / 21	70.5 / 552	1626
Bet $5K & $20K	26.4 / 470	19.4 / 7	23.1 / 181	658
Over $20,000	14.4 / 257	22.2 / 8	6.4 / 50	315

For Females Only

	Both Birth Parents	Intact Adopted	Step- and Other Families	Base N
Estimated market value of owned residential property **				
< $50,000	26.1 / 310	37.5 / 6	40.2 / 227	556
$51 to $100K	40.3 / 498	25.0 / 4	35.2 / 199	701
Over $100K	33.6 / 416	37.5 / 6	24.6 / 139	561
Total amount of money assets **				
< $5000	60.6 / 1092	64.0 / 16	73.4 / 680	1788
Bet $5K & $20K	26.3 / 475	24.0 / 6	18.6 / 172	653
Over $20,000	13.1 / 236	12.0 / 3	8.0 / 74	313

*   Chi square probability < .05
**   Chi square probability < .001

Source: National Longitudinal Study of Youth, 1992

TABLE 8. Fertility and Childbearing Among NLSY Female Respondents by 1992 Between Those Raised by Both Birth-Parents, in Intact Adoption Families and Children Raised in Step- and Other Families

Percentage / N

	Both Birth Parents	Intact Adopted	Step- and Other Families	Base N
Total number of pregnancies **				
None	24.0 / 613	24.2 / 8	13.4 / 217	838
One	18.6 / 475	21.2 / 7	16.1 / 261	743
Two or more	57.4 / 1468	54.5 / 18	70.5 / 1144	2630
Total number of children ever born ** (Z)				
None	35.7 / 1868	38.1 / 32	27.1 / 846	2746
One	21.5 / 1127	21.4 / 18	22.2 / 694	1839
Two	25.3 / 1322	29.8 / 25	27.2 / 852	2199
Three or more	17.5 / 914	10.7 / 9	23.5 / 735	1658
Total number of miscarriages/stillbirths **				
None	84.3 / 2157	78.8 / 26	80.3 / 1304	3487
One	12.3 / 316	15.2 / 5	14.4 / 234	555
Two or more	3.4 / 87	6.1 / 2	5.2 / 85	174
Total number of abortions **				
None	85.5 / 2185	78.8 / 26	77.2 / 1254	3465
One	9.8 / 250	12.1 / 4	15.3 / 249	503
Two or more	4.7 / 121	9.1 / 3	7.5 / 121	245
Age of respondent at first pregnancy **				
Not yet preg.	24.2 / 613	24.2 / 8	13.6 / 217	838
17 and under	14.1 / 358	12.1 / 4	34.3 / 546	908
18-21	26.1 / 661	33.3 / 11	32.0 / 510	1182
22 and over	35.5 / 900	30.3 / 10	20.1 / 321	1231
Non-biological children added to families by 1990 (Z) **				
Adopted	19.5 / 107	16.7 / 1	12.0 / 47	155
Step-child(ren)	80.5 / 442	83.3 / 5	88.0 / 346	793

(Z)   Among both males and females
*Chi square probability < .05   ** Chi square probability < .001

Source: National Longitudinal Study of Youth, 1992

and miscarriages (than those from intact bio-parent families) but none of these differences came close to achieving statistical significance. Related to their tendency to postpone child bearing, women raised by both birth parents were more likely (than those from step- and other families) to add children by adoption. However, given that the children from step- and other type families were somewhat more likely to have dissolved marriages, this too, increased their propensities to add children through step-parentage, rather than adoption.

This evidence is suggestive, because of the extremely small sample size of adoptees. It showed adoptees no more inclined than other groups of prospective parents to use adoption as a mode of family formation. (Even when all 195 adoptees from the entire sample were included in an analogous comparison, only 10 percent of females reported adopting a child compared to the remaining 90 percent who added children through step-parentage.

In each household where non-biological children were added, it could have been through adoption, step-parentage or both. Any mixed cases were omitted. Those cases counted were either by adoption only or by step-parentage only. Among all three groups of study respondents 155/948 or 16% added children by adoption and 793/948 (or 84%) added children through step-parentage. Overall, the data suggested those most inclined to rely upon adoption were those who deferred fertility and subsequently encountered problems in conceiving biological children.

Table 9 shows differences in marriage patterns among the three groups of respondents. Cohabitation prior to marriage was more common among adoptees and those raised in step- and other type families, than among those raised by both birth parents. Those raised in step- and other families showed the greatest tendency to remain never married, and they anticipated (more than any other subgroup) that they would never marry; they also showed the highest rates for divorce and separation. This group also showed the highest rates of premarital pregnancy; and 60 percent had their first child before being married for a full year; for the other subgroups less than 40 percent had responded similarly.

In the two group comparison with those raised by both bio-parents, adoptees were significantly more likely to live together with their partner prior to marriage. More than half of the adoptees reported getting married after age 22, the highest rate of late marriage of any of the other subgroups. Though, they did not differ significantly in this respect from those raised by both bio-parents. Another noteworthy difference among the adoptees was their tendency to report the lowest levels of marital happiness of all three subgroups.

TABLE 9. Marital Status, Cohabitation Prior to Marriage, and Marital Happiness Among NLSY Respondents, 1992, Between Those Raised by Both Birth-Parents, in Intact Adoption Families and Children Raised in Step- and Other Families

Percentage / N

	Both Birth Parents	Intact Adopted	Step- and Other Families	Base N
**Age at first marriage ** **				
Not yet	27.7 / 1432	20.5 / 17	33.6 / 1033	2482
17 & under	2.8 / 144	3.6 / 3	8.3 / 256	403
18-21	25.9 / 1338	24.1 / 20	25.9 / 797	2155
22 and over	43.6 / 2250	51.8 / 43	32.2 / 990	3283
Lived together with partner before marriage ** ++				
Yes	37.8 / 1490	51.4 / 36	51.9 / 1119	2645
No	62.2 / 2447	48.6 / 34	48.1 / 1040	3521
Timing of first birth in relation to 1st marriage **				
Before	17.7 / 508	18.8 / 9	30.5 / 522	1039
Within 1st yr	25.8 / 741	14.6 / 7	29.6 / 506	1254
Bet 1-3 yrs	31.7 / 910	39.6 / 19	23.0 / 393	1322
After 3 yrs	24.7 / 708	27.1 / 13	16.9 / 290	1011
Current marital status (1992) **				
Never married	27.6 / 1446	20.2 / 17	33.5 / 1046	2509
Married/rem	57.8 / 3026	65.5 / 55	46.6 / 1456	4537
Separated	4.5 / 236	2.4 / 2	7.3 / 228	466
Divorced	9.5 / 499	11.7 / 10	12.2 / 383	892
Widowed	.5 / 24	0.0 /	.4 / 14	38
Marital happiness (Y) ** +				
Very happy	75.7 / 1302	59.1 / 13	68.3 / 639	1954
Fairly happy	22.6 / 388	36.4 / 8	27.9 / 261	657
Not too happy	1.7 / 29	4.5 / 1	3.7 / 35	65
Expectations to eventually marry (Y) *				
Likely soon	29.5 / 249	9.1 / 1	22.3 / 152	403
Likely not soon	50.4 / 425	63.6 / 7	51.7 / 355	787
Not likely	20.0 / 169	27.3 / 3	26.1 / 179	351

(Y)   Among females only
*Chi square < .05   + Bivariate Chi square > .06 and < .15
**Chi square < .001   ++ Bivariate Chi square < .05

Source: National Longitudinal Study of Youth, 1992

Table 10 reflects responses to the CES-D depression scale, which was administered to respondents in the 1992 follow-up survey. The scale consists of 20 items referring to behaviors that have been experienced in the past year. Typical items include such questions as: "are you bothered by poor appetite," "do you have trouble keeping your mind on tasks," "do you feel depressed," "do you experience restless sleep," etc. Each item is graded on a four point scale depending upon the frequency of its occurrence. "Never" is graded as 0, "rarely" as 1, "sometimes" as 2, and "often" counts as 3, thus creating a possible score range between 0 and 60.

Table 10 divides all respondents into four relatively equal depression groups. Scale responses showed those growing up in step- and other type families significantly more likely to report depression than either of the other two subgroups. Because depression is gender related, and since there were somewhat unequal gender distributions among each family type

TABLE 10. CES-D Depression Scale Scores Among NLSY Respondents, 1992, Between Those Raised by Both Birth-Parents, in Intact Adoption Families and Children Raised in Step- and Other Families

Percentage / N

		Both Birth Parents	Intact Adopted	Step- and Other Families	Base N
Among all respondents: **					
Very Low	(0-3)	31.3 / 1610	29.3 / 24	24.9 / 766	2400
Low	(4-7)	24.1 / 1241	26.8 / 22	23.8 / 731	1994
High	(8-15)	26.4 / 1359	26.8 / 22	26.0 / 799	2180
Very High	(16-60)	18.2 / 934	17.1 / 14	25.3 / 777	1725
Among males only: **					
Low	(0-7)	59.5 / 1548	62.0 / 31	51.6 / 753	2332
High	(8-60)	40.5 / 1052	38.0 / 19	48.4 / 707	1778
Among females only: **					
Low	(0-7)	51.2 / 1303	46.9 / 15	46.1 / 744	2062
High	(8-60)	48.8 / 1241	53.1 / 17	53.9 / 869	2127

**Chi square probability < .001

Source: National Longitudinal Study of Youth, 1992

subgroup, I re-ran the depression scale among each gender group. Differences still remained significant with more of those growing up in step- and other type families more likely to report depression than any of the other subgroups. With so few adoptees in each separate gender subsample, the depression scale was recalculated into a two-fold division of high and low scores.

Those raised in step- and other families still reported higher levels of depression than any of the other subgroups of adoptees and those raised by both bio-parents. Adoptees were also statistically undistinguished when they were compared to those who were raised exclusively by both bio-parents till age 18.

DISCUSSION

These findings showing higher levels of youth dysfunctionality—greater criminal participation, drinking and drug use—among those raised in attenuated nuclear families, may come as no surprise. There is abundant past research evidence documenting that the experience of family breakup increases the risk of later difficulties and interferes with the fulfillment of conventional occupational, familial and economic goals (Wallerstein and Blakeslee, 1989; Furstenberg, 1990; Whitehead, 1993).

Again, and also not very astonishing, is the pattern linking early youth dysfunctionality to later adult problems and diminished achievement. Many studies attest to the association between early criminal participation and drug taking to later diminished educational attainment, higher unemployment, lower social status, greater marital discord, unhappiness and mood disorders (Chambliss, 1973; Maddux and Desmond, 1981; Vaillant, 1983).

Yet, as one looks over these findings one cannot but wonder how much of these differences might have been byproducts of the social class dissimilarities that were initially observed between those raised by both bio-parents and those from step- and other families. Table 1 demonstrated more children from attenuated nuclear families came from homes where fathers were less well educated and were more often employed as semiskilled manual workers, in contrast to the higher percentages of well educated, professional and managerial fathers among those raised in intact birth parent families.

To control for social class differences I re-ran each bivariate hypothesis (not presented here) splitting the sample up into two separate subgroups: those whose fathers completed a high school or less education, and those whose fathers finished some college or more education. Within each paternal education subgroup, those who grew up in step- and other families still showed higher teen crime and drug use, and later adult drug use and drug-related problems on all of the relationships shown in Tables 2 through 4. The step- and other raised children also showed fewer completing schooling, higher current rates of unemployment, lower social status and asset accumulations, greater marital discord, unhappiness and evidence of depression (compared with those raised in intact birth parent families), shown in Tables 5 through 10.

Regrettably, the NLSY surveys did not query respondents on their exposure to psychotherapy during their teen age years. Though the surveys extensively surveyed respondents' vocational counseling experiences and court-mandated counseling, this is not the same as when families and teenagers voluntarily seek and gain professional psychological help for the developmental problems of their teenage children. Most likely, in the families where psychological counseling was provided, higher percentages of troubled youth would eventually go on to achieve more education, higher job statuses, more assets, and all the rest, compared to the others who did not get counseling. Such evidence would probably suggest that opportunities for counseling (for those from attenuated nuclear families) would be especially helpful not only to relieve the turbulence of adolescence, but also, to reduce the likelihood of encountering later problems and diminished achievement during adulthood.

On the basis of this evidence, the availability of psychological counseling and social services seems to be equally essential for adolescent adoptees to help them cope with the stress producing changes that accompany their movement from childhood to adulthood. For the adoptee, counseling may be indispensable for dealing with the unique adoption-related stresses compounding this turbulent transition.

These results offer confirmation for the theories of adoption positing an identity crisis ordinarily emerging during adolescence with which the adoptee must cope. Such identity confusion issues apparently present special problems to the adoptee. Nearly a fifth (19%) reported running away from home during their adolescent years—three times the percent reporting such behavior among those raised in intact bio-parent families.

Most of the adoptees in the NLSY sample were placed in their adopted homes, as infants. Over four-fifths (84%) reported living in their adoptive homes by age 2. Thus, what we are reporting on here, are adoptees who have experienced minimal family disruption during their early childhoods, whose only known parents were their adoptive parents.

One of the more surprising results of the present investigation was the relative absence of problems reported in later lives of the adoptees, in comparison to the reports given by the children who grew up in step- and other families. Given the extremely wide range of comparisons that were made, one cannot but be impressed by the remarkable level of convergence between the adoptees and their counterparts raised by both bio-parents.

Yet, on the other hand, it might be presumptive to conclude that adoptees are fully successful at putting their adolescent turmoil behind them. The evidence at hand did show significantly more adoptees living in cohabitation relationships prior to marriage. And nearly a statistically significant number of the females reported being less happy in marriage; and the males, too, seemed to be more likely to report higher rates of recent unemployment. These trends could be indicative of possible adjustment deficits and lingering problems related to being adopted. These differences, and the potential indications of vulnerability associated with them to being adopted, should be investigated more closely in future research.

Yet, even though the adoptees may be afflicted by some lingering adjustment deficits, as a group they appeared to stand out in sharp relief to those raised in step- and other families, whose turbulent adolescent years seemed to have left a lasting negative impact on their lives in a wide variety of ways. The evidence at hand suggested on the whole that adoptees were able to reduce their past patterns of teen age delinquency and heavier drug use and were almost able to approximate the conventional goal attainment patterns exhibited by those raised in intact bio-parent families.

We can only speculate as to how adoptees, for the most part, were able to circumvent most problems that may have still plagued their step- and other raised child counterparts. Other studies show adoptive families relying more heavily upon supportive mental health services (Zinn, 1985; Warren, 1992). This may have helped parents restrain their troubled teenagers, eventually assisting them to succeed in the realization of conventional social goals. Yet, it remains to be documented whether the recipients of mental health care actually are more successful in the pursuit of prosocial goals than their counterparts who do not receive such psychotherapeutic aid. This will be a task for future researchers to substantiate.

As one may be struck by the level of convergence between the adult adoptees and those raised in intact bio-parent families, others may be less impressed by the number of such similarities. Keeping in mind that the adoptees were relatively more advantaged to begin with—more had well educated, professional and managerial fathers, then those from intact bio-parent families—one may claim that as a group they may have been collectively more downwardly mobile than the other groups of respondents. Yet, until we have baseline data on the level of difficulties likely to be encountered for people attempting to move into the highest status ranks during the late '80s, we can only wonder whether the obstacles confronted by these adoptees were similar or were any more difficult to surmount. Future researchers may want to address this issue, as well.

In any case, given the sparse number of cases of adoptees available for this study, we can only offer the findings suggestively. Hopefully, in the future similarly conceived research projects will be done with larger samples of adoptees, enabling us to make more definitive tests of the hypotheses presented here about adult adoptive outcomes.

REFERENCES

Bohman, M., & Sigvardsson, S. (1990). Outcome in adoption: Lessons from longitudinal studies. In D. M. Brodzinsky & M. S. Schecter (Eds.), *The Psychology of Adoption* (pp. 93-106). New York: Oxford University Press.

Brodzinsky, D. M., (1993). Long-term outcomes in adoption. *The Future of Children, 3*, 153-166.

Brodzinsky, D. M., Radice, C., Huffman, L., & Merkler, K. (1987). Prevalence of clinically significant symptomatology in a nonclinical sample of adopted and nonadopted children. *Journal of Clinical Child Psychology, 16*, 350-356.

Brodzinsky, D. M., Schecter, D. E., Braff, A.M., & Singer, L. M. (1984). Psychological and academic adjustment in adopted children. *Journal of Consulting and Clinical Psychology, 52*, 582-590.

Center for Human Resource Research (1994). *NLS User's Guide, 1994.* Columbus, OH: Center for Human Resource Research, Ohio State University.

Chambliss, W. J. (1973). The saints and the roughnecks. *Society, 2*, 24-31.

Furstenberg, F. F. (1990). Divorce and the American family. *Annual Review of Sociology, 16*, 379-403.

Lifton, B. J. (1994). *Journey of the Adopted Self,* New York: Basic.

Maddux, J. F., & Desmond, D. P. (1981). *Careers of Opioid Users,* New York: Praeger.

Mikawa, J. K., & Boston, J. A. (1968). Psychological characteristics of adopted children. *Psychiatric Quarterly Supplement, 42*, 274-281.

Norvell, M. & Guy, R. F., (1977). A comparison of self-concept in adopted and nonadopted adolescents. *Adolescence, 12*, 441-448.

Sorosky, A. D., Baran, A., & Pannor, R. (1978). *The Adoption Triangle,* Garden City, New York: Doubleday Anchor.

Stein, L. M., & Hoopes, J. L. (1985). *Identity Formation in the Adopted Adolescent,* New York: Child Welfare League of America.

Wallerstein, J. S., & Blakeslee, S. (1989). *Second Chances: Men, Women and Children A Decade After Divorce.* New York: Ticknor and Fields.

Warren, S. B. (1992). Lower threshold for referral for psychiatric treatment for adopted adolescents. *Journal of the American Academy of Child and Adolescent Psychiatry.* 31, 512-517.

Vaillant, G. B. (1983). *The Natural History of Alcoholism.* Cambridge, MA: Harvard University Press.

Whitehead, D. B. (1993). Dan Quayle was right. *Atlantic Monthly,* 271, 47-84.

Zill, N. (1985). Behavior and learning problems among adopted children: Findings from a U.S. national survey of child health. Paper presented at the Meeting for the Society for Research on Child Development, Toronto, April.

Search and Rescue:
A Belated Critique
of "Growing Up Adopted"

H. David Kirk

SUMMARY. This paper is a critique of a research program carried out by the Search Institute of Minnesota. The report, "Growing Up Adopted," was printed and distributed by the organization itself, and accompanied by grandiose media claims. "The Largest Study Ever of Adoptive Families in the United States," it promised to open new vistas on an old subject. Elegantly turned out, the 1994 report shows sets of data built on questionable research methods resulting in inapplicable if comforting conclusions.

At the heart of the report is a section specifically directed to ideas and concepts derived from Kirk's work. It highlights the questionable methodology and misleading conclusions of the report as a whole.

Whereas Part I of this critique deals with weaknesses in the Search Institute's current research, Part II looks back to data produced by an earlier research program carried out under the same auspices. A decade ago similar problems as those posed in the current study had been explored there. Not only were similar issues studied and approached with greater competence, but the conclusions drawn

H. David Kirk is Emeritus Professor of Sociology, University of Waterloo, and Visiting Scholar, University of Victoria.

Address correspondence to the author at P.O. Box 318, Brentwood Bay, B.C. Canada V8M 1R3 (e-mail address: <dkirk@pinc.com>).

The author wishes to thank Lois Melina, William Feigelman, and Randolph Severson for their kindness in reading and commenting on an earlier draft of this paper.

[Haworth co-indexing entry note]: "Search and Rescue: A Belated Critique of 'Growing Up Adopted.' " Kirk, H. David. Co-published simultaneously in *Marriage & Family Review* (The Haworth Press, Inc.) Vol. 25, No. 3/4, 1997, pp. 225-249; and: *Families and Adoption* (ed: Harriet E. Gross and Marvin B. Sussman) The Haworth Press, Inc., 1997, pp. 225-249. Single or multiple copies of this article are available for a fee from The Haworth Document Delivery Service [1-800-342-9678, 9:00 a.m. - 5:00 p.m. (EST). E-mail address: getinfo@haworth.com].

were more realistic if less comforting. Thus while Part I seeks principally to rescue the good reputation of Kirk's work, Part II seeks to rescue the good reputation of an organization which had evidently set aside earlier and more competent studies in favor of one with lesser credibility.

Indirectly this critique is also an indictment of the public granting agency that sees fit to finance research of this calibre. *[Article copies available for a fee from The Haworth Document Delivery Service: 1-800-342-9678. E-mail address: getinfo@haworth.com]*

PRELIMINARIES

Adoption is always news. Sometimes it is a romantic story of the young couple taking into their family a waif from a foreign country. Or it is the bitter-sweet "reunion" story of an adopted person meeting a birth parent or sibling. More often now it is an account of a dismal battle for custody between birth parents and adopters.

Underneath such reports, whether romantic, nostalgic, or acrimonious, is a darker and until recently more or less hidden theme. Actually it is a very old theme, here resurrected in a new guise: "blood is thicker than water" has become "what outcome for adoption?" That question is fed by recurring reports of adopted people being over-represented among the delinquent and the mentally disturbed.

Not surprisingly, there is pressure to deal scientifically with the "outcome" question, and public funding has been available for such research. One such study was initiated by the Search Institute of Minnesota and supported by the National Institute of Mental Health. Its positive, even euphoric, report "Growing Up Adopted"[1] is the focus of my critique.

Some details in brief: in 1989 the Search Institute launched a study of 715 families with adopted adolescents who had been adopted in infancy. Among issues it investigated were: How do adopted youth navigate through adolescence? How psychologically healthy are they? Does adolescence present greater risks for adopted youth than for their non-adopted counterparts? What factors promote or interfere with psychological health?

Here is what "Growing Up Adopted" says about the results:

> On a series of measures on the formation of identity (there was) little evidence that adopted adolescents are particularly vulnerable . . . (they) are as likely to report positive identity as their non-adopted siblings. . . . adopted adolescents are as deeply attached to their parents as are their non-adopted siblings. . . .

In this study, what we see is a preponderance of families who know both how to be good families and how to be good adoptive families. When this skill is combined with infant adoptions, the possibility of strong attachment, positive identity formation, and positive affirmation of adoption is likely.

It sounds very reassuring, and for people with children adopted in infancy it is. But bear this in mind; (a) the number of infant adoptions was long on the wane in 1989 when the Search Institute launched the study, and (b) for the large number of families with children adopted later in life, many of them children with disabilities, the findings reported in "Growing Up Adopted" do not apply. In "Limitations of the Study" (p. 14) the report says "Other types of adoption (such as older child) introduce new dynamics that would likely change the findings in significant ways." Thus this study cannot begin to address the question of adoption outcome. That question would have called for a very different research design.

WHY THIS CRITIQUE?

In a climate of questioning whether adoption, as presently practiced, is in the interest of children, the Search Institute's work could and should be scrutinized for the methods it employed and the conclusions it drew from its findings. Although this critique will deal with some such issues, its motivational thrust is personal: it is to protect the integrity of my work which in the report "Growing Up Adopted" has been distorted and misused.

Why should my work need rescuing from the Search Institute (here also called SEARCH) to which I had lent my name as a consultant?[2] Ordinarily, when my research is quoted incorrectly, the circumstances do not call for a public response.[3] That is not so in the case of the SEARCH report "Growing Up Adopted" (also called GROW); here the situation is different. If the report had appeared as an article in a professional journal, circulated among insiders, a rejoinder note would have sufficed. But elegantly designed, and with the trappings of a scientific report, GROW was widely circulated in places and among readers not given to scientific probity. Thus prominently mentioned, but fallaciously presented and interpreted, my work was used by the authors as a "straw man" to build their case. For these reasons my critique must now become a public document. But to be effective a critique must come close on the heels of the thesis it is meant to answer. This critique should thus have appeared soon after

"Growing Up Adopted" was issued. Having been unavoidably delayed, it must now make its case without the benefit of immediacy.

ORGANIZATION

"Search and Rescue" consists of two parts. Part I, "Rescuing the Shared Fate Theory,"[4] concerns itself principally with my work and the way the Search Institute's report misrepresents it. Part II, "Rescuing the Search Institute from Itself," shows that GROW short-changed the Search Institute's record of previous research. The implication of an apparent rupture between earlier studies and the present one raises serious questions. It raises questions about the judgments of those responsible for the research that led to GROW, and about the judgment of those who finance such research.

I. RESCUING THE SHARED FATE THEORY

Rescuing my work from SEARCH poses a dilemma: on the face of it I should be pleased that in the section called "Dealing with Differences in Adoptive Families" the authors devote four pages (56-59) principally to my work. But already on the first page they distort it:

> One of the more interesting debates in the adoption literature focuses on how families deal with differences inherent in the life of adoptive families. Kirk . . . advanced the notion that adoptive parenthood is marked by role handicaps. Among these are the stress of infertility, the stigma associated with adoptive parenthood, the lack of role models for parenting, the tension of disclosing adoption to their child and dealing with the child's inquiries and uncertainties about identity. Kirk posited two approaches to these tasks and challenges. Some families practice "rejection of difference" in which they take the sting out of adoption by denying that adoptive family life is different and suppressing communication about adoption. The approach seems to be that if we pretend our child is not adopted, everything will be o.k.

> In our study (not seeing adoptive family life as different and suppressing communication about and acknowledgment of adoption) are very different phenomena. But the conceptualization of rejection-of-

difference does not readily apply to the families in this research project. . . . *the two parts of the equation (not seeing adoptive family life as different and suppressing communication about . . . adoption) are not necessarily linked. In our study these are very separate phenomena.* [italics added for emphasis, HDK]

Here we have a straw man. Anyone who has read my work knows that I have never spoken of *suppression* of communication. Nor does my work posit a *necessary* link between "rejection of difference" and a low level of parent-child communication. Instead, what my studies have consistently shown is *statistically probable*[5] associations between parental "rejection of difference," little empathy, and inadequate parent-child communication. This misreading of the Shared Fate theory is not a lone error; GROW has built its case on more than errors of interpretation.[6]

The Search Institute researchers put before adopted youth and their parents questionnaire items ostensibly based on my work but actually derived from misinterpreted concepts and misapplied constructs. With invalid results thus obtained they declared the Shared Fate theory inapplicable to the families in their sample. While it may be true, as GROW asserts, that inferences from the Shared Fate theory are outdated and do not apply to the families in these studies, GROW's data fail to make that case.

A Principal Focus of Misinterpretation: Role Handicap

Sociological reasoning is often misunderstood, not only among uninitiated people but also in circles where technical or professional training and interests should make for greater sophistication. This may explain some of GROW's confusion about, and misinterpretations of, the concept "role handicap." Professionals whose work touches on adoption—especially psychologists, psychiatrists, and social workers—typically look at the subject of their inquiry through psychological lenses. Individual psychology tends to emphasize perceptions, dispositions, and feelings, often to the exclusion of structural factors of milieu. Sociological frames of reference on the other hand emphasize the social and cultural milieu, minimizing personal affect and cognition. Being sociology-based, the Shared Fate theory draws attention to two facets of milieu: (a) opportunities thought to be one's due become "normative" (i.e., culturally given) role expectations, and (b) by upsetting normative role expectations, drastic change puts a premium on innovation. Change-induced transitions from established to makeshift roles tend therefore to create barriers to satisfactory role performances. Such barriers are called "role handicaps,"[7] making up a key concept useful for studying the impact of drastic change on social relations.[8]

How does role handicap feature in the context of adoption? Involuntarily childless people will typically, at one time, have assumed themselves able to create offspring. Then, on top of the handicap of being unable to procreate, they find that their infertility is being judged invidiously. Failing to meet normative (culturally given) role expectations readily leads to stigma and self-deprecation. Misconstruing the meaning of role handicap, the authors of GROW treated it as a psychodynamic rather than the sociostructural concept it is meant to be. In that connection, inspect this paragraph:

> The adoption literature describes a number of "role handicaps" that are normative [sic] for adoptive parents. These include unresolved feelings about infertility, discomfort in talking about adoption with their children, feeling stigmatized, and experiencing hardship or trauma during the adoption process. Though each of these "handicaps" is a potentially serious dynamic requiring recognition and attention, each is relatively uncommon among these parents. (GROW, p. 7)

The claim that "the adoption literature describes . . . 'role handicaps' as normative for adoptive parents" is utterly alien to me, and I have not seen that use of "normative" in any sociological[9] work. If role handicaps were in fact *normative* in the sociological sense, it would mean that people had initially been taught to expect disappointing events, such as a inability to procreate, and its social *sequelae.* This kind of mixup between sociological and psychological definitions has elsewhere confounded the authors of this study. In that context it is instructive to compare three related issues that were turned into very different research questions: sociologically by me and psychologically by the authors of GROW (see Figure 1).

Note that *my* questions asked how parents initially experienced the milieu, whereas those phrased by the Search Institute dealt mainly[10] with long-term feelings. Milieu experiences imply an awareness of role handicaps (i.e., an awareness of structural barriers to role enactment) whereas long-term feelings focus on the consequences of role handicap. Since certain role handicap patterns (e.g., the inability to produce offspring) are closely linked to adoption, it is reasonable to suggest that in the Minneapolis of the 1990s my milieu questions would have been answered in the affirmative. But feelings, free of a particular context, might in 1961 have run a greater gamut, paralleling the results obtained by the Search Institute.

It may be true, as GROW claims, that as the culture has been changing,

FIGURE 1. Comparison of Sociological and Psychological approaches in operationalizing research questions.

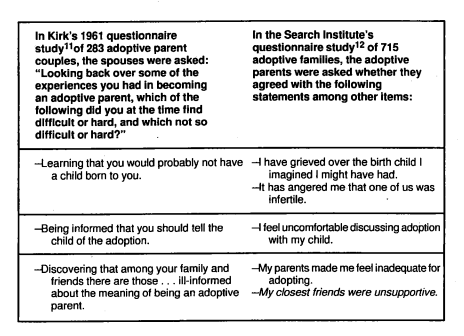

In Kirk's 1961 questionnaire study[11] of 283 adoptive parent couples, the spouses were asked: "Looking back over some of the experiences you had in becoming an adoptive parent, which of the following did you at the time find difficult or hard, and which not so difficult or hard?"	In the Search Institute's questionnaire study[12] of 715 adoptive families, the adoptive parents were asked whether they agreed with the following statements among other items:
—Learning that you would probably not have a child born to you.	—I have grieved over the birth child I imagined I might have had. —It has angered me that one of us was infertile.
—Being informed that you should tell the child of the adoption.	—I feel uncomfortable discussing adoption with my child.
—Discovering that among your family and friends there are those . . . ill-informed about the meaning of being an adoptive parent.	—My parents made me feel inadequate for adopting. —*My closest friends were unsupportive.*

some role handicapping conditions have lessened. If true, adoption may be "less stigmatized now." Adopters may in fact be receiving more support from fellow adopters and from their families and friends than did adopters in the 1950s and sixties. But on the basis of what is known about currently childless people who adopt, I question GROW's assertion that "very few of the parents in this study were saddled with a deep grieving about infertility, even though most adoptions in this study occurred as a partial result of infertility" (p. 56). Let the Search Institute check how today's husbands view involuntary childlessness as compared with the way their wives view it. In a phase of my 1961 studies 283 husbands and wives were given identical questionnaires,[13] simultaneously but separately administered. We found a vast difference between the wives' degrees and styles of grieving and those expressed by their husbands.

Even more problematic is the fact that the authors of "Growing Up Adopted" treat the absence of grieving over childlessness as an asset. In contrast, the Shared Fate theory sees the memory of grief, decontaminated of its nagging quality, to be capable of reminding the adopters to put themselves in the shoes of the child. The child, learning that adoption means having been given up, may need much empathic support. Thus the Shared Fate theory suggests that the adoptive parents' *memory* of grief can stimulate their empathy with the child's inchoate grieving, even anger, over a lost past. If the GROW parents had in fact not been grieving, then, in the light of the Shared Fate theory, they would have been less capable than the parents in my studies to put themselves empathically into their children's shoes.

"Rejection of Difference" and "Adjustment"

I have previously noted that, while my work is prominently displayed in GROW, it is also called not applicable to GROW's adoptive families. This occurs in the context of a discussion of rejection of difference which GROW treats as a monolithic concept. But in my work rejection of difference is part of a continuum from "acknowledgment" to "rejection of difference." Thus GROW not only truncates the concept itself but totally distorts its implication. To see what I am driving at, please recall this quote from GROW:

> Kirk posited two approaches to these tasks and challenges. Some families practice "rejection of difference" in which they take the sting out of adoption by denying that adoptive family life is different and suppressing communication about adoption. The approach seems to be that if we pretend our child is not adopted, everything will be OK.

Now comes the *corpus delicti [remarks of my own are shown in italics and brackets-HDK]:*

> One can imagine that this approach–posited to interfere with the healthy adjustment of adopted children *[this "adjustment" clause is spun out of thin air[14]]* could have been common when Kirk did his original research in the 1950s. But the conceptualization of rejection-of-difference does not readily apply to the families in this research project–*[by implication the Search Institute seems also to be saying that, in contrast with the families of my earlier studies, its parents now have "healthily adjusted" children].*
> In our study, these are very separate phenomena. . . . only a very small minority of families practice a communication pattern resembling suppression or denial. But nearly all parents and adopted adolescents see no significant difference between adoptive and other

families. Among the nearly 80 percent of families who do openly and comfortably discuss adoption, nearly all parents reject the view that adoptive families are different—*[and once again: misconstruing the meaning of "rejection of difference"]*. Even most adopted adolescents reject the view. These views are documented in Figure 4.7 *[see my notes on Figure 4.7, here shown as Figure 2.]* Hence, this renders the traditional concept of rejection-of-difference as an inappropriate construct for understanding our families *[a conclusion built on the false premise of a misconstrued concept]*.

What is of interest, though, is why today's adoptive families so easily reject the concept that adoptive families are different. *[Now the false conclusion is being explained.]* One can make the case that many of the things that challenged and stressed adoptive families decades ago are less visible today. Some of the stressors have changed meaning.[15]

In summary, it is not the rejection of the fact that adoptive families are different that is problematic. Nor is it the acknowledgment of adoptive families as different (Brodzinsky, 1987; Kirk, 1964) that promotes the healthy adjustment of adopted children *[there it is again: "healthy adjustment"]*. As we have seen, nearly all children and parents in this study downplay the differences (and . . . most adopted adolescents are thriving). So the issue of adoption can't be the issue. More predictive of the mental health of adopted children is the other part of the original formulation: the issue of open vs. closed communication. Combining the findings presented in the previous section with an adaptation of the conceptual language advanced by Kirk and Brodzinsky, it is proposed that families that practice *denial of child's difference* or *insistence on child's difference* interfere with healthy development, while those that *promote acceptance of child's difference* attitude promote it.

What are those "findings presented in the previous section"? In most of these families talking about adoption "is no big deal." But "we estimate, that in about 15 to 20 percent of families, communication is awkward, uncomfortable, and largely non-existent." Where adoption is stressed, or talked about frequently, things don't go so well.

Have these researchers read *Shared Fate* and *Adoptive Kinship?* Where do they find me arguing that "acknowledgment of difference" means stressing the fact of adoption, or talking about it frequently? In the Shared Fate theory, when adoptive parents acknowledge to themselves that their social position as parents differs from that of people who have produced offspring, they tend also to be sensitive to the child's untutored attempts at

FIGURE 2. As quoted from GROW (where it appears as Figure 4.7).

	ATTITUDE MEASURE	PERCENT AGREEING*	
		Father	Mother
PARENTS' ATTITUDES	I think being an adoptive parent is different than being a birthparent.	4%	5%
	I think that adoptive families are different from other families.	3%	4%
	I think that raising an adopted child is different than raising a non-adopted child.	5%	6%
		Boys	Girls
ADOPTED ADOLESCENTS' ATTITUDES	My mother thinks that raising an adopted child is different from raising a non-adopted child.	5%	4%
	My father thinks that raising an adopted child is different from raising a non-adopted child.	6%	4%
	I think adoptive families are different from other families.	8%	13%

*Agreement is defined as the percent who say the statement is often or always true.

This figure originally appeared as Figure 4.7 in "Growing Up Adopted," published in 1994 by the Search Institute. Reprinted with permission. For further information, see Note 16.

understanding the complicated facts of adoption. Such empathy helps the parents to be open to their child's groping for answers. That's what "communication" means in *my* work—it does not mean forcing the subject down the child's throat. And my dependent variable is not the global concept "healthy development," but the leaner concept "trust," measured by the number and kinds of questions the child feels free to ask the parents. The parents' readiness to listen to their child enhances the child's trust in them.[17]

Denial at SEARCH: The Case of the Ignored Caveat

On May 2, 1994 I received by courier a pre-publication package of the text and tables that a few weeks later would, almost identically, become the final "Growing Up Adopted" report. On reading this document marked "CONFIDENTIAL—do not reproduce or quote" I became sufficiently concerned about its contents that two days later (May 4), I sent by fax an urgent letter to the project's research directors, Drs. Benson and

Sharma. That letter expressed my deep misgivings about what I perceived as the blatant misuse of my ideas. Here is the principal paragraph of my complaint:

> Please refer to Figure 4.7. I have always defined "acknowledgment of difference" situationally and never categorically. Adoptive parents are not different from other parents *as persons;* neither are adopted children different from other children *as children.* What differs for them are the circumstances in which they find themselves, the thoughts they have about these circumstances, and how other people think about adoption. The indicators of Acknowledgment-of-Difference on pages 43-44 of my book *Adoptive Kinship* make that clear.

GROW was issued on June 24, but I had received no reply to my May 4 letter; my caveat had been ignored. In fact, the SEARCH team has never responded to my concern. That is why this section is called "Denial at SEARCH."

My defense of the Shared Fate theory is not an exercise in doctrine but in rescuing the sociological imagination. In the exploration of the human condition, explanations—sometimes called theories—are merely heuristic thresholds to the search for new knowledge. Theories attract competing ideas and in competition one must play by the rules. *The rules for testing human behavior theories require replication. The Search Institute did not even attempt to replicate the Shared Fate theory.*

The philosopher E.A. Burtt, in a preface to one of his books, says that an author should claim much for his work, whether he delivers what he claims or not. Others will soon judge if the work lives up to the claims.[18] On that note I rest my case against the Search Institute's misinterpretations of the Shared Fate theory.

This critique could have ended at this point. But who would then remember and rescue the solid work that had been done at the Search Institute in previous years? That second and final rescue attempt now follows.

II. RESCUING THE SEARCH INSTITUTE FROM ITSELF

When I first read GROW I kept thinking that something was missing. But what was it? Early on[19] in the text one finds the admission that the study lacks a control group of non-adopted youth. Nevertheless, much later some pseudo-control group data[20] show up. Interesting as these data, stemming from a concurrent but unrelated study[21] may be, they do not satisfactorily address the central issue identified in "Highlights of the Study." That issue, mentioned on the report's first page, refers to "the oft-cited dictum that adopted adolescents are over-represented in mental health treatment populations."

It turns out that my sense of something missing from GROW had this origin: a decade ago I had seen data from SEARCH studies that in retrospect seem highly pertinent to the persistent but unreliable[22] claim of over-representation. With "High-Risk Behavior" so prominently featured in GROW, why had the pertinent mid-1980s data not been included? Could they have been forgotten or lost? Unfortunately the authors of GROW do not tell us.

GROW'S Approach to Studying High-Risk Behavior

Of concern to public policy experts, parents and educators is the untenably high rate of health-compromising behaviors among American adolescents (Benson, 1993; Blyth, 1993, Dryfoos, 1990).[23] These come in many forms: binge drinking, illicit drug use, early sexual activity and adolescent pregnancy, violence and suicide. These behaviors have no economic, racial-ethnic, or town size boundaries. To understand adolescent well-being requires exploration of these issues.

Search Institute's on-going assessment of 6th-12th grade youth includes an index of 20 forms of high-risk behavior. These [24] are defined in Figure 5.3. This index was included in the current study, providing. . . . opportunity to compare adopted adolescents to . . . teenagers studied in . . . Colorado, Illinois, Minnesota, and Wisconsin. . . .

As shown in Figure 5.4, on nearly all high-risk indicators, percentages are lower for adopted adolescents than for the general public school sample. There are a few exceptions, including daily cigarette use for 16-18 year olds (23% for adopted adolescents, 20% for the comparison sample).

When comparing the overall index score (i.e., the average number of 20 high-risk behaviors), the mean for adopted adolescents (1.95) is appreciably below that for the comparison sample (2.89). For adopted adolescents there is an age difference but no gender difference (Figure 5.5). Both age and gender differences are found in the comparison sample. . . . we find no evidence that adoption is particularly problematic for boys.

Health-compromising behavior is untenably high for all adoles-

· *cents, both adopted and not. But it is, according to these data, no worse for adopted youth than their nonadopted peers.* [italics added for emphasis, HDK]

The emphasized paragraph points to a basic flaw in the Search Institute's studies of the 1990s. Its sample consists of families with children adopted below the age of 15 months. It represents that shrinking[25] number of adoptive families who start family life with infants. Adoption has changed; a decreasing proportion of adoptive families fit the pattern of the Search Institute's sample. Although the Search Institute cannot be faulted for its choice of that restricted sample, it can and must be faulted for unwarranted inferences drawn from that sample. Thus "Growing Up Adopted" cannot really tell about the risks that adoption poses to children and families in the current adoption scene.

Earlier Studies of High-Risk Behavior

During 1983 it was my good fortune to be in touch with Professor Arthur L. Johnson, a sociologist at the University of Minnesota who also served as a Search Institute research consultant. That is how I learned about two studies of adolescents, both of which provided comparison data for adopted and non-adopted youth. The unpublished abstract[26] of a descriptive paper on these studies is available to me and I will quote from it here:

> Two large data banks are utilized to compare the incidence of selected problem behaviors among adopted and non-adopted youth. From a representative sample of 10,342 Minnesota youth in grades 8, 10, and 12, we find slightly higher, but consistent incidences of chemical use by adopted boys, and particularly in 12th grade. Adopted girls report slightly lower incidence rates for legal drugs (alcohol, tobacco) and illicit drugs (cocaine, heroin, LSD, and PCP), and slightly higher usage of other drugs used unlawfully (amphetamines, aerosols, barbiturates, and tranquilizers). Though advantaged by higher education of their parents, higher marital stability of parents, and more involvement in organized youth activities, adopted youth were less likely than other youth to feel comfortable talking about drugs or alcohol with their parents and would be more likely to turn to an "adult friend" than a parent if they had a drug problem.
>
> Comparing adopted and non-adopted youth in a study of 8,162 young adolescents in grades five through nine and their mothers, we find the following:

1. No differences between youth adopted in early childhood and other youth on alcohol use, drug use, tobacco use, norm violations, and aggressive behavior.
2. Significantly higher rates of the above behaviors were found, however, for youth reporting later adoption by one or both parents or now living with a step-parent.
3. Slightly higher indicators of depression (suicide thoughts, alienation, low self-esteem) among early adoptees and stronger indications for later adoptees.
4. Substantially higher indicators of parent-youth conflicts and tensions among both early and later adoptees.
5. Mothers of adopted children (both early and later) perceive slightly more child handicaps (particularly learning disabilities or achievement.)

These findings suggest patterns of stress which may be more typical of some adopted youth and their parents. These data are unable to determine which differences may have linkages to genetic and congenital factors and which are related to the unique environment of being an adopted child or parent.

Further research is urgently needed to identify major elements accounting for these differences. [emphasis added-HDK]

Once again a final sentence has been emphasized. This time I want to draw attention to the fact that Drs. Johnson and Benson were calling for further research that might explain the differences obtained in the two mid-1980s youth studies. At this point in the story of the Search Institute's 1994 report, it should not be necessary to clarify that the studies reported in "Growing Up Adopted" do not continue the work done under Search Institute auspices in the 1980s. Why this break with the past work occurred is a question that the present critique cannot answer. All that we can do here is to elaborate on some of 1980s findings and wonder . . .

The Young Adolescence Study of 1984

Here I continue to quote from the summary by Drs. Johnson and Benson, with special reference to the younger group (grades five through nine).

The second data bank for re-analysis is the Young Adolescence Study, conducted by Search Institute in 1984, in collaboration with 13 national youth serving agencies, 11 national churches, some 4-H

Extension groups, and the National Society of Homes for Children. Over 8,000 youth in grades 5 through 9 completed a 319-item survey. Companion surveys were completed by over 6,000 mothers and 4,300 fathers. Youth survey findings, used in this analysis, focused on comparing four youth samples: total youth sample, youth living their first five years of life with both adoptive parents (Early Adoptees Sample), other youth reporting having lived with one adoptive parent and with adoptive parents or parent currently (later Adoptees Sample), and other youth not included in the above adoptive samples (Step-Parent Sample).

A few of the statistical tables showing data obtained in the early youth study are of special interest in the light of the data reported in "Growing Up Adopted." Tables shown in Figures 3, 4, 5, and 6 were prepared in January 1986 by Professor Arthur L. Johnson. Please note that the numbers in the cells indicate the percent of higher (+) or lower (−) scores obtained when the particular category (e.g., "Early Adoptees") is being compared with the summary score for the total group of 5th to 9th grade youth.

First a summary table for high-risk behavior. Note that this table is the only one to show totals for the number of young people in the four sub-samples: Early Adoptees (302), Later Adoptees (320), Step-children (704), Single Parent Youth (742).

IMPLICATIONS

(The reader is advised to study Figures 3-6 prior to, or in conjunction with, "Implications.")

Even a few data from the earlier studies of the Search Institute make for skepticism about the euphoria that emanates from GROW. While the "early youth" data from 1984 support the claim that youth adopted very early in life do generally well, a very different picture is obtained for young people who claim to have lived with one or more adoptive parents only after their first five years.[27] Since the data for late adoptees often resemble the data for stepchildren, I conclude that those children who have less firm "social ground"[28] under their feet are typically at greater risk in growing up, whether adopted or not.

The euphoria emanating from GROW may seem reassuring to some parents and certain professionals. But if the age-limited[29] interpretations proposed in GROW were taken as valid and applied to adoptions generally, they could have deleterious consequences. In an era of fiscal constraints there is a strong public policy urge to have dependent children of any age[30] placed for adoption, which appears like an inexpensive option

FIGURE 3. The Young Adolescence Study of 1984: Youth Behavior.

CONTENT DOMAIN: YOUTH BEHAVIOR
HYPOTHESIS: Adopted children are more likely than other children to have behavior problems, more anti-social behavior, and more chemical substance use.

DATA: AVERAGE PERCENT DIFFERENCES FROM TOTAL SAMPLE

BEHAVIOR CATEGORY	Early Adoptees (N = 302)	Later Adoptees (N = 320)	Stepchildren (N = 704)	Single Parent Youth (N = 742)
norm violation # of items = [3] (shoplifting, cheating, lying)	+1	+11	+7	+5
Aggressive Behavior [3] (vandalism, hitting, fighting)	+2	+16	+12	+5
Alcohol Use [2] (frequency, drunk)	0	+20	+14	+7
Drug Use [3] (Pot, Pills, hard drugs)	−2	+22	+14	+6
Cigarette Use [1]	0	+21	+17	+6
AVERAGE ALL CATEGORIES	0	+18	+14	+6

FINDINGS:

1. Early Adoptees—Hypothesis rejected—their anti-social behavior and chemical substances usage is similar to youth in the total sample.

2. Later Adoptees— Hypothesis is strongly confirmed. Of all groups compared, they are *most* likely to engage in these deviant behaviors. (An average of 18% higher on the 12 behaviors studied.)

3. Step-children average 14% higher, and Single Parent Youth are slightly higher than all youth sampled (6% higher).

COMMENTS:

1. Youth adopted by one parent or later appear especially vulnerable to various deviant behaviors, especially drug usage (over 20% higher).

2. These huge differences are expected to be reduced, when gender is controlled. This group has 11% more males, 58.6% vs. 47.4% in the total sample. Mean grade level in school, however, are very similar for groups compared.

3. It remains to test whether these deviant behaviors rise more rapidly with aging or school grade change, compared with other youth.

FIGURE 4. Life threatening attitudes.

CONTENT DOMAIN: LIFE-THREATENING ATTITUDES
HYPOTHESIS: Adopted children experience more trauma leading to more thoughts about suicide

AVERAGE PERCENT DIFFERENCE FROM TOTAL SAMPLE

DATA:	EARLY ADOPTEES	LATER ADOPTEES	STEP CHILD	SINGLE PARENT
1. Frequency of suicidal thoughts	+4	+10	+7	+2
2. Worry about killing self	+3	+11	+7	+1
3. Worry about dying soon	0	+8	+5	+3
AVERAGE [3]	+2	+10	+6	+2

FINDINGS:
1. Later Adoptees—Hypothesis strongly confirmed—data are consistent in showing more youth in this category express suicidal thoughts.
2. Early Adoptees—Hypothesis not clearly substantiated, only slightly higher.
3. Step-children also show somewhat higher rates of suicidal thoughts.

of care. It is likely that such policies would prove not only detrimental to many dependent children, especially those in their later teens, but also to adoptive families and in the long run to the institution of adoptive kinship.

There is another important implication that arises from the difference between children adopted early and late in their lives. The often repeated claim that adopted adolescents make up an undue proportion of clients of mental health services could at least partly be explained with reference to data from "early" vs. "late" adoptions. If the appearance and rising tide of this presumed fact were found to have coincided with a similar increase in the adoption of older and other special needs children, it should make for serious second thoughts. It might very well mean that the claim of over-representation is spurious, that it is not adoption but handicap that makes for whatever over-representation was shown to exist. To put such loose and potentially damaging claims to rest, relevant research ought to be undertaken soon, preferably by disinterested scholars applying demographic skills.

FIGURE 5. Developmental processes.

CONTENT DOMAIN: DEVELOPMENTAL PROCESSES–DEPRESSION, ETC.
HYPOTHESIS: Adopted youth are more vulnerable to personality stress, such as depression, alienation, low self esteem, isolation.

AVERAGE PERCENT DIFFERENCE FROM TOTAL SAMPLE

DATA:	EARLY ADOPTEES	LATER ADOPTEES	STEP CHILD	SINGLE PARENT
1. SOCIAL ALIENATION (lonely, misunderstood, kids tease) [3]	+4	+11	+5	+4
2. LOW SELF-ESTEEM [5]	+3	+10	+7	+1
3. WEAK FRIENDSHIP NETWORK [3]	−5	+6	+4	+1
AVERAGE	+1	+9	+5	+2

By adding LIFE THREATENING ATTITUDES, we approximate a depression scale

LIFE THREATENING ATTITUDES [3]	+2	+9	+6	+2

FINDINGS;

1. Later Adoptees–Hypothesis is consistently supported by all of the measures, indicating lower self-esteem, higher social alienation, weaker friendship ties, and more life threatening attitudes, thus indicating more symptoms of depression.
2. Early Adoptees–Data not fully consistent with hypothesis. They have an above average friendship network, rather than a weak one, that could partly compensate for slightly more alienation and slightly less self-esteem.

COMMENT:

1. Controlling on gender, grade, and possibly other variables might clarify these relationships, as well as more closely identify those youths most vulnerable to these patterns.

FIGURE 6. Family climate.

CONTENT DOMAIN: FAMILY CLIMATE
HYPOTHESIS: Adoptive homes will have less harmony and warmth among family members and between the parents.

AVERAGE PERCENT DIFFERENCES FROM TOTAL SAMPLE

DATA	EARLY ADOPTEES	LATER ADOPTEES	STEP CHILD	SINGLE PARENT
Family members not close [2]	+2	+13.5	+10	+6.5
Low harmony between parents [3]	−2	+7.0	+9	+27.0

FINDINGS: Hypothesis supported for later adoptees and step children, with less harmony among family members, including spouses. Early adoptees show harmony between the parents and generally close bonds among family members. This supports other findings that they receive more affection from their parents, even though they are also held to perceived impossible standards and unrealistic or oppressive control and discipline techniques.

Statistical significance data concerning the above tables (supplied by Professor Johnson) will be found in Note 31.

WHO PAID THE PIPER?

It is probably not fair to lay all the blame for its poor performance on the Search Institute. Some blame surely belongs to those in NIMH who apparently vote continuing financial support for research without a final quality control check. This information derives from a September 23, 1993 memorandum sent by the Search Institute's Jean Wachs to "project agencies and consultants": "We have learned recently that the National Institute of Mental Health does not require an end-of-project technical report; rather, they prefer that we disseminate information through scholarly articles."[32]

Usually it takes many months, sometimes years, for research information to be published in refereed journals. The Search Institute, however, did not wait for the publication of the research papers it had submitted, but independently issued its own GROW report. It happens that quite recently there appeared a critical review[33] of GROW with specific reference to the Search Institute's self-publication of that report. That review said:

Often with such a study, the scientific debate over the validity of the findings would take place before they are released to the public. The findings would be evaluated when the articles on the research were submitted to professional journals for review prior to publication. Once the scientific community gave its approval to the data and its interpretation by agreeing to publish the findings, they would be released to the public.

However, the report of this study was self-published and released simultaneously to a presentation at a nationwide adoption conference.

Whatever re-interpretation of the data there may be is unlikely to receive as widespread publicity as the original report. [emphasis added, HDK]

The same issue of *Adopted Child* also censured other aspects of GROW, among these the large number of non-respondents (approximately half of the sample of 715 families) and that these were not followed up. If you have a million dollars to spend on a survey, you should be able to follow-up and learn at least something about the families who failed to, or refused to, answer the survey forms. In one such follow-up study of non-respondents I made discoveries that shed new light on the investigation. Among other things it was found that the response rate went up steeply among couples who had adopted more than one child,[34] and that non-respondents had remained mainly one-child adopters.

As my critique of even small parts of the methodology underlying GROW showed, its competence leaves much to be desired. In an interview with *Adopted Child,* Anu Sharma, one of the principal investigators, said "I feel comfortable with the methodology, but the interpretation of the data is open to debate. . . ."[35] One wonders what the scientists who reviewed the project's methodology thought—did they share her methodological comfort? They must have done so, for why else would NIMH have awarded the Search Institute a million dollars, a not inconsiderable sum for this kind of research. They must have known that the emperor had no clothes to start with, and that he would not likely be clothed later.

AUTHOR NOTE

H. David Kirk attended high schools in Germany and England and came to the USA in 1938. At that time his parents changed the family name from Kirchheimer. After the war Kirk completed an undergraduate degree at the City College of New York and went on to study at Cornell

University. Having been a refugee from Nazi persecution, he used his sociological training to explore issues in social mobility and integration. At first he did so in the context of people made homeless in their own country: Japanese-Americans forcibly "relocated" during World War II. This study of "the loyalties of men in crisis," alerted Kirk to other instances of forced migration and its consequences. Noting that such issues can be studied in the context of kinship and, defining adoption as attempts at integrating previously unrelated "migrants," it led to his Ph.D. In 1954, on the faculty of the McGill University School of Social Work, he launched a program of "Studies in Group and Family Life," incorporating the Adoption Research Project. In 1964 this resulted in the now classic *Shared Fate.* That year Kirk left McGill University to join the University of Waterloo. He continued to pursue his old interest in adoption along somewhat different lines. Studies of family law and policy resulted in 1981 in *Adoptive Kinship.* Two years after his retirement from teaching (1988) appeared *Exploring Adoptive Family Life,* a collection of his adoption papers and research instruments. Currently Kirk lives with his wife on Vancouver Island and retains links to the world of learning as a visiting scholar at the University of Victoria.

NOTES

1. "Growing Up Adopted: A Portrait of Adolescents and their Families," by Peter L. Benson, Anu R. Sharma, and Eugene C. Roehlkepartain, SEARCH INSTITUTE, Minneapolis, 1994.

2. Mostly unpaid: in 1992 I received a cheque for $300, after which there was no further payment. This is not a complaint, just a memorandum of fact.

3. One example of incorrect interpretations of my work to which I did not respond occurred in a scholarly paper by Kenneth Kaye and Sarah Warren (1988, June), Discourse About Adoption in Adoptive Families, *Journal of Family Psychology,* pp. 406-433. There the views erroneously attributed to me were reaching a relatively small number of specialists, whereas in the case of GROW, that report was widely distributed, especially among agencies whose personnel would not likely distinguish between genuine and spurious references.

4. The Shared Fate theory of adoptive relationships, developed in my book *Shared Fate,* 1964, 1984, has become widely accepted as correctly describing and explaining the dynamics of adoptive parent-child relations.

5. Rather than a *necessary* association.

6. Part II of this critique will show serious flaws of commission and omission in the design and execution of the study. To be worth its salt, any study of atypical families would require a control group of families of the mainstream. But no planned-for control group is found in "GROW" even though a kind of pseudo-control group suddenly surfaces well past the middle of the report (p. 67). There,

in a footnote, we discover that this supposed "control group" stems from an altogether separate study, with a different sampling base. In addition there is the problem of a large number of non-respondents, larger even than is typically found in survey research. One would think that the SEARCH team would have made preparation to follow up at least a random sample of non-respondents. However, no attempt at following-up non-respondents was made by the people who produced GROW.

7. "role-handicap." A term introduced into sociological literature by H. D. Kirk (see his *Shared Fate: A Theory of Adoption and Mental Health.* 1964) to point [sic] the contrasts between people in certain kinds of situations, where the culture provides in the one case for behavioural expectations, and in the other case it does not do so, or does so inadequately . . . Again, the situation of people facing disaster is different if the disaster occurs during war-time, when the populace is prepared for hardships, than it is in peace-time, when they are less prepared psychologically, and we may say that the latter represents a case of role-handicap. Mitchell, G. D. (Ed.). *(1979). A New Dictionary of Sociology* (p. 162) London.

8. H. David Kirk, "The Impact of Drastic Change on Social Relations–A Model for the Identification and Specification of Stress," in G.K. Zollschan and W. Hirsch, *Explorations in Social Change,* 1964.

9. The sociological meaning of the term "normative" refers to cultural norms or rules of behavior, i.e., to what 'ought' to exist or be done. In experimental psychology, on the other hand, "normative" denotes a statistical norm, i.e., an average test score.

10. Because the questionnaire item *"My closest friends were unsupportive"* is an exception in this list, it is shown in italics. It refers not to a feeling state but to a socially structured event.

11. See *Shared Fate* pp. 14-15.

12. See "Growing Up Adopted" pp. 84-85.

13. That study is reported in *Shared Fate* pp. 2-4.

14. Nowhere in my writings will one find a reference to adopted children's–or for that matter non-adopted children's–"healthy adjustment." But in the context of an agenda to invalidate the Shared Fate theory, the notion of "healthy adjustment" becomes a useful ploy. By introducing "Adjustment" (instead of "Trust"– see *Adoptive Kinship* pp. 46-47) as the ultimate dependent variable, a foreign body has been smuggled into the Shared Fate theory. For readers who view human development through strong psychological lenses, introducing an "adjustment" variable can serve as a veritable Trojan Horse.

15. There follow four examples of "former" stresses: the "once-upon-a-time" stigma, the former grieving about infertility, the former lack of role models, and the former (!) stress of telling the child about the adoption–lately eased by "effective assistance and counsel provided by adoption professionals."

16. The serious reader is also referred to the following journal articles:
McGue, M. K., Sharma, A. R., & Benson, P. L. (1996). The effect of common rearing on adolescent adjustment: Evidence from a U.S. adoption cohort. *Developmental Psychology, 32,* 604-613.

McGue, M. K., Sharma, A. R., & Benson, P. L. (1996). Parent and sibling influences on adolescent alcohol use and misuse: Evidence from a U. S. adoption cohort. *Journal of Studies on Alcohol, 57,* 8-18.

Sharma, A. R., McGue, M. K., & Benson, P. L. (1996). The emotional and behavioral adjustment of United States adopted adolescents: Part I. An overview. *Children and Youth Services Review, 18,* 77-94.

Sharma, A. R., McGue, M. K., & Benson, P. L. (1996). The emotional and behavioral adjustment of United States adopted adolescents: Part II. Age at adoption. *Children and Youth Services Review, 18,* 95-108.

Sharma, A. R., McGue, M. K., & Benson, P. L. (1996). *The psychological adjustment of United States adopted adolescents and their nonadopted siblings.* Manuscript submitted for publication to *Child Development.*

17. See *Adoptive Kinship* Chapter 4: "A Theory of Bonding," pp. 39-54.

18. This is an excerpt from the preface to his *Beyond Alienation,* 1967, by Ernest Becker, author of the famous *The Denial of Death.* E.A. Burtt, to whom he refers, is best known for *The Metaphysical Foundations of Modern Physical Science,* 1932.

19. See "Limitations of the Study" in GROW, p. 13.

20. See "Indications of Well-being" and "High Risk Behavior," pp. 66-73.

21. A footnote in figure 5.1 (GROW, p. 67) says "Based on analysis of 51,098 6th-12th grade, non-adopted public school students in Colorado, Illinois, Minnesota, and Wisconsin. Data collected by Search Institute since 1990 as part of its ongoing national assessment of students in public school districts."

22. See H.D. Kirk, K. Jonassohn, and A.D. Fish, "Are Adopted Children Especially Vulnerable to Stress?", *Archives of General Psychiatry.* Vol. 14, March 1966.

23. Once again something is missing. Why no mention here of the published (Harper & Row) work by Benson, Williams, and Johnson, *The Quicksilver Years— the Hopes and Fears of Early Adolescence,* 1987? Instead, in "References" (pp. 121 ff.) Benson appears twice, but only as author of in-house publications. Williams and Johnson are not referenced at all.

24. The At-Risk Indicators are classed under: Alcohol, Tobacco, Illicit Drugs, Sexuality, Depression/Suicide, Anti-Social Behavior, School Problems, and Vehicle Safety.

25. As the authors of GROW themselves realize, one limitation of their study is that their sample is decreasingly characteristic of adoption as it is being practiced in North America. With fewer and fewer women relinquishing children to adoption shortly after birth, and more and more "special needs," including older children being adopted, applying the GROW data to other groups of adopted children would probably be misleading.

26. Arthur L. Johnson and Peter L. Benson, "An Epidemiological Study of Selected Problem Behaviors in Adopted and Non-adopted Youth," Search Institute, 1986.

27. Professor Johnson warns that the category "later adoptees" may be a mixed category, since the young people supplying the information may have here

added other categories like foster parents or relatives with whom they lived. It seems likely that many of the "later adoptees" are in fact mostly stepchildren, who have been adopted by the new spouse.

28. The concept "social ground" derives from the work of Kurt Lewin and served me in my adoption studies as a dependent variable. As previously indicated here, I have not made use of the concept of "adjustment" when looking at the outcome of an adoptive parent-child relationship, but rather the "social ground" on which a child stands.

29. As previously noted, the authors of GROW were careful to limit their report's implications to adoptions made in the child's infancy. In a final introductory note under "Limitations of the Study" (p. 14) GROW says "Our study only examined a certain type of adoption: agency-placed infants below the age of 15 months. Thus the data are best interpreted within that focus. Other types of adoption (such as older child) introduce new dynamics that would likely change the findings in significant ways." The authors should thus not be held responsible for misinterpretations made by others.

30. For age differences in children's readiness for adoption see: H.D. Kirk, "Growth, Crises, and Integration in Adoptive Childhood" in B.J. Tansey (Ed.), *Exploring Adoptive Family Life,* 1988.

31. In these tables the statistical significance (T-tests for comparing two percentages) is very consistent. With a total sample of 8,162 and 302 in the early adopted group and 320 in the later adopted group, the appropriate standard errors are rather small when comparing either adopted group with the total sample. Given the fairly standard levels of expressing statistical significance as probabilities of less than .05, .01, or .001, we can conclude:

–The Early Adopted Group does not differ significantly from the Total Sample.
–The Later Adopted Group differs highly from the Total Group, with significance levels of less than $P < .001$ for every item, with the possible exception of two items significant at the $P < .01$ level. Weak Friendship Network (6% higher) and Low Parental Harmony (7% higher).

–Comparisons between the two adopted samples are also very consistent:
–The twelve Youth Behavior items are all significant at the $P < .001$ level.
–The three Life Threatening items are significant at the $P < .05$ level.
–Developmental Processes–

      Friendship Network–items significant at the $P < .01$ level.

      Alienation and Self Esteem items significant at the $P < .05$ level.
–Family climate
      Family Not Close–significant at the $P < .001$ level.
      Low Parental Harmony–significant at the $P < .01$ level.

To summarize, the 31 relevant items clearly show distinctly different patterns for early adopted youth and later adopted youth. Early adopted youth are very similar to youth in the total sample, whereas later adopted youth are not.

32. Who in the scientific community is not expected to disseminate information through scholarly articles?

33. *Adopted Child,* August 1995, p. 4. *(Adopted Child* is a monthly newsletter edited and published by Lois Ruskai Melina, P.O. Box 9362, Moscow, Idaho.)

34. See *Shared Fate,* pp. 79-81, especially p. 80, Table 5.

35. As quoted in *Adopted Child, op. cit.* p. 4.

Index

251

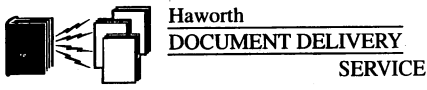

Haworth
DOCUMENT DELIVERY
SERVICE

This valuable service provides a single-article order form for any article from a Haworth journal.

- *Time Saving:* No running around from library to library to find a specific article.
- *Cost Effective:* All costs are kept down to a minimum.
- *Fast Delivery:* Choose from several options, including same-day FAX.
- *No Copyright Hassles:* You will be supplied by the original publisher.
- *Easy Payment:* Choose from several easy payment methods.

Open Accounts Welcome for ...
- Library Interlibrary Loan Departments
- Library Network/Consortia Wishing to Provide Single-Article Services
- Indexing/Abstracting Services with Single Article Provision Services
- Document Provision Brokers and Freelance Information Service Providers

MAIL or *FAX* THIS ENTIRE ORDER FORM TO:

Haworth Document Delivery Service
The Haworth Press, Inc.
10 Alice Street
Binghamton, NY 13904-1580

or FAX: 1-800-895-0582
or CALL: 1-800-342-9678
9am-5pm EST

PLEASE SEND ME PHOTOCOPIES OF THE FOLLOWING SINGLE ARTICLES:

1) Journal Title: _____
    Vol/Issue/Year:_____Starting & Ending Pages:_____
Article Title:_____
_____

2) Journal Title: _____
    Vol/Issue/Year:_____Starting & Ending Pages:_____
Article Title:_____
_____

3) Journal Title: _____
    Vol/Issue/Year:_____Starting & Ending Pages:_____
Article Title:_____
_____

4) Journal Title: _____
    Vol/Issue/Year:_____Starting & Ending Pages:_____
Article Title:_____
_____

(See other side for Costs and Payment Information)

COSTS: Please figure your cost to order quality copies of an article.

1. Set-up charge per article: $8.00

                ($8.00 × number of separate articles)   _____

2. Photocopying charge for each article:

                1-10 pages: $1.00   _____

                11-19 pages: $3.00   _____

                20-29 pages: $5.00   _____

                30+ pages: $2.00/10 pages   _____

3. Flexicover (optional): $2.00/article   _____

4. Postage & Handling: US: $1.00 for the first article/

                $.50 each additional article   _____

              Federal Express: $25.00   _____

              Outside US: $2.00 for first article/

                $.50 each additional article _____

5. Same-day FAX service: $.35 per page   _____

                            GRAND TOTAL: _____

METHOD OF PAYMENT: (please check one)

❑ Check enclosed   ❑ Please ship and bill. PO # _____

                (sorry we can ship and bill to bookstores only! All others must pre-pay)

❑ Charge to my credit card: ❑ Visa; ❑ MasterCard; ❑ Discover;

                ❑ American Express;

Account Number: _____ Expiration date: _____

Signature: ✗ _____

Name: _____ Institution: _____

Address: _____

        _____

City: _____ State: _____ Zip: _____

Phone Number: _____ FAX Number: _____

MAIL or *FAX* THIS ENTIRE ORDER FORM TO:

Haworth Document Delivery Service	**or FAX:** 1-800-895-0582
The Haworth Press, Inc.	**or CALL:** 1-800-342-9678
10 Alice Street	9am-5pm EST)
Binghamton, NY 13904-1580	

❏ YES, please send me **Structured Exercises for Promoting Family and Group Strengths**

—— in hard at $39.95 ISBN: 1-56024-978-1 (Outside US/Canada/Mexico: $48.00)

—— in soft at $19.95 ISBN: 0-7890-0224-8 (Outside US/Canada/Mexico: $24.00)

- Prices subject to change without notice.
- Individual orders outside US, Canada, and Mexico must be prepaid by check or credit card.
- Discount not good on 5+ text prices and not good in conjunction with any other discount.
- 5+ text prices are not good for jobbers and wholesalers.
- Postage & handling: In US: $3.00 for first book; $1.25 for each additional book. Outside US: $4.75 for first book; $1.75 for each additional book.
- NY, MN, and OH residents: please add appropriate sales tax after postage & handling.
- Canadian residents: please add 7% GST before postage & handling.
- If paying in Canadian dollars, use current exchange rate to convert to US dollars.
- Please allow 3–4 weeks for delivery after publication.

❏ **BILL ME LATER** ($5 service charge will be added).

(Not good for individuals outside US/Canada/Mexico. Service charge is waived for booksellers/jobbers.)

❏ Check here if billing address is different from shipping address and attach purchase order and billing address information.

Signature —————————————————

❏ **PAYMENT ENCLOSED $** ——————————————

(Payment must be in US or Canadian dollars by check or money order drawn on a US or Canadian bank.)

❏ **PLEASE BILL MY CREDIT CARD:**

❏ Visa ❏ MasterCard ❏ American Express ❏ Discover ❏ Diners Club

Account Number ——————————————

Expiration Date ——————————————

Signature ——————————————

FAX

NAME ——————————————————

INSTITUTION —————————————————

ADDRESS —————————————————

—————————————————————

CITY —————————————————————

STATE ————————————— ZIP —————————

COUNTRY —————————————————

COUNTY (NY residents only) ——————————

E-MAIL —————————————————————

May we use your e-mail address for confirmations and other types of information? ( ) Yes ( ) No

❏ **YES**, please send me **Structured Exercises for Promoting Family and Group Strengths (ISBN: 0-7890-0224-8)** to consider on a 60–day examination basis. I understand that I will receive an invoice payable within 60 days, or that **if I decide to adopt the book, my invoice will be cancelled.** I understand that I will be billed at the lowest price. (Offer good only to teaching faculty in US, Canada, and Mexico.)

Signature ——————————————————

Course Title(s) ——————————————

Current Text(s) ——————————————

Enrollment ——————————————————

Semester ——————————— Decision Date ——————————

Office Tel ——————————— Hours ——————————

FAX

THE HAWORTH PRESS, INC., 10 Alice Street, Binghamton, NY 13904–1580 USA

⑤ 06/97 BIC97

Please remember that this is a library book,
and that it belongs only temporarily to each
person who uses it. Be considerate. Do
not write in this, or any, library book.

DATE DUE
